# Rock Climbing Northwest California

Steven Mackay

Guilford, Connecticut
An imprint of The Globe Pequot Press

A FALCON GUIDE®



**Library of Congress Cataloging-in-Publication Data**

Mackay, Steven, 1949-

Rock climbing northwest California/by Steven Mackay.

p. cm.

ISBN 1-56044-768-0

1. Rock climbing—California, Northern—Guidebooks. 2. California, Northern—Guidebooks. I. Title.

GV199.42.C2 M33 2001

917.94—dc21

00-051869

♻ Text pages printed on recycled paper.

Manufactured in the United States of America

First Edition/First Printing

# Rock Climbing
# Northwest California

## WARNING:
## CLIMBING IS A SPORT WHERE YOU MAY BE SERIOUSLY INJURED OR DIE. READ THIS BEFORE YOU USE THIS BOOK.

This guidebook is a compilation of unverified information gathered from many different climbers. The author cannot assure the accuracy of any of the information in this book, including the topos and route descriptions, the difficulty ratings, and the protection ratings. These may be incorrect or misleading and it is impossible for any one author to climb all the routes to confirm the information about each route. Also, ratings of climbing difficulty and danger are always subjective and depend on the physical characteristics (for example, height), experience, technical ability, confidence, and physical fitness of the climber who supplied the rating. Additionally, climbers who achieve first ascents sometimes underrate the difficulty or danger of the climbing route out of fear of being ridiculed if a climb is later down-rated by subsequent ascents. Therefore, be warned that you must exercise your own judgment on where a climbing route goes, its difficulty, and your ability to safely protect yourself from the risks of rock climbing. Examples of some of these risks are: falling due to technical difficulty or due to natural hazards such as holds breaking, falling rock, climbing equipment dropped by other climbers, hazards of weather and lightning, your own equipment failure, and failure or absence of fixed protection.

**You should not depend on any information gleaned from this book for your personal safety; your safety depends on your own good judgment, based on experience and a realistic assessment of your climbing ability. If you have any doubt as to your ability to safely climb a route described in this book, do not attempt it.**

The following are some ways to make your use of this book safer:

**1. Consultation:** You should consult with other climbers about the difficulty and danger of a particular climb prior to attempting it. Most local climbers are glad to give advice on routes in their area and we suggest that you contact locals to confirm ratings and safety of particular routes and to obtain first-hand information about a route chosen from this book.

**2. Instruction:** Most climbing areas have local climbing instructors and guides available. We recommend that you engage an instructor or guide to learn safety techniques and to become familiar with the routes and hazards of the areas described in this book. Even after you are proficient in climbing safely, occasional use of a guide is a safe way to raise your climbing standard and learn advanced techniques.

**3. Fixed Protection:** Many of the routes in this book use bolts and pitons which are permanently placed in the rock. Because of variances in the manner of placement, weathering, metal fatigue, the quality of the metal used, and many other factors, these fixed protection pieces should always be considered suspect and should always be backed up by equipment that you place yourself. Never depend for your safety on a single piece of fixed protection because you never can tell whether it will hold weight, and in some cases, fixed protection may have been removed or is now absent.

Be aware of the following specific potential hazards which could arise in using this book:

**1. Misdescriptions of Routes:** If you climb a route and you have a doubt as to where the route may go, you should not go on unless you are sure that you can go that way safely. Route descriptions and topos in this book may be inaccurate or misleading.

**2. Incorrect Difficulty Rating:** A route may, in fact, be more difficult than the rating indicates. Do not be lulled into a false sense of security by the difficulty rating.

**3. Incorrect Protection Rating:** If you climb a route and you are unable to arrange adequate protection from the risk of falling through the use of fixed pitons or bolts and by placing your own protection devices, do not assume that there is adequate protection available higher just because the route protection rating indicates the route is not an 'X' or an 'R' rating. Every route is potentially an 'X' (a fall may be deadly), due to the inherent hazards of climbing—including, for example, failure or absence of fixed protection, your own equipment's failure, or improper use of climbing equipment.

THERE ARE NO WARRANTIES, WHETHER EXPRESS OR IMPLIED, THAT THIS GUIDEBOOK IS ACCURATE OR THAT THE INFORMATION CONTAINED IN IT IS RELIABLE. THERE ARE NO WARRANTIES OF FITNESS FOR A PARTICULAR PURPOSE OR THAT THIS GUIDE IS MERCHANTABLE. YOUR USE OF THIS BOOK INDICATES YOUR ASSUMPTION OF THE RISK THAT IT MAY CONTAIN ERRORS AND IS AN ACKNOWLEDGMENT OF YOUR OWN SOLE RESPONSIBILITY FOR YOUR CLIMBING SAFETY.

# CONTENTS

# ACKNOWLEDGMENTS

Many individuals contributed to the compilation of this guide, whether by patiently enduring my telephone calls, providing much-needed route information, or patiently belaying me while I did firsthand "research." I would especially like to thank the following climbers and climbing supporters for their help and encouragement: Alan Vick, Bruce Nyberg, and John Hauter for the great decades of enthusiastic climbing partnership; Paul Humphrey and Randy Adrian for their invaluable store of information on North Coast and Trinity limestone climbing; Roosbeh Narazi and Amaera Bay Laurel for sharing their knowledge of Grizzly Dome; Jake Palazzo for providing one of the few extant copies of Hutchinson's bouldering guide to Big Bald Rock; Scott Morris for persuading me to visit Natural Bridge; my father-in-law Leon Hutchinson for enthusiastically exploring the Feather River region with me; John Bald for encouraging me to write this book and for sharing his extensive knowledge of Castle Crags and Lassen Volcanic National Park; John Burbidge, Jessica Solberg, and Brynlyn Lehmann of Falcon Publishing for their faith in this guide; and the many climbers with whom I've shared these crags—especially Nate Manley, Jeff Czemanski, Ivan Prochaska, Clint and Jay Edwards, Christian Butler, Jordan Brown, Ron Howe, Angela Howe, Nate Coffin, David Perez-y-Cabrera, Jorge Medina, Greg Poulton, Ken Kehoe, and Mark Duden. Finally, I want to extend a special and heartfelt thank you to my wife Cara Lou for sharing so many adventures with me, and for continually believing in me and my love of climbing.

# MAP LEGEND

| | |
|---|---|
| Interstate Highway | |
| Paved Road (major) | |
| Paved Road (minor) | |
| Gravel Road | |
| Tunnel | |
| Dirt Road | |
| Trail | |
| Railroad | |
| Railroad Tunnel | |
| Forest/Park Boundary | |
| Fence | |
| Gate | |
| River/Creek | |
| Lake | |
| Marsh/Wetland | |
| Camping | |
| Building | |
| Parking | P |
| Interstate Highway | 5 |
| U.S. Highway | 2 395 |
| State/County Roads | 23 166 |
| Forest Service Road | 4420 |
| City/Town | Eureka |
| Bridge | |
| Peak/Elevation | x |
| Crag/Boulder | |
| Cliff | cliff face |
| Talus | |
| Pitch Number | 28 |
| Compass | N |
| Scale | 0 1 2 Miles |

# NORTHWEST CALIFORNIA CLIMBING AREAS

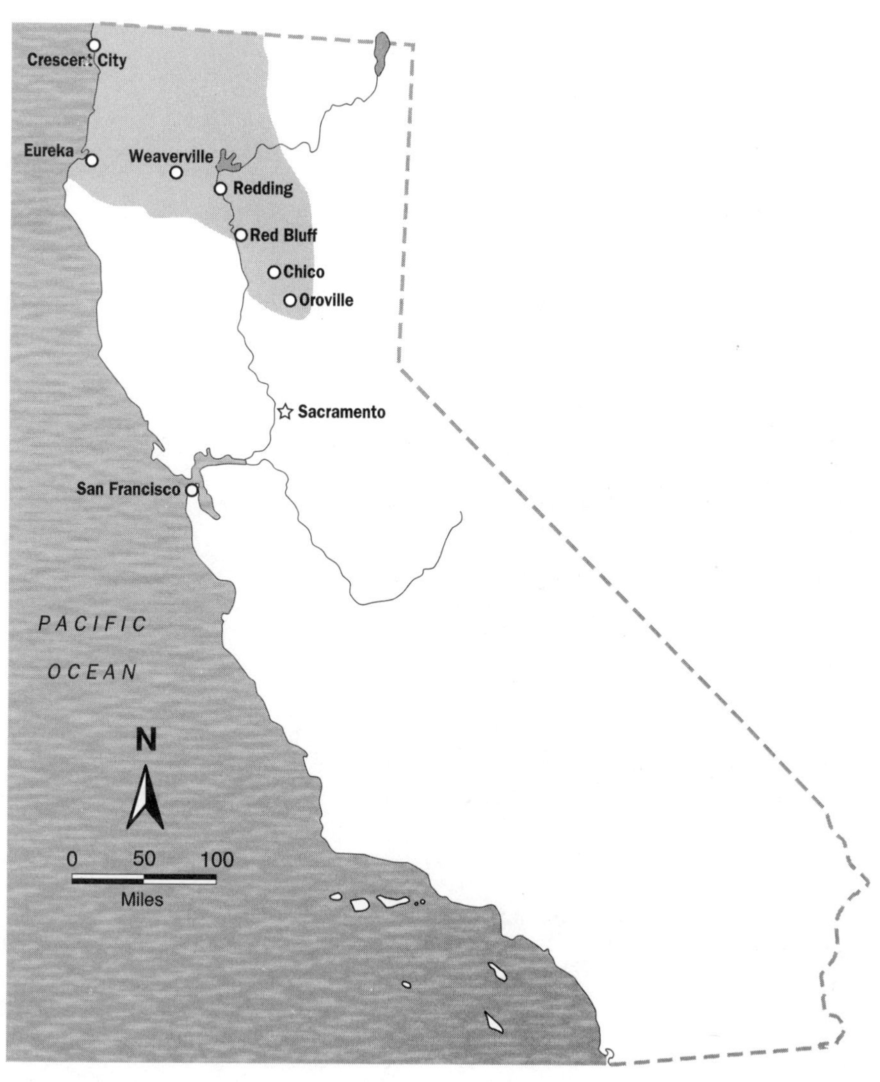

# NORTH COAST AND WESTERN KLAMATH MOUNTAINS CLIMBING AREAS

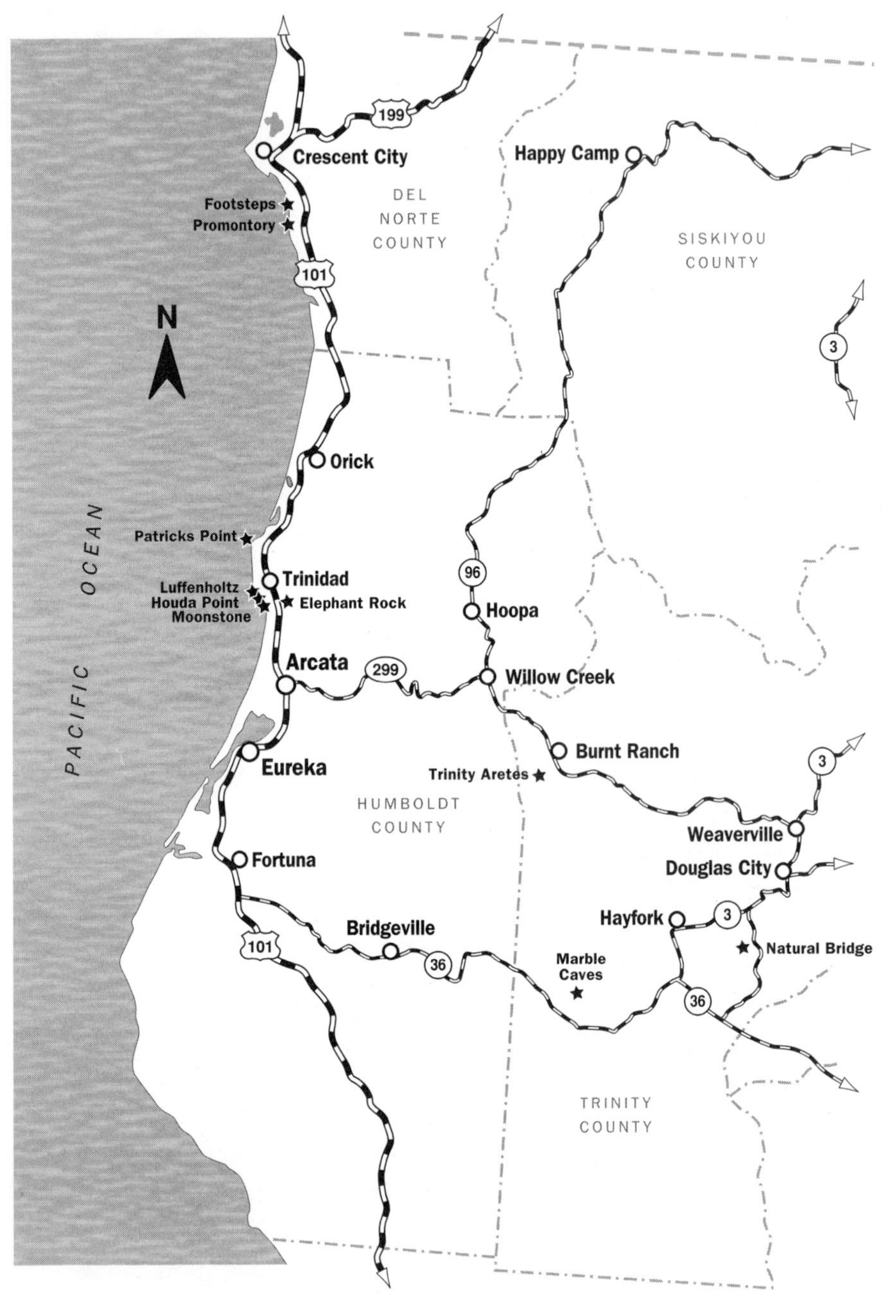

# EASTERN KLAMATH MOUNTAINS AND SOUTHERN CASCADE RANGE CLIMBING AREAS

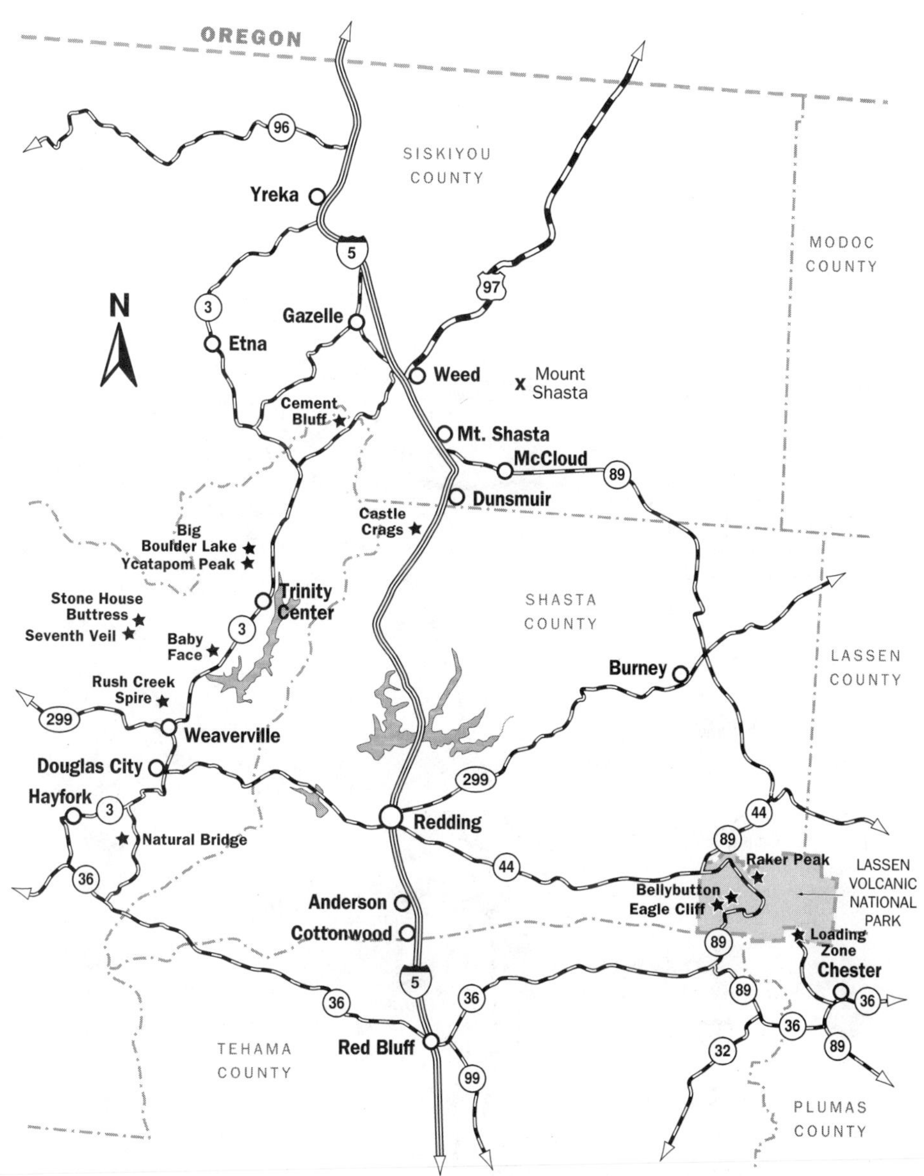

# SOUTHERN CASCADE RANGE AND NORTHERN SIERRA NEVADA RANGE CLIMBING AREAS

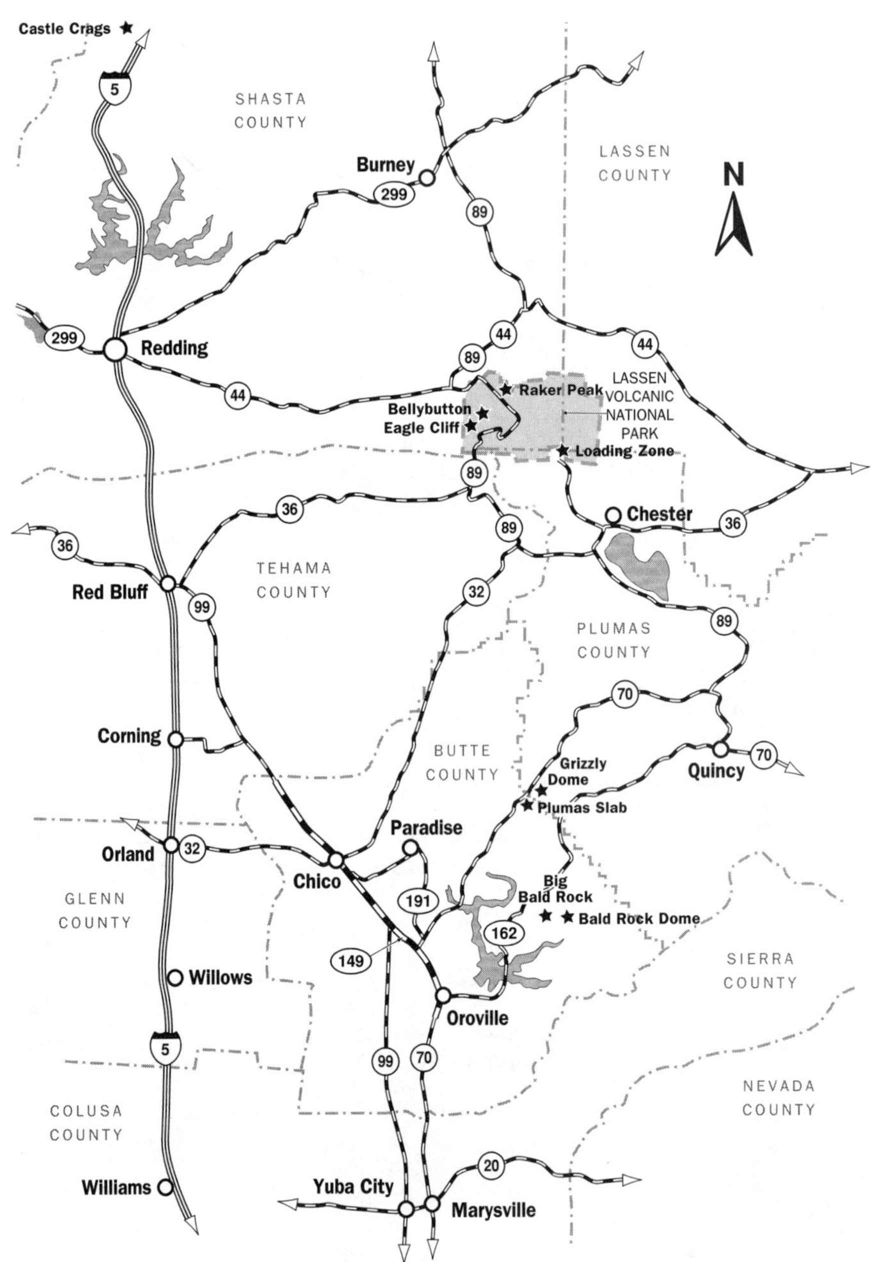

# KEY TO TOPO DRAWINGS

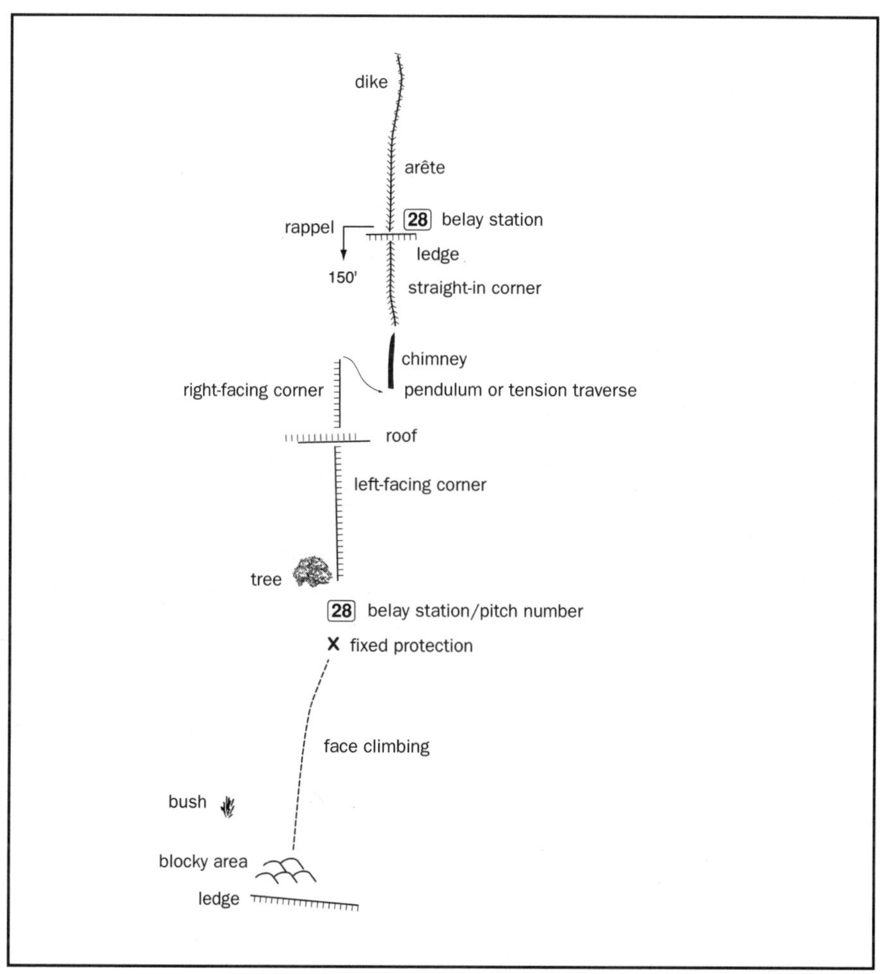

# INTRODUCTION

*Darest thou now . . . walk out with me toward the unknown region?*
WALT WHITMAN

*And he climbed and he climbed and he climbed, and as he climbed, he sang a little song.*
A. A. MILNE

California is the most geologically complex region of its size in the United States. This complexity has created a variety of climbing experiences for climbers that is second to none. Climbers here can enjoy quality climbs on sandstone, limestone, granite, and volcanic rock, in the form of sea cliffs, boulders, desert outcrops, mountain peaks, big walls, and crags of every size and description.

Strangely, in a state that boasts over 16,000 named climbs (a total that continues to grow each year) the northwest part of the state has been largely overlooked by the climbing world. This becomes all the more curious when one considers that this region-within-a-region offers virtually every type of climbing found elsewhere in California, with the exception of desert climbs and Yosemite-type big walls. Instead, climbers in northwest California can choose from sandstone sea cliffs that offer the best sea-cliff climbing in the state, limestone outcrops that host sport climbs rivaling the best in the country, granite domes reminiscent of those in Tuolumne Meadows, spires of granodiorite, wilderness peaks, lava cliffs offering superb climbing on the flanks of active volcanoes, and countless opportunities for quality bouldering. It is no exaggeration to say that an active climber could climb somewhere in northwest California every day of the year and never exhaust its store of climbs. Moreover, new-route fanatics would find a new world of possible climbs on literally square miles of unclimbed rock. Add to this the additional delight that nearly all the routes described in this book are situated in settings of great natural beauty, with many offering superb vistas that, on a clear day, can span 100 miles.

This guide covers the major crags and climbing centers of northwest California, from the Oregon border south along the Pacific coast to California Highway 36, east across the Klamath Mountains and Sacramento Valley to the Sierra crest, then south along the west side of the crest to the Middle Fork of Feather River. This region can be conveniently divided into four distinct geographical areas.

*Climbers on Karen Rock enjoying the sun on a winter afternoon.*

The North Coast, unlike the common impression of California beaches, is cool, rocky, and wild, with scores of secluded coves and beaches. Offshore rocks, inshore stacks, sea cliffs, and bluffs lie strewn about in picturesque disarray. Unlike the crumbly and disappointing rock found farther south, the North Coast rock tends to be satisfyingly hard—though sometimes brittle—and offers many opportunities for climbing and bouldering. Those who have visited northern California often mistakenly assume that the coast weather consists of one endless fog bank during summer and continual rain and wind the rest of the year. Although the North Coast is California's wettest area, hosting a substantial temperate rainforest, it does see sunny days, especially during May–June and September–October. On such days, the area practically sparkles with color, and climbing becomes a not-to-be-missed experience.

Farther inland, between the North Coast and the Sacramento Valley, lie the Klamath Mountains, the name collectively applied to numerous small mountain ranges that twist this way and that, making this region one of the state's wildest and least populated. The western Klamath Mountains are mainly forested ridges ranging up to 5,000 feet. These ridges harbor many outcrops of limestone, some of which attain sufficient size to have been developed as climbing areas. In general, the limestone is of excellent quality: quite hard, with an abundance of small holds and big overhangs—just the sort of architecture to appeal to sport climbers. It comes as no surprise then that these have become the region's primary sport-climbing venues. Farther east, the mountains, now named the Salmon Mountains, the Scott Mountains, and the Trinity Mountains, much more closely resemble the High Sierra, with glaciated granite peaks, alpine lakes, and a wealth of wilderness. Although the highest peaks barely pass the 9,000-foot mark, it is easy to believe they are 3,000 feet higher, judging by the scenery. The half-million-acre Trinity Alps Wilderness Area protects much of this area, and it contains hundreds of excellent faces and formations. Climbing in this area—and in the Castle Crags area farther east—consists of long moderates in wilderness settings or shorter test-pieces on small outcrops closer to the road.

Separated from the Klamath Mountains by the Sacramento Valley is the southern end of the Cascade Range, which terminates geologically at Lassen Peak. Although the high-desert plateau country north of Lassen Peak contains little to interest climbers, the country surrounding the peak holds several cliffs and outcrops—some of considerable size—that offer quality climbing and some of the best views of any crags in the state. The crags here lie at a much higher elevation, with some reaching nearly 10,000 feet. As a result, the climbing season, though short, is delightful, with cool, sunny days throughout the summer, interrupted only by occasional thunderstorms. The rock is dacite, a volcanic rock of surprising hardness and an almost ceramic look and feel, and the climbs range from Yosemite-like cracks to sport routes on sharp-cut aretes. Most of these crags lie within Lassen Volcanic National Park.

*Pondering the moves at the top of* Space Bucket *(I 5.10a), Grizzly Dome.*

South of Lassen Peak, the mountains become granitic and form the northernmost reaches of the Sierra Nevada. Though not the High Sierra, these wooded hills and low peaks (up to about 8,500 feet) are the source of the mighty Feather River, which, in terms of volume of water carried, is one of the largest in California. Aided by the area's abundant winter precipitation, the Feather River has carved magnificent canyons, especially along its north and middle forks. Here, the canyon walls harbor numerous impressive walls and slabs of clean, glittering granite and dark swirls of diorite. These formations offer interesting and easily accessible traditional and sport climbs, most within a very short stone's throw of the road. The mild climate makes possible a nearly yearlong climbing season on these low-elevation crags.

Put together, these distinct environments combine to make northwest California one of the country's finest climbing areas, rivaling the best anywhere. This book is both a menu of choices and an invitation to try some of these outstanding climbs. As one climber so aptly put it, "The only bad thing about climbing here is that you eventually have to go home."

## WHAT'S COVERED

In compiling this book, the author had to tread a rather narrow and dodgy path. Not all climbs were worth including in a book. Other climbs, though of high quality, were simply too far away from the road to appeal to the majority of climbers. Still others ascended rocks located on private land.

With these considerations in mind, the author chose to leave out all climbing areas that have little to offer in terms of quality rock and interesting climbs. All those located on private land or that require crossing private land were also excluded. Because most climbers dislike long approaches, climbs farther than three miles from the road were left out (although a few get pretty close to that limit).

Local climbers who frequent some of the crags in this book may question why it does not describe every route. This less-than-absolutely-comprehensive coverage reflects the comparative scarcity of route information for some areas, respect for the wishes of some local climbers to keep certain projects secret, and respect for local climbers and guidebook authors, most of whom freely shared valuable information. Where locally published guidebooks exist, they have been cited in the text and listed in the Appendix. Out-of-area visitors are encouraged to purchase copies of the local guidebooks when available.

Where it is available, first-ascent information is included in the climbing history section for each area; however, in some cases this information is sketchy or nonexistent.

# GEOLOGY

Climbers in northwest California can sample routes on several different kinds of rock, including igneous (both plutonic and volcanic), sedimentary, and, to a much lesser extent, metamorphic rocks. Although these are all present today, they represent far different ages and conditions of formation. The oldest rocks in the region—over 250 million years—are the limestone outcrops. They represent the floor of a shallow, ancient sea. Eastward movement of the earth's crust at the western edge of the continent pushed successive sections of the sea floor upward, jamming it against the coast, folding it into mountains and taking the peridotite basement rocks of the sea floor with it. These remnants of the sea floor are visible today as the isolated limestone outcrops and the abundant red peridotite rocks and soils visible throughout much of the Klamath Mountains. The pressure of the earth's crust pushing eastward and downward created considerable heat beneath the crust farther east, causing molten granite to push upward, taking the older rock up with it. Later erosion revealed the granite in large, isolated batholiths. At the same time that this was happening, the crust was also moving in the east, and similar forces created the Sierra Nevada batholith. This huge block of granite was thrust upward on its eastern edge, creating the ancient Sierra Nevada Range at about the same time as the Klamath Mountains. All this up-and-down movement created additional pressures under the earth's crust. These were relieved through vulcanism, and the volcanic rock of the Cascade Range was formed after the Klamath Mountains and the Sierra Nevada.

## IGNEOUS ROCKS

Igneous rocks are those formed by the melting of part of the earth's crust. Geologists group them into two categories: extrusive rocks and intrusive, or plutonic rocks. Extrusive rocks are those formed when melted material reaches the surface of the earth in a liquid state. Depending upon local conditions, the rock may explode from a volcano as ash, cinders, volcanic "bombs," or masses of lava. Generally speaking, the more slowly lava can cool, the better it becomes as a climbing medium. In northwestern California, the most common volcanic rock for climbing is dacite. Dacite is a fine-grained extrusive rock that is generally medium-to-light gray or brown with flecks of lighter-colored feldspar in it. It does not form the columns usually associated with basalt, but frequently offers sharp-edged pockets created by gas bubbles present when the rock was molten. In appearance and general technique requirements it resembles a cross between granite and sandstone.

In contrast, intrusive rocks form below the surface of the earth. As a result, they cool very slowly, and the individual mineral grains can usually be discerned without magnification. These rocks reach the surface by uplift of the earth's crust. Subsequent weathering away of the overlying rock layers exposes these formations. Granitic rocks are the most commonly encountered of intrusive rocks. Strictly speaking, granite refers to a specific mixture of minerals of a certain grain size included within a continuum of rocks ranging from pale aplite and rhyolite, through tonalite, granite, monzonite, granodiorite, diorite, diabase, porphyry, and gabbro. Most of the granitic rock that climbers encounter in northwestern California is either granite or granodiorite—the rock that makes up about half of the Trinity Alps and all of Castle Crags, as well as most of the formations along the tributaries of Feather River.

Peridotite is another type of intrusive rock that is generally associated with the ocean floor, and it is encountered throughout much of the region. Unlike the granitic rocks, peridotite contains only iron-rich dark minerals, such as serpentine, augite, hornblende, and olivine—minerals usually associated with the earth's mantle. Though often found as brick-red rock, peridotite is actually a deep, greenish gray-black. It achieves its red color from the oxidation of the iron in its surface. Peridotite, though not as aesthetic or durable as granite, makes an acceptable climbing medium in many places. Differential weathering of its surface often creates small solution pockets or rough, raised surface grains reminiscent of the rough quartz monzonite found in Joshua Tree National Park.

### SEDIMENTARY ROCKS

Sandstone, and its finer-grained counterpart siltstone, are formed when the sand of beaches, riverbars, or sand dunes is consolidated and later cemented together by a combination of pressure and chemical bonding among grains. Often, the bonding agent is a thin coating of calcium carbonate (limestone) which weakens when it is wet. Climbers should therefore avoid climbing sandstone during or immediately after wet weather to avoid damaging the rock. The sea stacks and formations of the North Coast region are made of a fine-grained marine sandstone.

Graywacke is a sandstone composed of a combination of both sand and bits of other sedimentary rocks, such as shale. The dark brown or gray color is typical of this type of rock. Many of the exposures of sedimentary rock in coastal Humboldt County are graywacke.

Tillite is a curious rock that differs from other sedimentary rocks in that its constituent particles are deposited by glaciers and glacial meltwater. Because of the quarrying power of the ice, these sediments do not display the usual sorting by grain size apparent in stream-deposited rocks. Typically, the finer grains contain enough lime to form a passable natural cement, gluing the larger rocks into a hard matrix. Cement Bluff is an excellent example of this type of rock.

### METAMORPHIC ROCKS

Metamorphic rocks are those that have been altered from their original forms through such geological processes as mountain-building, exposure to extreme heat via volcanic action or magmatic intrusion, or the extreme pressures resulting from subduction (the downward movement of a portion of the earth's crust under another portion). When any of these conditions occur, the mineral grains that make up the rocks may become distorted or recrystallized.

Where movement is involved, the rocks frequently become striated or even layered. The schists and slates visible in roadcuts along California 299 display considerable alteration of their parent material. Here, the slabby appearance usually resulted from side-to-side tension accompanied by extreme pressure from below as the nearby granite bodies pushed up from the earth's mantle—not from the layering usually associated with sedimentary rocks. This type of rock is usually brittle and unreliable, and it rarely forms outcrops suitable for climbing.

Under circumstances that do not involve movement, such as the intrusion of molten rock to form dikes, recrystallization is the usual result. A fine example of this phenomenon is the metamorphism of the granodiorite adjacent to quartz dikes at Castle Crags State Park: the recrystallization has made the rock bordering dikes much more solid and erosion-resistant.

## EQUIPMENT

For most of the climbs included in this book, your standard free-climbing rack should prove adequate. For traditional routes, this gear selection would include a selection of 6 to 8 wired stoppers from 3⁄16" to 1", 6 to 8 hexes from ½" to 1½", and 6 to 10 SLCDs (either TCUs or FCUs) from ⅝" to 3". For sport climbs, a dozen quickdraws and a few of the smaller SLCDs should suffice. For either kind of climbing, your rack should also include a number of runners to reduce rope drag, and webbing and rappel rings for bailoffs. Where other equipment is required for a particular climb, a listing is included in that route's description.

The routes described can be climbed with a single rope, but a few are most easily descended via a two-rope (i.e., double-rope) rappel. This practice saves time, saves gear, and, in the event of an emergency or bad weather, generally proves safer because of the need for fewer rap-station setups. Your rope should be treated for what it is: Your opportunity to live and learn from your mistakes instead of being killed by them. Treat it with the respect you deserve.

Regardless of the style of climbing you favor, there are other equipment recommendations to consider. For starters, a helmet is a vital piece of gear, particularly when climbing at higher elevations where loose rock on ledges, or decomposing rock are commonplace. For long routes, such as those on Ycatapom Peak or farther into the Trinity Alps in Canyon Creek, a good, working headlamp can be worth its weight in gold. The same can be said for a good set of rain gear. Although most storms in the region give ample advance warning, your descent and escape to camp or car can take longer than expected. Why risk hypothermia needlessly? A final addition to the gear list would have to be a pair of lightweight trail shoes for descents. Anyone who has suffered through a long descent in climbing shoes or socks will agree.

## CLIMBING DANGERS AND SAFETY

The popular perception most non-climbers have of climbing is that it is an inherently dangerous activity pursued by irresponsible thrillseekers with latent or not-so-latent suicidal tendencies. Although most climbers would agree that this generalization is laughably inaccurate, it does get reinforced in the public's consciousness when a member of the climbing community is injured or killed while climbing. Although we take care to minimize the actual risk—as opposed to perceived risk—when we climb, we cannot ignore the obvious fact that people and objects in high places fall farther and land harder than those in low places, and it is this inescapable fact that creates the risk in climbing. To minimize this risk, all climbers must be constantly aware of the potential sources of danger: objective dangers—those we cannot control (but strive to minimize); and subjective dangers—those we bring with us.

Objective dangers include such sources of injury as being struck by falling rock or other debris; falling because of a hold breaking off; being struck by lightning; being weakened or debilitated by extremes of heat or cold; being bitten or attacked by venomous insects or rattlesnakes; or drowning during stream crossings or as a result of being struck by ocean waves. Subjective dangers include such sources of injury as falling due to equipment failure, falling due to failure of technique, and falling due to improper use of equipment. We cannot eliminate these dangers completely, but we can minimize them by observing the following cautions:

1. **Your brain is your first line of defense against accidents.** Use it all the time to watch for potentially dangerous situations and to take the measures necessary to minimize or eliminate them. Pay attention to your intuition or "gut-feelings." Most of us pick up subtle "danger" signals from stimuli we are not consciously aware of. Pay attention to these feelings; if you get "bad vibes" about a climb, turn back. Do not forget to protect your brain with a good helmet; a fall from even shoulder height onto your unprotected noggin can be fatal.
2. **Dress appropriately for the conditions.** The weather may look calm, but it is not a given—a rain parka and sweater take up little space in your pack.

3. **Inspect your gear before, during, and after each climbing trip.** Retire or discard any piece of hardware that is obviously worn, cracked, or has been dropped. Exposure to dirt and ultraviolet light weaken ropes and webbing. Do not be such a cheapskate that you climb on old cord. If you climb a lot (i.e., at least three times a month) outdoors—and especially if you fall a lot—retire your rope after a season. More occasional climbers can stretch this to a couple of years, but beyond that, it becomes pretty iffy. In this vein, never trust rappel webbing you find in place, no matter how fresh it looks. Take off and pack out the old and replace it with fresh webbing before you rappel.
4. **Take a first-aid kit.** Something as simple as a bit of adhesive tape on a cut finger can mean the difference between completing the climb of a lifetime and turning back. Do not risk further injury or infection by leaving your first aid kit at home. If you have allergies that could be life-threatening, take a kit for treating respiratory emergencies.
5. **Take a headlamp.** Delays are difficult to prevent, but a reliable headlamp can be a godsend on long climbs. In general, a headlamp will be much easier to work with than a flashlight, although a spare flashlight in the bottom of your pack is not a bad idea, either.
6. **Know those you climb with.** Make sure you can count on everybody in your party in the event of an emergency. Big talk in the parking lot is no substitute for experience.
7. **Always assume there is a party below you.** Never throw material down a cliff, and try to avoid dislodging any loose material with your feet or the rope.
8. **Avoid "summit fever."** It can be almost overwhelmingly tempting to push on late in the day or in the face of changing weather, especially when close to the top of a climb. Unless topping-out provides a safer and easier way down for tired and potentially inattentive climbers, turn back at a decent time to avoid being caught by darkness or bad weather.

## ACCESS: CLIMBING STYLE AND ETHICS

In climbing, "style" refers to the manner in which a route was established, or how it is climbed, while "ethics" pertains to how we treat the rock and its associated community of plants, animals, and other climbers. Although climbers often use the terms interchangeably, they really refer to two entirely different things, each having different potential impacts on the individual climber and on the climbing community as a whole.

Style issues typically involve such considerations as the "purity" of an ascent—that is, how much assistance the leader used in terms of aid, route information, pre-inspection, or type of protection; how much time was involved; the line of ascent; and other matters. Style underlies the debate between so-called "traditional" climbers and "sport" climbers.

Traditional climbing is rooted in the idea of getting to the top of a rock or mountain from the ground up, placing all protection along the way. As the game is played, each party attempts to satisfy a number of stylistic requirements: getting to the top, using as little aided climbing as possible, using as little protection as absolutely necessary (including a few runouts to keep things interesting), and striving for fast times (a carryover from mountaineering, where speed means safety when the weather is unsettled). In addition, traditional climbing embraces the philosophy of "clean" climbing, favoring modes of protection according to the following order: runners, stoppers and cams, pitons, fixed pitons, runouts (of a length determined by the leader's ability and confidence), and bolts. Once a climb has been established, subsequent ascent parties are expected to observe the level of style established by the first ascent team as a minimum standard. If the first team used aid on a particular pitch, another party may use aid, but they may also climb it with less aid, or they may eliminate the aid. Once aid has been reduced or eliminated by a majority of climbers, the route's rating is usually revised to reflect the change in standards. At no time is it considered acceptable to use more aid than the first ascent team.

In contrast to traditional climbing, sport climbing places its emphasis on the skilled performance of the leader in negotiating a difficult, strenuous, and often intricate series of moves. The goal of sport climbing is not merely completing a climb, but achieving a "redpoint" or "flash," a lead completed without stopping or falling, and without the use of pre-placed gear other than fixed protection. Because the technical difficulties encountered in sport climbing are usually greater than those on traditional climbs (often beginning at the 5.11+ level), most leaders prefer to concentrate on completing the moves, rather than on placing protection. Thus, most sport climbs employ bolted protection at appropriate intervals and rarely extend into multiple pitches. The leader typically rappels or lowers off after the lead. Unlike traditional climbing, where all protection is placed while climbing, sport climbing, because of the technical difficulties of the routes, accepts practices that would be heresy in traditional climbing: pre-inspection, rappel-bolting, use of power drills to place the many bolts found on sport crags, and rehearsals prior to a redpoint attempt.

Because traditional climbing and sport climbing emphasize different things, and because each requires the complete focus and determination of the climber, neither is better or worse than the other. They are both climbing, and the sooner adherents of each accept the validity of the other, the better off climbing and climbers will be.

Where style relates to the intangible "rules" of climbing, ethics relates to our behaviors relative to other climbers, to the rock, and, in many cases, to the landowners and agencies with whom we as climbers interact. Our behavior should respect other climbers. Never add permanent protection (such as bolts) to an established climb without the permission of the first ascent party, or, if they are impossible to contact, without the consensus of the local climbing community. If you must place or replace a bolt, remember that a bolt hole lasts for millennia; drill only after you have determined that a bolt is both needed and appropriate. Make sure each bolt you place is a good, appropriate-sized anchor in a fully-drilled hole. Use stainless steel bolts of at least 3/8 inch diameter and hangers made for climbing—no angle-iron! Don't try to place bolts on-lead unless you can do so safely—and at appropriate intervals and locations. Otherwise, rap-bolt in the interests of the safety and enjoyment of those who will be using your bolts in the future.

While climbing, never consciously dislodge rocks, sticks, or other debris unless you can do so without endangering anyone below. While it is ethically justifiable to carefully pull off a loose flake in order to make a climb safer, it is not acceptable to do so in order to create a hold where the flake previously attached to the rock. If a climb is just too blank for you, resist the temptation to chip or enlarge holds—or worse, to bolt on or glue on a hold. There are climbing gyms for that sort of thing. Enjoy and measure yourself against the rock as it is. Resist the temptation to steal bolt hangers or fixed protection; someone else's life may depend on their presence. And finally, do not pirate someone else's project. Any climb in the making is a labor of love belonging to another climber.

Ethical behavior goes beyond merely climbing. For example, it is okay to "garden" dead pine needles or dirt out of a crack to place protection, but uprooting live plants or cutting trees and shrubs that are "in the way" is definitely taboo. Avoid the temptation to remove moss and other "nuisances" on shaded faces in order to reveal clean rock to climb on. In many areas, the micro-habitats of rock fissures and shaded, moss-covered faces provide the only homes for rare and sometimes endangered species of plants and animals. If we fail to observe these considerations, we place ourselves and others at risk of being "managed" out of legal access to the very rocks we treasure.

Finally, we must recognize that, for the most part, the climbing resource is owned or managed by non-climbers who, in most cases, accept us with a certain degree of skepticism. We must always respect landowner and agency concerns. Never climb on private land or even cross private land to get to a climb unless you have first secured the owner's permission. The biggest threat to access is not liability; it is bad behavior on the part of climbers. To safeguard access to climbing areas, we must be proactive in our approach to climbing by cooperating fully with land managers, by "adopting" areas (i.e., performing trail maintenance, litter pickup, or other public service activities), and by joining and supporting local and regional advocacy groups such as The Access Fund and The American Alpine Club (see Appendix D).

# Using This Guide

*Rock Climbing Northwest California* is a guide to over 550 climbs at 22 different climbing areas. These climbs have been described using text, maps, photographs, and topos. A series of overview maps at the beginning of the book and more localized maps accompanying each chapter aid in locating each climbing area.

Each area's chapter includes an **Overview,** which incorporates a general description of the area, its history and local ethics, and the usual gear requirements; **Trip planning information,** which includes brief summaries of the information necessary for a successful visit; **Directions to the crag,** which gives driving and hiking directions to the rocks, often accompanied by local maps; and **Route descriptions** of the climbs themselves, accompanied for clarity by photos and/or topos.

As mentioned previously, the **Overview** section of each chapter provides a thumbnail sketch of the area's setting, type of rock encountered, general length and difficulty of climbs encountered, and any particular style or ethical considerations. The area's history, if known, is recounted, and most first-ascent information is given at this point, rather than cluttering up the route descriptions with these credits. A list of recommended gear accompanies the other information. If a particular climb requires additional or different gear from this norm, some mention of the fact has been included with its route description. If no special mention is made, the standard selection should be adequate. If the same descent route is used for all climbs on the formation, it is included here; otherwise, descent descriptions are given for each group of climbs, as appropriate.

The section concerning **Trip planning information** includes data in the following categories:

**Area description:** A bare-bones summary of the area.

**Location:** A general description of where the area is located relative to the nearest town (or easily-located geographical feature).

**Camping:** The names, locations, and descriptions of the nearest campgrounds. In general, only federal and state campgrounds have been described in detail; private campgrounds and other lodgings, if any, may be mentioned, but not described.

**Climbing season:** A description of the best times to visit the area, including note of any conditions that should be anticipated.

**Restrictions and access issues:** A description of any physical, social, or managerial considerations that could affect current or future access to the area, including issues of special concern to climbers.

**Guidebooks:** A listing of any guidebooks or journal articles describing the area, whether published or unpublished. Complete bibliographical information is included in Appendix A.

**Nearby mountain shops, guide services, and gyms:** A listing of those sources for gear, local beta, and instruction nearest the area being described. Complete name and address listings are included in Appendix C.

**Services:** A list of any amenities or services available at the crag or within a short distance of it.

**Emergency services:** A listing of whom to contact in the event of an emergency, as well as a listing of the nearest hospitals. Complete hospital information is listed in Appendix E.

**Nearby climbing areas:** A list and capsule description of the nearest climbing areas, if any.

**Nearby attractions:** For non-climbing days, a list of additional points of interest.

**Finding the crag:** A brief but complete set of driving and hiking directions to the crag, usually beginning at the nearest town or highway junction.

The **Route descriptions** section of each chapter identifies each route numerically and lists the routes in either left-to-right or right-to-left order, whichever sequence is appropriate for clarity. Generally, the routes appear in the order they would be encountered along the usual approach route. Each description gives the route's name, its difficulty rating, a brief description of how to find the starting point, a description of the actual climb, a list of any additional gear needed, and other information considered helpful in the interests of safety. In many cases, photos or topos depict the routes being described. Multi-pitch routes are described pitch-by-pitch whenever possible. If a crag is very complex, or if a climbing area consists of several separate formations, the route descriptions are grouped for ease of use. A key to topo symbols used in these descriptions is located in the front of this book.

An **Honorable Mention** section has been included at the end of each chapter. Here, other climbing areas or potential climbing areas are listed and very briefly described. Some of these may be included as full chapters in later editions of this guidebook.

At the end of the book comes a series of Appendices. Appendix A is a bibliographic listing of other sources of information. Appendix B is a comparison chart of several different systems of rating climbing difficulty. Appendix C is a city-by-city listing of the names, addresses, and telephone numbers of mountain shops, guide services, and climbing gyms. Appendix D is a listing of the names, addresses, and telephone numbers of service providers and resource management agencies. Appendix E is a city-by-city listing of the names, addresses, and telephone numbers of hospitals.

An index at the end of the book provides page references for all proper names of people, areas, and climbs listed alphabetically.

This book covers a very large and diverse region, and in several cases represents the first written description of some of the crags. Climbs vary greatly in both length and difficulty, and nature itself can create changes in routes. It is therefore inevitable that some errors will find their way into print. Although the author has personally visited and climbed on every crag described here, it is physically impossible to have climbed all the routes. Therefore, the reader should not accept all the information presented here at face value. What seems do-able in print can take on a different face entirely in the field. This book is intended to direct you to climbing opportunities and give you some idea of which way to go. Beyond that, you must rely on your own skill and experience to safely make the climb. This book is not a substitute for experience and good judgement; only you can determine what you can safely do.

Those who have used other climbing guides may note that this book does not use "star ratings" to indicate the relative quality of climbs. So often, one person's "quality" route is another person's "ho-hum" scramble. It is also tempting to equate quality with difficulty, which is completely illogical. Suffice it to say that every route listed is worth doing. Those that the author found to be excessively dangerous, dirty, or uninteresting were omitted.

## RATING SYSTEM

The rating system used in this guide is the time-honored Yosemite Decimal System (YDS), which, cumbersome as it is, has gained nationwide acceptance. One should note at this point that there is no absolute measure of climbing difficulty; each climb's rating is the result of local consensus. While there is a general correlation of ratings among areas, the nature of the rock and the abilities of the climbers who habituate any given area can affect that area's rating. As a result, the "moderate" routes at Grizzly Dome tend to be somewhat more difficult than their counterparts at Castle Crags, and a muscular and acrobatic 5.10d at Moonstone may seem easier or harder than a 5.10d friction climb at Bald Rock Dome, depending upon the climber's past experience.

The YDS is an outgrowth of an earlier system developed by German climber Willo Welzenbach, who described mountain travel ratings so:

**Class 1:** Easy walking, hands-in-the pockets, no special footwear required.

**Class 2:** Off-trail hiking requiring boots; hands occasionally used for balance.

**Class 3:** "Scrambling;" handholds and footholds come into play; exposure increases, making a rope a good idea for less experienced members of the party.

**Class 4:** Smaller holds and steeper terrain encountered; anchored belays are necessary for the safety of all members of the party. Descents may require rappels.

**Class 5:** Steeper rock, smaller holds, and the need for more specialized technique are encountered, necessitating anchored belays and the use of specialized hardware to safeguard the leader. Descents may require rappels.

**Class 6:** Rock unclimbable by use of the holds available; the party must resort to the use of specialized hardware and slings for progress (i.e., "aided," or "aid" climbing).

American climbers in the 1930s discovered that most of their climbing was "Class 5," but that there was a big range of difficulty within that class. They therefore subdivided the class into decimals to produce 5.0 to 5.9 climbs. Similarly, they determined that Class 6 was inappropriate in this system because it was not necessarily harder than Class 5, just different. They accordingly replaced the Class 6 with Class A1 to A5, which signified climbs that required direct aid. (Note that, with rare exceptions, there are no aid climbs listed in this book.)

In 1960, climbs were accomplished that were distinctly harder than 5.9, but were not "aided" climbs. The climbing community jokingly referred to these as "5.10" climbs. With the psychological and logical rating barrier broken, the former decimal-based Class 5 became an open-ended system that currently stops at 5.15. To further complicate matters, in the early 1970s, climbers in Yosemite Valley began to further subdivide routes at and above 5.10 into sub-grades of a, b, c, or d to indicate relative difficulty within the rating. We now must deal with ratings such as 5.11c, which, according to the original proponents, is as much harder than a 5.11b as a 5.9 is than a 5.8.

Most of the routes in this guide are one-pitch climbs, but some run into many pitches. Clearly, this has some bearing on the overall seriousness of the climbs. A simple difficulty rating (i.e., 5.7) suffices for a single-pitch route. Longer climbs also include a Roman numeral prefix to indicate their seriousness. This system of co-rating was developed by California climber Mark Powell and can be interpreted as follows:

**Grade I:** A climb of a couple of hours.

**Grade II:** A climb that would take all morning or all afternoon.

**Grade III:** A climb that takes an all-day effort.

**Grade IV:** A climb requiring an early start and a descent after dark.

**Grade V:** A climb that lasts a full day plus a morning.

**Grade VI:** A climb requiring at least two full days, more often three or more.

Thus, a climb like *Orion* on Ycatapom Peak carries a rating of III 5.7, while a one-pitch route, such as *Centipede* at Promontory is rated 5.9.

Finally, some indication of a climb's ease of protection—or lack thereof—can be helpful. Colorado climber Jim Erickson developed his own system based on motion picture ratings, which has been adopted (in abbreviated form) for use here. An "R" rating indicates that at least one pitch on a climb requires a long runout without protection, or that the protection may be sketchy or hard to place. An "X" rating signifies a route for experienced climbers only, one on which a fall would almost certainly result in the death or serious injury of the climber. A "TR" rating signifies that the climb is normally climbed with a toprope. **Please note that due to changing conditions and/or incorrect information, any climb has the potential to be rated "R" or "X," even if it is not indicated as such in this guidebook.**

As a final ethical note, each climber is the best judge of what is the appropriate amount of protection necessary for his or her safety on a climb of a given rating. Each should strive to climb in the best style possible, always seeking to equal or improve on the standard set by the first ascent party. Above all, make this your goal: "Everybody has fun, nobody gets hurt."

# THE NORTH COAST

California's North Coast, from Humboldt Bay to the Oregon border, has long been a popular tourist destination, famous for its forests of giant coast redwood trees, its sport fishing for salmon and deepwater species, its art community, and its quaint and colorful, turn-of-the-century, gingerbread houses and commercial buildings. Over the past forty years, and especially over the last twenty, climbers have discovered the North Coast as the site of California's finest sea cliff climbing. Promontories, stacks, and isolated outcrops of marine greenstone, graywacke, and sandstone abound along the miles of uncrowded beaches, offering interesting and demanding climbs over a broad range of difficulties. Picturesque settings and easy access make these crags especially attractive, and guarantee their contribution to the enjoyment of a visit to this area.

Climbs in this region include both traditional and sport routes of all degrees of difficulty and seriousness, and the potential for new routes remains high. All the formations described lie on public land, so legal access is not a problem. However, the ocean here is deep, cold, and prone to big waves during high tide, creating the potential for access and safety problems for inattentive climbers. Fortunately, the most popular crags lie above the reach of the sea and tend to be dry and generally sound. In addition, while the ocean can create some problems, it also tends to moderate the weather. When the inland crags swelter in 100-degree heat, the coastal rocks remain a pleasant 60–70 degrees. In winter, a sunny day can provide shorts weather at the beach while crags elsewhere are closed due to snow.

## FOOTSTEPS AND PROMONTORY

Rising virtually from the edge of the sea and flanked by beautiful, driftwood-strewn, black sand beaches, Promontory and its more northerly neighbor Footsteps provide not only California's northernmost rock climbing, but also some of its best. On these sea stacks, climbers can come to grips with marine sandstone climbing at its best: sharp-edged cracks, porous walls laced with countless pockets from monodoigts to whole-hand jugs, serrated aretes, and looming overhangs that must be seen to be believed—all against a background of the roar of pounding surf. Routes range in length from less than 25 feet to nearly 80 feet, and in difficulty from 5.0 to 5.13, with the majority at or above 5.10. The climbing is interesting, subtle, and demanding—not suitable terrain

## FOOTSTEPS AND PROMONTORY

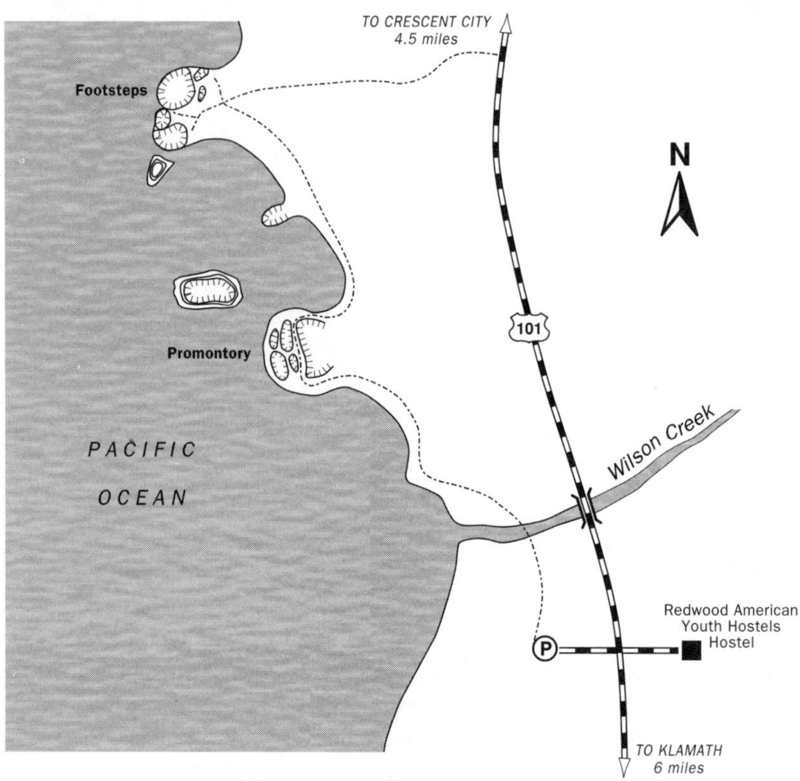


for inexperienced leaders moving up the scale of difficulty. More than one visitor has insisted that these routes are under-rated.

The rock on these formations is a gray-to-yellow, fine-grained sandstone, streaked with brown or varnished with black. Though surprisingly sound, it will not withstand rough treatment, so visitors should avoid climbing immediately after a rain. The tops of the rocks support a lush community of bushes and flowers, but the soil is thin and adheres poorly to the underlying rock; therefore, most routes do not top-out, but end at double- or triple-bolt anchors well below the summits.

**Climbing history:** The native people of the area, the Yuroks, were no doubt the first to explore these formations, although it is highly unlikely that they did any actual rock climbing, preferring to devote their energies to finding food and avoiding enemies. The construction of U.S. Highway 101 not only brought these picturesque rocks to the attention of Anglo-Europeans, but also provided convenient access.

Climbing as such did not begin here until the late 1980s and early 1990s. Local climbers in search of more sea cliff climbing than was offered farther south at Patricks Point or Moonstone headed north and were pleasantly surprised to discover the potential of this area. Matthias Halladay first tapped the rocks' potential with his early-1980s ascent of *Blackbeard's Tears* (II 5.11a A3) at Promontory. Paul Humphrey, Eric Chemello, Sean Leary, and their friends established many local classics, such as *Swallow the Sea* (5.12b) and *Pelican BVDs* (5.11b) at Footsteps, and *Great White* (5.12b/c) and *Redwood Burl* (5.12d) at Promontory. These sea cliffs came to the attention of the general climbing public with an illustrated article in the December 1998 issue of *Rock and Ice,* creating a new and broader climbing population. There is much here to challenge casual visitors and locals alike, and neither area is close to being "climbed-out."

**Rack:** Most routes here are sport climbs, although bolts are often supplemented with traditional gear. A selection of nuts and cams from ¼ inch to 2½ inches should suffice. In addition, take 14–15 quickdraws, runners, cordelette material, 6–8 removable bolts (RBs), and an adjustable wrench to test and tighten bolts. All climbers should note that the marine environment is very hostile to bolts. Even those marked "Stainless" lose strength after a few years. Every bolt should be treated as potentially unsound. To avoid this problem, the newer routes are making use of RBs.

**Descent:** In most cases, walking off or scrambling down is not an option. The leader simply lowers off or rappels from the anchors at the tops of the routes.

## TRIP PLANNING INFORMATION

**Area description:** Promontory is a compact group of large boulders and an amazing, almost continuously overhanging wall 100' high. Footsteps consists of two large stacks and two smaller stacks. The longer climbs reach about 120'. The rock is a fine-grained mixture of sandstone and graywacke. At present, no routes ascend the seaward faces of the outlying rocks, due to the potential tide and surf hazards.

**Location:** On California's north coast, approximately 13.4 miles north of the Humboldt/Del Norte county line.

**Camping:** There is no established camping available at either Promontory or Footsteps, although some hardy souls have camped at the foot of Promontory's main wall. Those wanting to spend more than a day here can make arrangements to stay at the American Youth Hostels Redwood Hostel, which lies just east of US 101 from the Promontory parking area. Other lodging and camping is available in the nearby town of Klamath (6 miles south) or in Crescent City (5 miles north).

**Climbing season:** All year, although long rainy periods from late October through April and foggy mornings from June through August limit activity; best in May and September.

**Restrictions and access issues:** Footsteps and Promontory are located on public land managed under the auspices of California State Beaches and Parks and the National Park Service. There are no managerial restrictions on access. The primary caution visitors should observe, however, is to remember that these are *sea cliffs* and present unique, physical access concerns. The shoreline access to both Promontory and Footsteps is safe only during low tide. The damp and mild climate fosters a luxuriant growth of plants on and atop these crags. Parties should try to avoid the urge to "garden" routes, especially as some harbor poison oak. These crags share a shortcoming common to sandstone outcrops elsewhere: during or immediately following wet weather, the rock can be soft or brittle, prompting special care to avoid damage to both rocks and climbers. The corrosive effects of the marine climate can seriously weaken bolts over a period of only a few years, and visitors should treat all bolts as suspect until satisfied that they are not.

**Guidebook:** There are two guidebooks for this area: Douglas W. LaFarge's self-published *Climbing Notes for the Humboldt County Coast* (1996), which includes numerous additional routes and variations not described in this guide, and Eric Chemello's beautifully-drawn, self-published collection of topos *Sandstone Supplement—Topographic Maps of Rock Climbs on the North Coast* (1998). Look for copies of these at area outdoor shops. Local climber Paul Humphrey is currently compiling a comprehensive guide to the area.

**Nearby mountain shops, guide services, and gyms:** The nearest mountain shops are Northern Mountain Supply in Eureka, and Adventure's Edge in Arcata. There are no guide services available for climbing at these crags. A small climbing wall has been installed at Humboldt State University. Visitors should contact the university's physical education department for more information.

**Services:** There are no services of any kind at either area, so visitors should plan to bring everything they plan to eat or drink. The lack of restrooms dictates care in choosing bathroom sites. Unfortunately, the most private ones lie at or near the foot of most of the climbing. The best approach is to visit the restrooms at the Lagoon Creek Picnic Area, which is located 0.5 mile south of the Promontory parking area.

**Emergency services:** In the event of an emergency, call 911 to summon an ambulance or rescue personnel. The nearest hospitals are Sutter Coast Hospital in Crescent City, Mad River Community Hospital in Arcata, and General Hospital and Saint Joseph's Hospital in Eureka.

**Nearby climbing areas:** Footsteps and Promontory are rather distant from any other developed climbing areas. The nearest is the Lost Rocks bouldering area, which is situated approximately 0.5 mile south of the mouth of the Klamath River and is accessed via a 1-mile drive along the coastal access road that leaves US 101 immediately south of the Klamath River bridge.

**Nearby attractions:** Crescent City, which lies 5 miles or so north of the crags, offers fine dining, antique shopping, and sport fishing. All along this section of coast lie the splendid redwood groves of Prairie Creek Redwoods and Jedediah Smith Redwoods State Parks and Redwood National Park. One can often watch whales or seals from the rocks, and the sunsets can be lovely.

**Finding the crags:** To reach Footsteps, drive north on US 101 from the junction of US 101 and California Highway 299 (just north of Arcata) for approximately 50.5 miles to the Humboldt/Del Norte County line. Continue another 13.5 miles to a signed vista point on the left. (Note that there are several pullouts in the area. The correct one has interpretive signs.) Pull off and park. From here, go north from the pullout about 20 yards, looking over the side for the faint and often overgrown trail. Once you find it, descend 0.5 mile, eventually arriving near the foot of North Rock. If you miss the trail (which is not unusual), avoid bushwhacking down to the rocks, as much of the undergrowth here is stinging nettle. Instead, approach along the beach by scrambling down a steep and exposed trail from the north end of Promontory's main wall, then pick your way over boulders and driftwood for 0.5 mile to the rocks. *Make sure you plan your day to avoid trying to return this way during high tide.*

For Promontory, drive north on US 101 as though going to Footsteps. Thirteen miles north of the Humboldt/Del Norte County line, and shortly after gaining your first view of the rock, reach a left-turn pocket just before the highway rises to a bridge over Wilson Creek. Turn left into a paved parking area at the edge of the beach. From here, walk north; wade across wide, shallow Wilson Creek; then continue along the beach on the other side. Where the way is blocked by a small, rocky bluff, take the trail up to and across its brow, then down its other side. Another quarter-mile of walking and boulder-hopping leads to the south end of the corridor whose overhanging east wall is Promontory's main climbing wall.

## FOOTSTEPS

Footsteps is the northernmost coastal climbing area in California and a worthy destination. The four rocks that make up its main climbing area—Shark Fin, North Rock, Center Rock, and South Rock—offer some of the finest maritime/sport climbing in the state, with most routes at or above the 5.10 level. Descend all climbs described by lowering off or rappelling. *For safety's sake, do not try to top out on the larger rocks, as they are heavily vegetated on top and descending safely would be a problem.*

# FOOTSTEPS

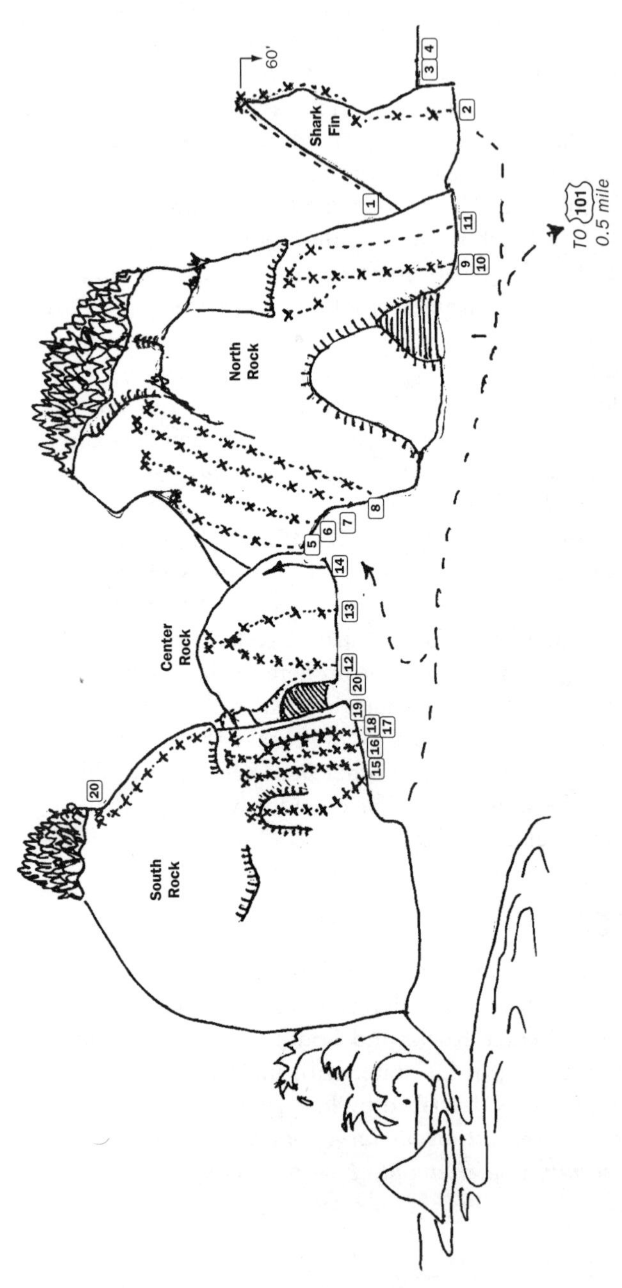

60'
Shark Fin
North Rock
Center Rock
South Rock
TO 101
0.5 mile
1
2
3
4
5
6
7
8
9
10
11
12
13
14
15
16
17
18
19
20
20

## SHARK FIN

At just over 60 feet high, aptly-named Shark Fin is the smallest of the rocks, yet it is perhaps the most distinctive. *Pelican BVDs,* which follows the rock's northeast arete, is a local classic. Descend by lowering off.

1. **Solo** (5.3 X) Make a scary climb of the comparatively low-angle but unprotected south arete of Shark Fin. It is possible to use *Solo* as a means of rigging a toprope for Route 2.
2. **Pelican BVDs** (5.11b) Follow the steep, narrow, and leaning northeast arete of the formation, clipping 6 bolts before reaching the 2-bolt anchor on top. Although the technical crux lies just past the first bolt, beware of tricky ground near the top.
3. **Tippy Toes** (5.10b) Around the corner to the right from Route 2 are two bolted sport routes. Ascend the left-hand climb up the increasingly overhanging face; 6 bolts to a 2-bolt anchor.
4. **Tap Dance** (5.10a) Climb the face right of *Tippy Toes* past 6 bolts to a shared anchor with Route 3.

## NORTH ROCK

North Rock is the largest of the formations that make up Footsteps, and it offers numerous interesting routes on its north, east, and south sides. The top is heavily vegetated, so all descents require lowering or rappelling. If you use a 60-meter rope, this becomes easier.

5. **Weltering Splash** (5.9) This is the bolted line at the far-left edge of the south face. Begin on the seaward side of a low ridge, then head up past 3 bolts to a 2-bolt anchor.
6. **Land Shark** (5.10d) Start about 35' right of Route 5, at the lowest point on the south face. Move up past 2 bolts, then encounter more challenging climbing as you work up the face, clipping 5 more bolts before reaching the 2-bolt anchor. Meet the crux just above the second bolt.
7. **Tsunami** (5.11c/d) Begin about 15' right of *Land Shark.* Proceed up similar, but trickier climbing protected by 8 bolts. Lower off (80') from the 2-bolt anchor. For a milder (i.e., 5.11b) version of this route, climb *Tsunami* to its third bolt, then move up left to join *Land Shark* at its fourth bolt. Continue up *Land Shark* to its next-to-last bolt, then face-climb up right to the anchor atop *Tsunami.* Save some strength for the crux; it lurks just below the anchors.
8. **Cutlass Supreme a.k.a. Radical Mass Movement** (5.11b) Locate this, the third major line on the south face, about 10' right of *Tsunami.* Clip a procession of 7 bolts on your way to the 2-bolt anchor 80' up. As on *Tsunami,* you must do the crux moves right at the end.

9. **Poison Oak** (5.11b) Find this nifty, overhanging climb on the east face, just right of a prominent cave. Climb the overhanging wall, clipping 5 bolts, then move up left past 2 more to the lower-right corner of a slab. Without a second bolt at this point to safeguard a lower-off descent, you must either traverse right to the anchors at the top of *Whales Brow* or climb the unprotected slab to an easy groove and follow it to a pair of bolts just below the summit gardens.
10. **Whales Brow** (5.11b) Begin this more direct and popular version of *Poison Oak* as though you are climbing that route. Follow *Poison Oak* to its fifth bolt, then continue directly upward on continuous 5.11 climbing past another bolt to a 2-bolt anchor.
11. **Lurch** (5.11c TR) Set up the toprope anchor for this route by using a single bolt 15' right of the anchor for *Whales Brow.* (For added safety, use the *Whales Brow* anchor as an additional anchor point.) This done, ascend the overhanging face midway between Route 10 and the northeast buttress of the rock.

## CENTER ROCK

Center Rock is the smallest of the three main stacks, but it offers several good climbs, including some interesting toprope routes on the seaward face. The routes described all lie on the rock's north and east faces. By climbing *Loner,* you can establish a toprope for *Drilling Me Softly* and *Bolt 45.*

12. **Drilling Me Softly** (5.11a) Begin this route about 8' right of a boulder cave between South Rock and Center Rock. Face-climb up and gradually right, clipping 6 bolts, then move directly upward to the 2-bolt anchor. Surmount the crux just below the third bolt.
13. **Bolt 45** (5.10d) Start this easier version about 15' right of Route 12. Climb past 2 bolts, pull the crux, then continue past 2 more bolts. Work up left to a fifth bolt, then straight up to the anchor shared with Route 12.
14. **Loner** (5.2 X) For this dangerously unprotected route, head right from *Bolt 45,* passing around the corner to the north face. Follow the obvious line to the top.

## SOUTH ROCK

South Rock provides some of the area's best climbing and its sunniest rock—a real godsend on a chilly, windy day. These routes are a little bit shorter than those on North Rock, but they are no less charming or challenging.

15. **Swallow the Sea** (5.12b) Look for an obvious line of many bolts that leads up to a conspicuous arch about halfway up the rock's east face; these mark this local classic. Climb up left past 3 bolts, then climb directly up

past 6 more before moving up to and over the roof at the top of the arch to reach the 2-bolt anchor. The crux, which occurs both above and below the route's sixth bolt, requires very difficult and continuous climbing.

16. **Sprinkling Pockets** (5.12b) Start this route just right of the arch climbed by Route 15. Climb very steep rock past 4 bolts to the first really hard section, move up past 2 more bolts, pull the second "crux," then keep on past 2 more bolts to the 2-bolt anchor.
17. **Osteoporosis** (5.11b) Begin this slightly longer route 8' right of Route 16, at a point directly below the left end of a small roof that lies about halfway up the rock on its northeast side. Climb rock that begins as overhanging and gradually eases to merely vertical by the time you have clipped the fourth bolt. Face-climb past one more, then begin a long, difficult crux section with a bolt in the midst of it. Two more bolts take you to the 2-bolt anchor under a small roof.
18. **Porifera** (5.10d) Find this route 15' right of *Osteoporosis* and just left of a conspicuous flake on the rock's northeast buttress. Climb parallel to the flake's left edge. After clipping the route's sixth bolt, move up left (5.10c/d) to the last bolt on *Osteoporosis,* clip it, then move up to that route's 2-bolt anchor.
19. **Hammer Toes** (5.8 A2 or 5.9 R) Start below a prominent groove 10' right of *Porifera.* Climb into the groove, then ascend the groove and continue up the face above to a 2-bolt anchor below the right side of the *Osteoporosis* roof.
20. **Toe Hold** (I 5.9) Begin this, the longest route at Footsteps, by climbing to the first bolt of *Drilling Me Softly* on Center Rock's east face. Work up left to a short ramp that slants up left. Follow it, gradually working up and over a boulder jumble between South Rock and Central Rock. Scramble through this section, then head up left to the north face of South Rock. Regain solid rock again, then face-climb past 7 bolts to a 2-bolt anchor just below the cap of summit vegetation.

## PROMONTORY

Promontory is a compact group of rocks clustered at the seaward terminus of a point of land between two lovely, black-sand beaches. Though fairly easy to reach, the area retains a marked sense of remoteness and seriousness. Promontory's main climbing wall is its primary attraction, and what an attraction it is: almost 90' high and overhanging its base by nearly 20'! On this semi-enclosed, concave marvel lie nearly a dozen fabulous climbs. By scrambling onto the enormous boulders opposite the wall, you can gain an

# PROMONTORY, MAIN WALL

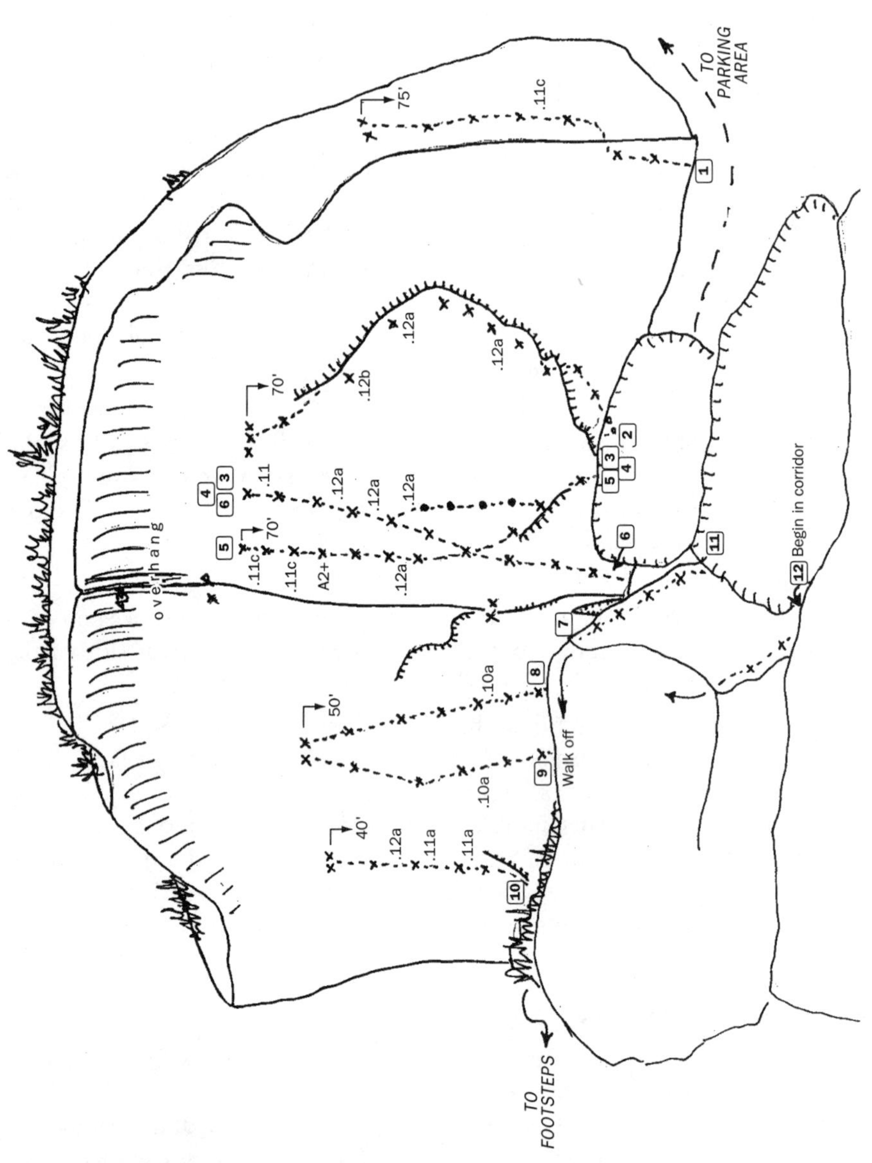

uninterrupted view of the face and of the efforts of those on it. Several of the routes on the main wall follow zones or streaks of strangely porous, pocketed rock resembling a giant Swiss cheese. With no sight of beach or highway, and no sound but the muted roar of the surf and the steady pat-pat-pat of dripping water, this is a very other-worldly place. Due to the abundance of wet, shallow-rooted vegetation on the very top of the Promontory formation, no routes actually go to the summit. Successful leaders lower off from single-, double-, or triple-bolt anchors; a 50-meter rope is adequate for doing so. Routes are listed from right to left, in the order they are encountered when coming from the south.

1. **Shrapnel** (5.11c/d) Start just left of the arete formed by the junction of the main wall's west and south faces. Ascend the arete to the upper of 2 bolts, then swing around the corner onto the bald, black-varnished south face. Using friction and thin crimps, climb past another 4 bolts right of the arete to a double-bolt anchor.
2. **Redwood Burl** (5.13a) Begin near a fire ring situated at the foot of an amazing flake crack that begins as a low-angle ramp that sweeps up to the right, eventually turning into a thin dihedral and winding up as an arch—all on an overhanging, pocketed wall. Follow the ramp up right past 3 bolts, then more directly up, passing a 5.12a section above the next bolt. Four bolts higher still, begin a long section of continuous 5.12b–5.12d with a bolt in the middle. After clipping 2 more, you reach the 3 bolts of the anchor.
3. **Straight White** (5.12c/d) Start just left of the base of the *Redwood Burl* ramp. Climb up left, following the course of *Great White*. When you reach the second bolt, head directly up the wall, using ⅜-inch RBs to plug 4 holes as you make the crux moves. Join *Albino* at its sixth bolt, then follow it to a single-bolt anchor. Gingerly lower off.
4. **Great White** (5.12b/c) Start this local classic as for *Straight White*. Make a rising traverse left past 3 bolts, then move more steeply up left to a fourth bolt, which is shared with the next three routes. Now work up and slightly right for the rest of the climb, using another 5 bolts to protect tricky moves on pocketed rock. A final bolt provides the lower-off anchor.
5. **White Flight** (5.12c) Climb *Great White* until you reach the fourth bolt, then continue up left to a fifth bolt before striking out directly upward past 5 more bolts before reaching the single-bolt anchor.
6. **Albino** (5.12c) Find the start of this route 20' left of the starting point of *Great White*. Look for the first 2 bolts, which are placed just left of a large flake. Face-climb and lieback the flake, using the 2 bolts for protection, then move up right past 2 more bolts, where you join *Great*

*White* for the rest of the way up the face; 10 bolts.

MAIN WALL, PROMONTORY

7. **Blackbeard's Tears** (II 5.11a A3+) You will have no trouble identifying this intimidating line, which follows a remarkable single, thin crack up the wall. Unfortunately, you will also notice that this crack is a drainage for moisture above, and water seeps out of it continually, often dripping free to land an amazing distance away from the wall. **Pitch 1:** Beginning at a wide, flared crack with a flake jammed in the bottom, climb past the flare, then continue up a 5.11a fingertip crack to a double-bolt anchor. Most parties lower off from here, but if you feel brave, go on to **Pitch 2:** Using stoppers and small TCUs to ¾", aid up the A2/A3 crack to a fixed pin and bolt, from which you can lower off. You can top out on this route, but to continue the crack requires A3+ aid climbing over the summit roof with an unpleasant and dangerous finish.
8. **Ride the Woody** (5.10c) Look for another section of pale, pocketed wall about 35' left of Route 7. Climb the right-hand series of 6 bolts 50' to a 2-bolt anchor.
9. **Humboldt Current** (5.10a) Beginning about 10' left of Route 8, ascend the left side of the pocketed streak. Pass the crux just beyond the second of 5 bolts that lead to the 2-bolt anchor shared with Route 8.

10. **Pulling Teeth** (5.12a) Start at a left-facing flake close to the ground, about 15' left of *Humboldt Current.* Climb the flake, then follow a line of 4 bolts leading to the 2-bolt anchor. You meet the crux above the third bolt.

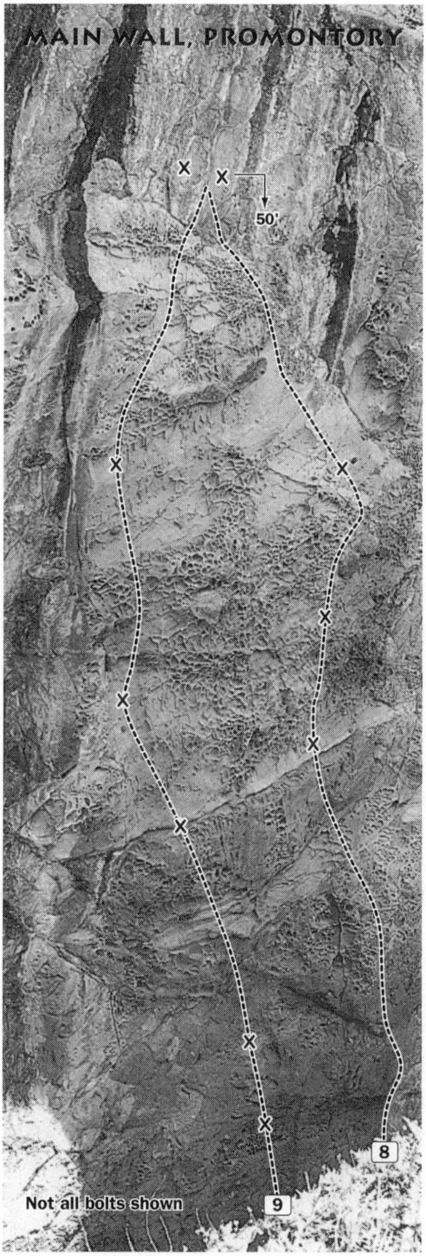

The following routes ascend the giant boulder northwest of the main wall. From the vicinity of the fire ring, a narrow, damp corridor leads seaward. The routes follow the aretes at the beginning and end of this corridor. A trail leads down to the fire ring area from the top of this rock.

11. **Centipede** (5.9) Almost immediately after entering the corridor, you can spot this route's 4 bolts just left of the right-hand edge of a very steep, smooth slab. Chimney up out of the corridor to reach the first bolt, then continue up the face, pinching and occasionally liebacking the arete on the right as you work you way to the top of the rock. For a trickier start, begin in the small, right-facing dihedral just right of the bolted face. From the top of the dihedral, make an awkward move left around the corner to the first bolt.



12. **Tentacle** (5.8 R/X) Reach the start of this route by going through the corridor (watch out for wet, slippery rock underfoot) to its far end. Chimney and face-climb up out of the corridor and onto angular, broken rock right of the arete. Clip a meager 2 bolts on your way to the top.

## PATRICKS POINT STATE PARK

One of the most popular places on California's north coast for camping, hiking, sightseeing, and climbing is Patricks Point State Park, located on a prominent headland 6 miles north of the city of Trinidad. Here, visitors can hike through dense, temperate rainforest of Sitka spruce and western hemlock; admire beautiful wild rhododendrons; watch gray whales, seals, and even orcas; look for wave-polished agates on rocky beaches; and enjoy some excellent rock climbing. The rocks consist of cliffs and stacks of brown, Franciscan formation sandstone and darker greenstone and graywacke. Some, such as Ceremonial Rock and Mussel Rock, stand atop old marine terraces, far removed from the ocean, while others rise practically from the water's edge. This range of settings creates a very different climbing atmosphere at each formation. The inland crags are usually drier, but they are also more vegetated. The crags on the shore tend to be cleaner and more solid, but also more brittle. As is the case elsewhere, the salt spray creates a harsh environment for fixed protection, so climbers should treat all fixed anchors as suspect and test them accordingly. The climbs offer a full spectrum of difficulties from easy, low-fifth-class routes to exposed, challenging outings for the most experienced. Most climbs are one pitch in length, and many can be toproped.

**Climbing history:** The first climbers in this area were the native people. Foraging parties often scrambled and climbed in their search for shellfish or seabirds' eggs. Early white settlers concerned themselves more with farming, fishing, or logging than to bother with the challenges or "nuisance" of sea cliffs or rock outcrops. Recognizing the almost universal appeal of high rocks, the management of Patricks Point State Park constructed stairways and scenic overlooks on Wedding Rock and Ceremonial Rock. No doubt these improvements sparked the imaginations of latent climbers.

During the 1950s and 1960s, most climbing activity focused on aid climbing in preparation for more ambitious routes elsewhere. Records of these climbers and their exploits are scant at best. It was not until the late 1970s that rock climbers from nearby Humboldt State University began to explore the free climbing possibilities these crags offer. Concentrating initially on toproped climbs, habitués realized that, with proper preparation, they could forge quality climbs capable of being led and protected. Most of the early free climbs may be repeated at the inland formations of Patricks Point State Park: Ceremonial Rock and Mussel Rock.

The 1980s and 1990s marked the golden age of climbing development on the North Coast. Local climbers recognized the area's value and potential as a climbing destination in its own right, instead of merely as a substitute or training ground for "the real thing." Some of these quality routes, many of which were established by such local aces as Paul Humphrey, Eric Chemello,

# PATRICKS POINT STATE PARK

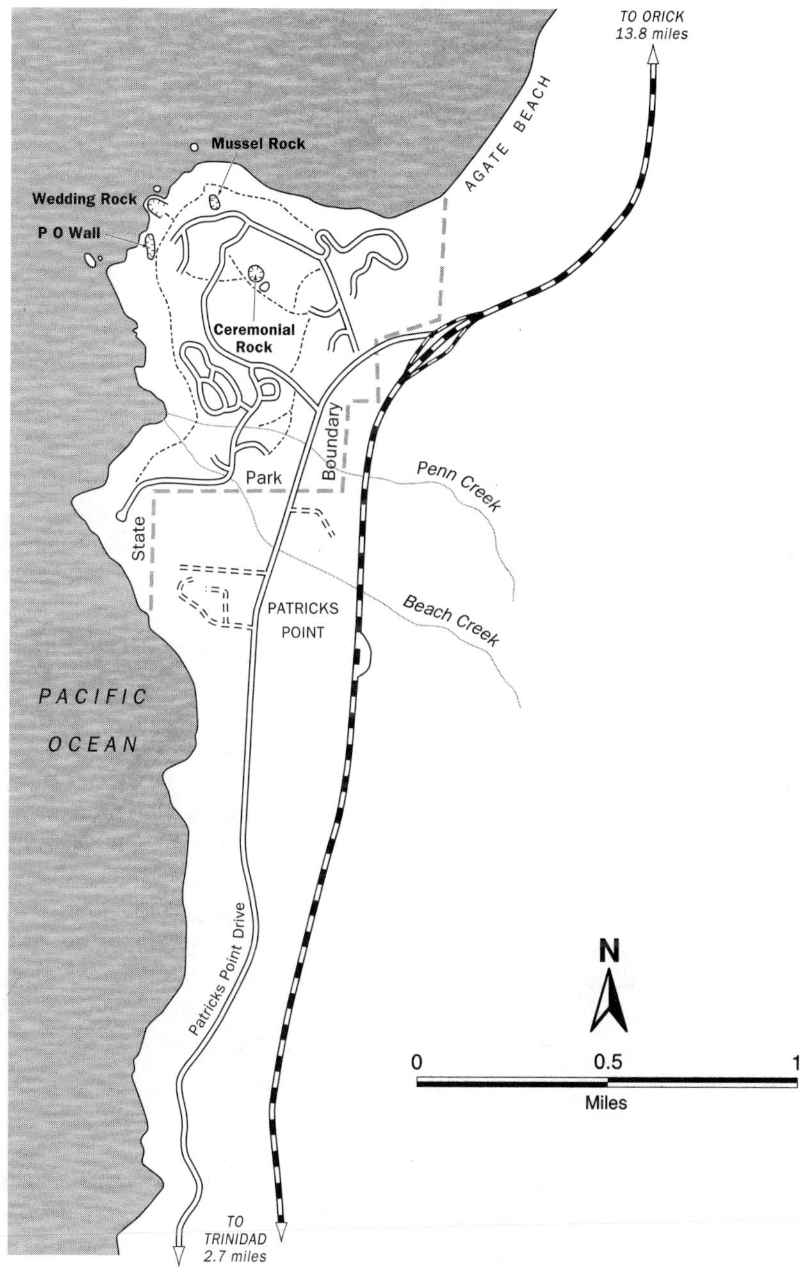

David LaFarge, Randy Adrian, and Sean Leary, include *Dizzy Dial* (5.12a), *Whale Nation* (5.11c), and *Superstitious* (5.12b). With the discovery of the climbing potential at Footsteps and Promontory, new route development at Patricks Point has languished for the past few years, but considerable potential for quality routes remains.

**Rack:** A light rack of 8–10 stoppers and hexes and a few cams to 2" suffices for most climbs. Supplement these with several runners, 8–10 quickdraws, and a small adjustable wrench for testing and tightening fixed anchors.

**Descent:** Descents from the rocks at Patricks Point are as varied as the formations themselves: some can be scrambled down from, while others require rappels or lowering off. Specific descent directions accompany the description of each crag.

## TRIP PLANNING INFORMATION

**Area description:** Crags consist of sandstone, graywacke, and fine-grained conglomerate bluffs, stacks, boulders, and dry-docked outcrops on forested or brush-covered marine terraces. Many formations rise directly from the water's edge, adding both interest and potential hazard due to tidal fluctuations and occasional storm surf.

**Location:** On or near California's north coast, 20 miles north of Arcata in Humboldt County.

**Camping:** The park offers a nice, 123-space campground with flush toilets, piped water, showers, fire rings, and picnic tables for $12–$15 per night. Reservations should be made through DESTINET at 800-444-7275. There are also many private campgrounds, RV parks, and motels south of the park, along Patricks Point Road.

**Climbing season:** All year, although long rainy periods from late October through April and foggy mornings from June through August limit activity; best in May and September.

**Restrictions and access issues:** There is a $5.00 per vehicle day-use fee for Patricks Point State Park. Pedestrians and cyclists pay less, but climbers should not attempt to park along the frontage road to save money; the shoulder is simply too narrow to safely do so. The crags at Patricks Point State Park are *sea cliffs* and present unique, physical access concerns. Some, such as Wedding Rock, are most easily and safely accessed during low tide. At high tide, or during unsettled weather, waves become dangerously large, making merely getting wet the least of one's worries. The damp and mild climate fosters a luxuriant growth of plants on and atop these crags. Parties should control the urge to "garden" routes, especially as some harbor poison oak. These crags share a shortcoming common to many sandstone outcrops elsewhere: during or immediately following wet weather, the rock can be soft or brittle, prompting special care to avoid damage to both rocks and climbers.

There are two primary access issues in the park. First, even though many routes have been established as sport routes, the park managers have banned the bolting of new routes. Park visitors should plan to toprope most climbs. Elsewhere, bolts have been placed on a number of climbs. Because of the softness of the rock and the corrosive nature of the marine environment, climbers should remember that any anchor is potentially suspect and climb accordingly. Any new or replacement bolts should be of stainless steel with stainless steel hangers. Second, the park has a duty to safeguard historical and prehistoric artifacts. One of the latter, a Native American midden, or rubbish-heap, lies just south of P O Wall. Previously, the climbers' trail passed over this site, and the trail has been closed. Climbers should respect this closure and use the longer approach described in this guide.

Finally, climbers need to keep in mind that this park is heavily used by visitors of all kinds, each of whom expects a pleasant experience. Please respect the other park users by keeping a low profile and by acting as goodwill ambassadors for climbing. A little consideration can repay big dividends in public support.

**Guidebook:** There are two guidebooks for this area: Douglas W. LaFarge's self-published *Climbing Notes for the Humboldt County Coast* (1996) and Eric Chemello's *Sandstone Supplement—Topographic Maps of Rock Climbs on the North Coast* (1998). Look for copies of these at area outdoor shops. Paul Humphrey is currently compiling a comprehensive guide to the area.

**Nearby mountain shops, guide services, and gyms:** The nearest mountain shops are Northern Mountain Supply in Eureka, and Adventure's Edge in Arcata. While there are no guide services available, Center Activities, a student outing and recreation program at Humboldt State University in Arcata, offers climbing instruction. A small climbing wall has been installed at Humboldt State University. Visitors should contact the university's physical education department for more information.

**Services:** Visitors have access to piped water, restrooms, campgrounds with showers, and interpretive services. Lodging, food, and other supplies can be obtained in the communities of Eureka, Arcata, McKinleyville, Trinidad, Orick, and Crescent City.

**Emergency services:** In the event of an emergency, call 911 to summon an ambulance or rescue personnel. If you are climbing at Patricks Point State Park, contact park personnel for assistance. The nearest hospitals are Sutter Coast Hospital in Crescent City, Mad River Community Hospital in Arcata, and General Hospital and Saint Joseph's Hospital in Eureka.

**Nearby climbing areas:** Just south of Trinidad lie the beach crags and boulders of Luffenholtz Beach, Houda Point, Moonstone Beach, and Elephant Rock.

**Nearby attractions:** The North Coast offers many attractions for visitors, including the spectacular redwood forests of Prairie Creek Redwoods State

Park and Redwoods National Park; the beautiful, "lost world" atmosphere of Fern Canyon; black sand beaches; whale watching from several scenic overlooks; sea kayaking at Big Lagoon and Freshwater Lagoon; and fine dining and shopping in the Victorian towns of Eureka, Arcata, and Ferndale.

**Finding the crags:** From the junction of U.S. Highway 101 and California Highway 299 just north of Arcata, drive north on US 101 for 18 miles to the signed Patricks Point State Park exit. From Crescent City, drive south on US 101 for 48 miles to the Patricks Point exit. Either way, leave the freeway and head west, then south on the frontage road (Patricks Point Road) for 0.5 mile to the park entrance on the right.

## CEREMONIAL ROCK

Ceremonial Rock is the park's oldest sea cliff, a fact demonstrated by the fact that it no longer stands beside the ocean, but instead lurks among the trees on a marine terrace high above its former place on shore. The rising coastal lands carried Ceremonial Rock up with them, and it now stands as a sentinel overlooking a large meadow. The view from the top is quite good, which prompted the state park managers to construct a wood-and-stone staircase up the formation's south and east sides. The stairs provide easy access for establishing toprope anchors, as well as a convenient way down. This crag is popular with climbers and non-climbers alike, so climbers should be cautious and courteous, and remain aware of the risk of falling debris from both groups.

Though not immediately obvious, Ceremonial Rock is the nearest crag to the park entrance. Shortly after passing the entry booth, the road forks. About 0.3 mile along the right-hand fork is a parking lot on the left. From this lot, a short trail, which begins across the road, leads through dense forest for 0.25 mile to the south side of the rock. If this parking area is full or is missed, continuing along the road for another 0.3 mile leads to another fork in the road. From here, a footpath leads back southeast across the meadow to the rock. Routes are listed from left to right, beginning with the northwest buttress, the high prow visible from the meadow.

1. **No New Tale to Tell** (5.12a TR) Beginning directly below a jutting block at the top of the rock's north buttress and right of an obvious, vegetated crack, climb steep rock to a horizontal break, then continue up the smooth face just right of the jungle-crack. A final pull over the summit block takes you to a 2-bolt anchor.

2. **Regular Route** (5.10a) Start below a line of bolts 12' right of Route 1. Chase a series of 6 bolts up the face to the right end of a horizontal break, then follow a crack on the right that gradually curves back left. Either continue up left to the anchor atop Route 1, or head up right along another crack to the summit guardrail. Take several small stoppers

NORTH FACE, CEREMONIAL ROCK
Walk off
1
2
3

and TCUs to ¾". For a more demanding variation, try *Headstrong* (5.11a TR). Follow *Regular Route* to its last bolt, then head up left, following a shallow 5.11a groove up the wall about 6' right of Route 1.

3. **Secret Ceremony** (5.10b TR) Begin about 15' right of *Regular Route* and below a series of small overlaps. Thread your way up to, and through the overlaps, then head up the face to a shallow crack and follow it to the top.
4. **Southwest Buttress—Left Side** (5.6–5.8 TR) Climb any of several possible routes on the west side of the buttress at the right edge of the rock's west face.
5. **Southwest Buttress—Right Side** (5.7) Face-climb up the left edge of the crag's concave south face.
6. **South Face** (5.11c TR) Ascend the overhanging dihedral in the middle of the south face.
7. **South Buttress** (5.2 TR) Begin about 10' right of Route 6 and climb the right side of the south face, staying left of the actual buttress.
8. **Mosey Mantle** (5.10a TR) Locate this route on the smooth, slabby southwest face of a companion formation right of the staircase and separated from Ceremonial Rock by a shallow notch. Scramble across the notch to set up or retrieve your toprope. Basically, climb the middle of the face. You can make many variations to this route, some of which may be easier.

## MUSSEL ROCK

Although it lies conveniently close to parking and picnic facilities, Mussel Rock has not seen the degree of development shown on nearby Wedding Rock or Ceremonial Rock. The rock's name is a mystery, as it lies high above the ocean, well away from any place a mussel could live. The climbing is actually pretty good, especially on the 30-foot west face of the rock. There are no fixed anchors, so nearly all routes require topropes manned by belayers stationed on the flat top of the crag. Approach the rock by either hiking across the meadow from Ceremonial Rock, hiking on the park's perimeter trail, or by driving on the paved loop toward the interpretive center and parking in a paved parking area near the restrooms adjacent to the Mussel Rock picnic area. Descend by scrambling down the somewhat mossy northeast side. The following routes are described from left to right, beginning at the mossy, overhung north face.

9. **North Overhang** (5.9/5.10a TR) Ascend the scooped-out north face of the rock—many variations are possible.

10. **Drumroll** (5.7 TR) Start below the left end of an obvious, small roof visible a few feet above a small ledge. Pass left of the roof, then head up left to the top.
11. **Farewell to Arms** (5.8) Begin below a small roof above a ledge near the left-central part of the face. Climb to the roof, traverse left under it, then angle up right and follow a flared groove to a higher, smaller roof just below the summit. Pull the roof to reach the top. Take protection to 1½".
12. **Southwest Corner** (5.0) Begin a few feet right of *Farewell to Arms,* then head up right to a small platform halfway up the southwest corner of the rock. Follow a short dihedral to the top.
13. **George of the Jungle** (5.2 TR) Climb the center of the face visible above the park road.

## WEDDING ROCK AND THE STACKS

One of the most famous, and certainly the most photogenic, of the crags at Patricks Point State Park is Wedding Rock, a large sandstone bluff that rises from the edge of the blue Pacific at the end of a short finger of land flanked by rocky beaches. The spectacular view and the opportunity to watch for whales led to the construction of a trail to the shoulder below the top of the rock, where a stone guardrail protects the thousands of summer visitors who make the short ascent. North of the hulking mass of the main rock stand two slender sea stacks, both of which offer exciting and very photogenic climbing. Route development has concentrated on the stacks and on the south face of Wedding Rock. Worthwhile routes could be worked out on the seaward face, but the prospect of getting slapped by a big wave while climbing has justifiably curtailed exploration.

To reach Wedding Rock, take the right-hand fork where the road splits shortly after passing the entry booth to the park. About 0.6 mile later, where the road again splits at the northwest end of a broad, lush meadow, take the left-hand fork and follow it as it curves left for another 0.3 mile to a large parking area on the right, overlooking the cove south of Wedding Rock. From the north end of the parking area, follow a short, obvious trail out to the saddle east of the rock. For the south side routes, head left down a strange "ladder" of timbers connected by steel cables to the cove. For the stacks, take a narrow, but obvious path downhill to the north, eventually curving left. Access the climbs by passing through the notch between the two pinnacles. You can walk off from the top of Wedding Rock, but you must rappel from the stacks. The following climbs are listed from right to left.

14. **Zigzag Crack** (5.7) Starting at the base of the rock's somewhat sheltered southeast face, follow an obvious finger-to-hand crack that switchbacks up the face. Where the crack breaks into two parallel fissures, take your

EAST SIDE OF THE STACKS

pick; the upper one is slightly harder. When the crack ends, face-climb up right to the trail. Take a selection of gear to 2".

15. **Lost Sailor** (5.10a) Start at the left edge of the southeast face, at a point below a right-slanting flake/ramp. Face-climb to the flake, then follow it up right to its end and join *Zigzag Crack*.
16. **Riptide** (I 5.10a R) Right of the huge dihedral that splits the south side of the rock, look for a smaller, clean-cut, overhanging dihedral. **Pitch 1:** Lieback and jam the dihedral to a sloping belay spot at its top. **Pitch 2:** Either exit left onto a run-out slab leading to the top, or follow the crack up right, then climb a short wall and friction up right, then up to the top.
17. **Wedding Rock Dihedral** (I 5.9) Ascend the obvious, huge dihedral by any of many possible variations.

*The following two routes should not be attempted during heavy surf or high tide.*

18. **Keel Haul** (I 5.9) Begin about 50' left of the huge dihedral. **Pitch 1:** Climb broken rock along a line of weakness, eventually working up left into a small, right-facing corner. Ascend it, then proceed a bit higher to a belay stance. **Pitch 2:** Climb the steep, orange wall above, then head up right on easy ground to the guardrail. Take gear to 1".

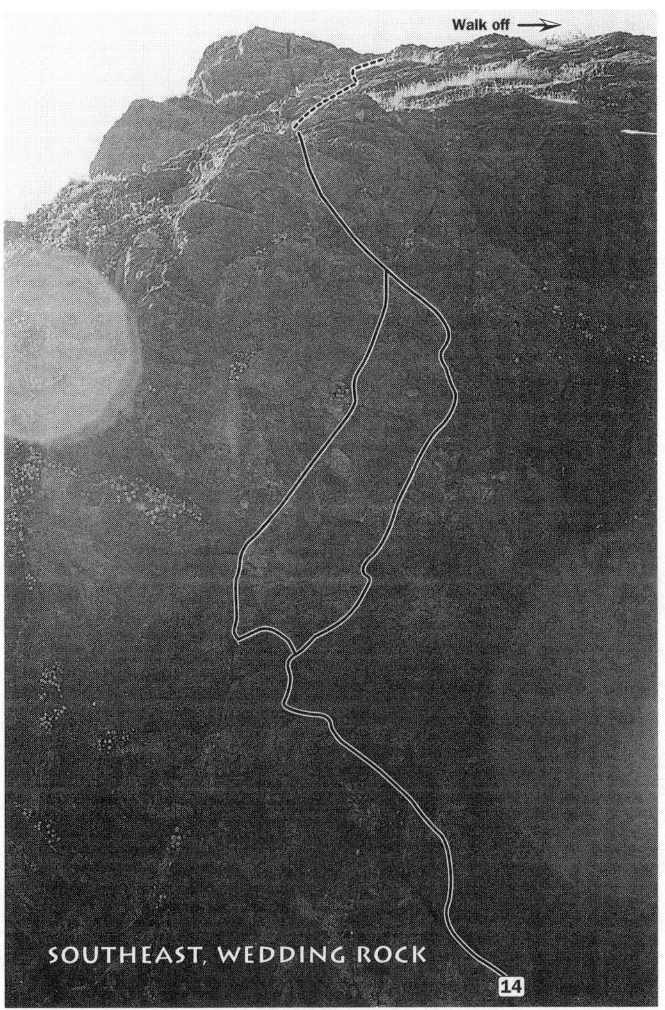

SOUTHEAST, WEDDING ROCK

19. **Out to Sea** (I 5.10b) Start 25' left of *Keel Haul,* at the foot of a face seamed by many thin cracks. **Pitch 1:** Climb the 5.10b face to a diagonal crack, follow it up right into a niche, then move up left to a belay stance. **Pitch 2:** Climb a short, right-facing corner to a sloping ledge, traverse left, then climb a short corner to reach easy ground at the top.

SOUTH FACE, WEDDING ROCK

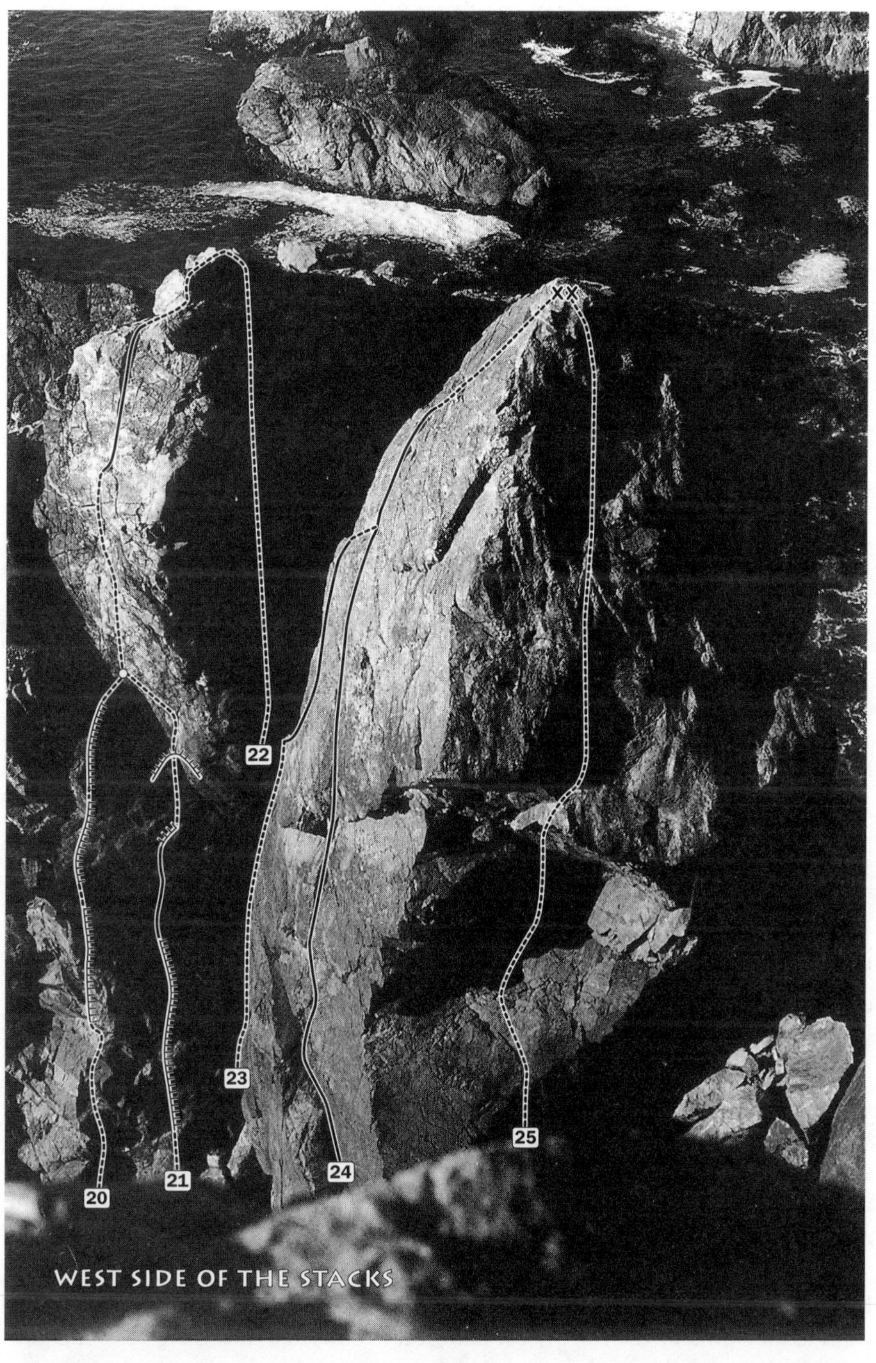
22
23
24
25
20
21
WEST SIDE OF THE STACKS

The next several routes lie on the west and south faces of the sea stacks north of Wedding Rock.

20. **Nautilus** (I 5.9) After passing through the notch between the two stacks, drop down a gully to the boulders at the foot of the crags. Begin this route practically at the water's edge, below a series of left-facing flakes. **Pitch 1:** Face-climb to the flakes, then lieback and jam to their top, move right, and belay at a very small stance. **Pitch 2:** Face-climb to a short 5.6 crack, then scramble to the top from its upper end. Rappel from slings to return.

21. **Seawolf** (I 5.10b) Start 10' right of *Nautilus.* **Pitch 1:** Climb a difficult, offset crack. From its top, head up to a small arch, then pull over and head up left to join *Nautilus* at its belay stance. **Pitch 2:** Finish as for *Nautilus.*

22. **Slip Sliding Away** (5.11a TR) After climbing one of the two preceding routes, leave your rappel rope in place and try your skill on the south face of North Stack, climbing directly up from the notch.

23. **High Tide Crack** (5.10d TR) Begin in the notch separating the two stacks. Climb a good, but strenuous crack out of the notch. From its upper end, make a short, scary traverse right to connect with the upper part of *Low Tide Crack* and follow it to the summit of South Stack.

24. **Low Tide Crack** (5.9) Ascend the quality jams on this classic crack on South Stack's west face. When the crack ends, face-climb to the 2-bolt anchor. Rappel down the south side of the rock.

25. **South Stack—South Face** (5.11a TR) Climb the face from the notch between South Stack and Wedding Rock.

## ROCKY POINT

Rocky Point is the next headland south of Wedding Rock. Although it is higher than Wedding Rock, it lacks the other rock's isolated atmosphere, and the view from its top is not nearly so expansive. Nevertheless, it offers some excellent climbing, free of most of the tidal considerations that limit access to portions of Wedding Rock. The climbs on Rocky Point ascend two primary formations: Black Rock, a small, dark wall on the north side, which forms the south enclosing wall for the cove between Wedding Rock and Rocky Point; and P O Wall, a steep, west-facing wall that lies just south of the lookout point atop the promontory. Climbs range up to 150' in length.

To reach Rocky Point, take the right-hand fork where the road splits shortly after passing the entry booth to the park. About 0.6 mile later, where the road again splits at the northwest end of a broad, lush meadow, take the left-hand fork and follow it as it curves left for another 0.3 mile to a large parking area on the right, overlooking the cove south of Wedding Rock. For Black Rock, follow a short, obvious trail from the north end of the parking area to

the saddle east of Wedding Rock, then head left down a "ladder" of timbers connected by steel cables, to the cove. The routes lie on the dark, 50-foot wall on the left. For P O Wall, take the Rim Trail from the south end of the parking area south past the spur that leads out to the overlook. About 0.12 mile past the overlook trail, head down right on a narrow path to the beach, then walk and scramble back north (right) to a large boulder at the foot of the wall. Head directly up to the wall from here.

To descend the routes on Black Rock, scramble down toward the ocean and circle back around to the right. From the climbs on P O Wall, you can follow the overlook path back to the parking area from the routes that top out; otherwise, you will need to trail a second rope and rappel your route.

## BLACK ROCK

The following routes lie on Black Rock and are listed from left to right.

26. **Bon Voyage** (5.9) Climb the left-hand of three wide cracks that split the wall, converging near the top. Take pro to 6", or set up a toprope.
27. **Clipper Ship** (5.6) Jam the center crack, a fine, easy offwidth. Take pro to 4".
28. **Schooner** (5.7) Start at the foot of a left-facing dihedral 15' right of *Clipper Ship*. Climb the left-leaning corner to the ledge at the top of the wall.

## P O WALL

These routes ascend P O Wall and are described in left-to-right order.

29. **Dizzy Dial** (5.12a) Locate the start of this local classic by heading directly toward the cliff from the large boulder. Begin at the lower-left corner of a smooth slab that ends under a right-slanting roof. Climb the left margin of the slab past 5 bolts to the roof. Pull through a break at the left end of the 5.10a roof to a bolt, then make some tricky 5.12a moves up left to another bolt. Climb the continuous 5.11c face to the last bolt, then brave more 5.11 climbing to the 2-bolt anchor. Using a second rope, rappel the route.
30. **Whale Nation** (5.11c) Begin at the right edge of the slab that starts *Dizzy Dial.* Face-climb along the slab's right margin, then pass over the upper-right end of the slanting roof and angle up right to a pair of belay bolts. Use 8 bolts along the way for protection. With a second rope, rappel from here.
31. **Whale Nation Continuation** (5.12c TR) If you don't mind the complex logistics, this is a worthwhile outing. Begin by climbing *Whale Nation.* From the belay bolts, charge up a strenuous, overhanging dihedral/groove that only gets harder the higher you go. From its top, stagger up to a belay bolt near a tree on the top of the crag.
32. **California Coast** (A3+) Look for a thin crack that slices up through the steep wall 70' right of *Whale Nation.* Using thin stoppers, many pins, hooks, and anything else that works, nail up the crack to the top of the crag.
33. **Superstitious** (5.12b R) Begin this challenging route at the foot of an indentation shaped like an inverted triangle that lies at the southern end of the wall. From a conspicuous hole at the lowest point of the indentation, face-climb up the face and left-leaning seam above, eventually passing up and out of the indentation at its upper-left corner. Clip 8 bolts to protect this route. Be aware, however, that the face climbing near the top is run-out.

# P O WALL

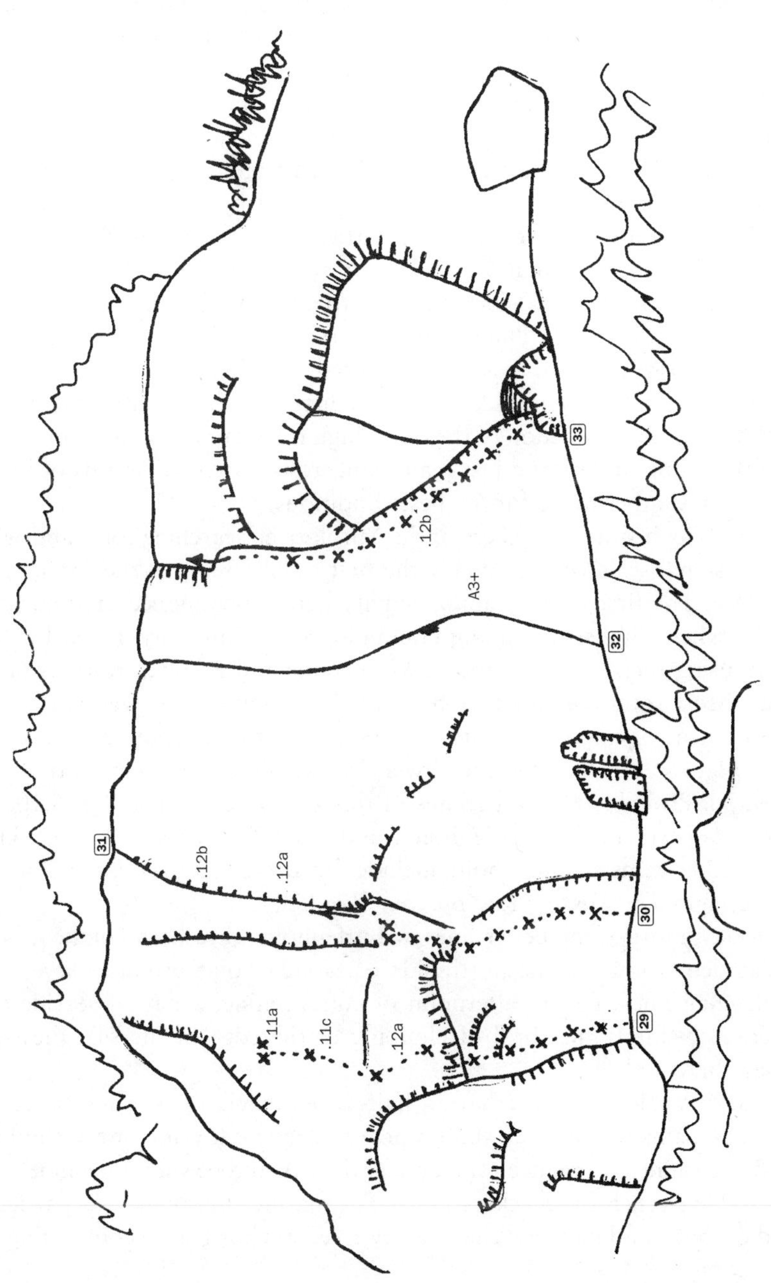

# LUFFENHOLTZ BEACH AND HOUDA POINT

Less than a mile north of the community of Westhaven, beachgoers, artists, and climbers have discovered a pair of charming, secluded coves, each carpeted with fine, gray-brown sand and framed by cliffs of dark Franciscan sandstone and greenstone. Luffenholtz Beach, the more northerly of the two, offers bouldering and short climbs on a sea cliff and cluster of large boulders at its north end, while Houda Point provides some of the area's most strenuous and demanding bouldering. Though scenic and easily accessible, neither of these beaches sees nearly as much traffic as nearby Moonstone Beach, making either one a good bet for a concentrated session of climbing. Climbs at Luffenholtz Beach begin at 5.7 and go up from there to 5.11c on formations ranging in height from 10-foot boulders to an impressive 60-foot wall traced by sport routes. Houda Point's boulders require no gear other than a chalk bag and brush; the sand makes for generally gentle landings (although using a spotter is always a good idea). The quality and accessibility of climbing at both locations is a function of the tides; high tides can make the climbing dangerously damp at best and just plain dangerous at worst. Periods of low tide and good weather make for the best conditions.

**Climbing history:** Members of the Yurok tribe searching for seabirds' eggs or occasional seals were probably the first to climb any of the formations in this area. The first rock climbing activity here probably occurred during the 1970s, when climbers attending Humboldt State University in nearby Arcata began using the rocks here and at Moonstone and Patricks Point as practice crags. Most routes were either bouldered or toproped. It was not until the development of improved bolts and the popularity of sport climbing in the mid-to-late 1980s that the rocks were re-examined for their sport-climbing potential. Probably the best routes of this period are *Think Big* (5.10a) and *Shit Kebobs* (5.11a) at Luffenholtz, and *She's Got Jugs* (5.11a) at Houda Point. Later gems at Luffenholtz include *Sea Breeze* (5.10a), *Back Door Man* (5.10c), and *The Missing Red Banana Slug* (5.11c).

Today, most of the better lines at Luffenholtz have been climbed, but the big, undercut cliff on the north side of Houda Point promises several very challenging lines. For an afternoon of conditioning, a day of seaside camaraderie, or simply the thrill of climbing at the edge of the sea, these crags remain hard to beat.

**Rack:** A selection of perhaps a half-dozen quickdraws, a few small stoppers, and cams to about 2" should prove adequate for any of the climbs listed. Bring runners to reduce rope drag and wear, and be sure to include a small adjustable wrench for checking bolts. The marine environment is particularly hard on bolts and hangers; check every fixed anchor before committing to its protection.

# LUFFENHOLTZ BEACH AND HOUDA POINT

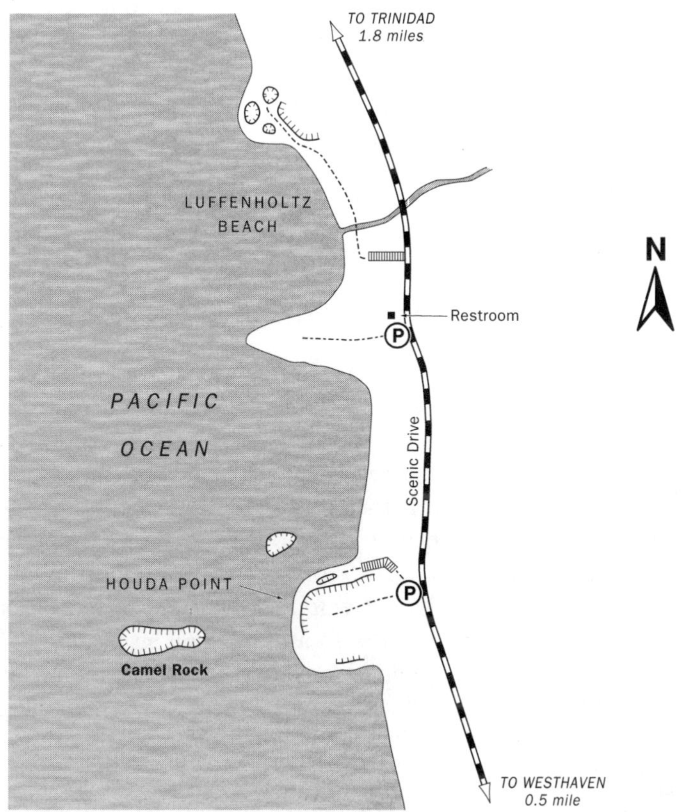


**Descent:** You can scramble down from the boulder climbs at Houda Point. The longer routes at Luffenholtz Beach require either lowering or rappelling, as the tops of the rocks can be vegetated, loose, and slippery. Look for specific descent and approach directions accompanying the description of each rock.

## TRIP PLANNING INFORMATION

**Area description:** Small sea cliffs and boulders flanking attractive, secluded, sandy beaches. Climbs range from 5.7 to 5.11c in difficulty and from 10 to 60 feet in height.

**Location:** On California's north coast, between the communities of Westhaven and Trinidad in Humboldt County.

**Camping:** Luffenholtz Beach and Houda Point are day-use areas that do not offer camping; however, motels and camping facilities are available close by. Six miles north of Trinidad, visitors can camp at Patricks Point State Park. The park operates a 123-space campground. Farther north, at scenic Prairie Creek Redwoods State Park, located 5 miles north of the town of Orick, climbers can stay in a 100-space campground. Both offer piped water, picnic tables, and toilets. Other, private campgrounds and a plethora of motels can be found all along U.S. Highway 101, from Eureka to Crescent City.

**Climbing season:** All year, although long rainy periods from late October through April and foggy mornings from June through August limit activity; best in May and September. Even when the weather is conducive to climbing, climbers should always keep an eye on the tide to avoid getting wet, stranded, or worse.

**Restrictions and access issues:** These crags are all located on public land managed by California State Beaches and Parks. There are no managerial restrictions on access, but climbers should be aware of a few conditions that could affect present enjoyment and future access. First, these beaches get plenty of use, mostly by non-climbers. It is therefore important to present a good image of climbers as responsible, socially-conscious recreationists. The crags lie within the coastal rainforest, and the tops of many rocks support mini-jungles. Cleaning off holds is acceptable, but wholesale removal of vegetation is definitely out. Installation of new anchors should be made using only stainless-steel bolts and hangers, and should be undertaken only if the resulting route is important enough that it will see enough traffic to warrant the permanent alteration of the rock. If it does not, the climb should be left as a toprope problem. Climbers visiting the city of Trinidad will no doubt be tempted by the impressive sea cliffs of Trinidad Head, but this area, managed as a lighthouse site by the United States Coast Guard, is off-limits to the general public.

**Guidebook:** There are two guidebooks for this area: Douglas W. LaFarge's self-published *Climbing Notes for the Humboldt County Coast* (1996), which includes numerous additional routes and variations not described in this guide, and Eric Chemello's beautifully-drawn, self-published collection of topos *Sandstone Supplement—Topographic Maps of Rock Climbs on the North Coast* (1998). Look for copies of these at area outdoor shops. Local climber Paul Humphrey is currently compiling a comprehensive guide to the area.

**Nearby mountain shops, guide services, and gyms:** The nearest mountain shops are Northern Mountain Supply in Eureka, and Adventure's Edge in Arcata. While there are no guide services available, Center Activities, a student outing and recreation program at Humboldt State University in Arcata, offers climbing instruction to enrolled students. A small climbing wall has been installed at Humboldt State University. Visitors should contact the university's physical education department for more information.

**Services:** There is a portable toilet installed at the Luffenholtz Beach parking area; Houda Point has no facilities. Neither site has piped water. Visitors must bring whatever they plan to eat or drink, or they can retire to one of the local eateries after climbing. Lodging, food, and other supplies can be obtained in the communities of Eureka, Arcata, Trinidad, McKinleyville, Orick, and Crescent City.

**Emergency services:** In the event of an emergency, call 911 to summon an ambulance or rescue personnel. The nearest hospitals are Sutter Coast Hospital in Crescent City, Mad River Community Hospital in Arcata, and General Hospital and Saint Joseph's Hospital in Eureka.

**Nearby climbing areas:** The nearest climbing areas are Moonstone Beach, a short half-mile south, and Elephant Rock, located across US 101 from Moonstone.

**Nearby attractions:** The North Coast offers many attractions for visitors, including the spectacular redwood forests of Prairie Creek Redwoods State Park and Redwoods National Park; the beautiful, "lost world" atmosphere of Fern Canyon; black sand beaches; whale watching from several scenic overlooks; sea kayaking at Big Lagoon and Freshwater Lagoon; sport fishing for salmon, ling cod, and halibut from Trinidad, Eureka, and Crescent City; and fine dining and shopping in the Victorian towns of Eureka, Arcata, and Ferndale.

**Finding the crags:** From the junction of US 101 and California 299 just north of Arcata, proceed north on US 101 for 10.2 miles to the signed Westhaven exit. Leave the freeway, and turn left at the stop sign. At a T-intersection with a frontage road on the west side of the highway, turn right. Follow the narrow, winding road along the tops of bluffs for 0.5 mile to the signed parking lot for Houda Point on the left. Walk around or step over a low fence made of retired anchor chain and follow the trail and stairway down the north side of the point to the beach. For Luffenholtz Beach, pass the Houda Point parking area and continue another 0.3 mile to the signed parking lot for Luffenholtz State Beach on the left. From the parking area, head north along the road for 200 yards, then descend 100 wooden stairs to the beach. Cross a small creek, then continue north for a few hundred yards to the obvious cluster of rocks.

## LUFFENHOLTZ BEACH

At the north end of Luffenholtz Beach, an appealing, steep, 60-foot wall stands, accompanied by a cluster of large boulders. These provide interesting and varied climbing, including several quality, moderate routes. Rappel or lower from bolts at the tops of the rocks.

## CENTIPEDE ROCK

Centipede Rock is the farthest north of the rocks at Luffenholtz. There is a 2-bolt anchor on top for descents or toproping.

1. **Hangover** (5.11a TR) Climb the overhanging, seaward face of the rock, then exit onto the arete that leads to the top.
2. **Centipede** (5.7) Face-climb past 3 protection bolts on the left side of the rock's south face.
3. **East Africa** (5.8 R) Begin about 8' right of Route 2. Climb up to a bolt, clip it, then head up and over a sloping shelf to a second bolt and on to the top. Be careful—if you miss the second clip, you risk a groundfall.

## SEA BREEZE ROCK

Sea Breeze Rock is the tall, tombstone-shaped rock between Centipede Rock and Main Wall. Routes ascend the north, west, and south faces, and all offer interesting climbing. There are two 2-bolt anchors on the west end of the sloping summit.

4. **Local Motion** (5.11a) Start near the left (landward) side of the gently overhanging north face. Pinch the arete and crimp small edges as you work past 3 bolts, then swing onto the summit.
5. **Sea Breeze Variation** (5.7 R) Beginning near the right side of the north face, work up right along a poorly-protected ramp to join *Sea Breeze* at its third bolt. Finish via that route.

6. **Sea Breeze** (5.10a) Climb the right side of the northwest arete, using 3 bolts for protection. Higher, swing left onto the north side of the rock to a fourth bolt, then continue to the summit.

7. **Back Door Man** (5.10c) After a bouldery, overhanging start, ascend the narrow west face of the rock; 3 bolts.

8. **Missing Red Banana Slug** (5.11a) Just around the corner to the right of Route 7, look for a bolt beneath a curving, overhanging flake. Climb up to the bolt, pull over the flake to a second bolt, then continue past 2 more widely-spaced bolts to the top.

9. **Macintosh** (5.9) Start from a detached flake in the gully separating Sea Breeze Rock and Main Wall. Climb the right side of the south face, clipping 4 bolts along the way to the top.

## MAIN WALL

Main Wall offers the longest routes at Luffenholtz, and—a plus for climbers—the rock least affected by incoming surf. These routes all require 6–8 quickdraws, a couple of runners, and webbing for rappels. It is possible, though not recommended, to scramble down the south end of the cliff. Because the top-out area is covered with vegetation, most climbers lower off.

10. **Succulent Mank** (5.9) Begin in the gully separating Main Wall from Sea Breeze Rock. (Look for the clump of ice-plant that gives the route its name.) Climb to a bolt at the base of a right-facing flake, then climb the flake to a second bolt. Work up left to a third bolt, mantle a left-slanting shelf to a fourth, then head directly up to a 2-bolt anchor.
11. **Unnamed** (5.11a TR) Start at a short, overhanging section of rock 25' right of Route 10. Climb directly up the face to the anchor atop Route 12.
12. **Think Big Variation** (5.10a) Locate the start of this route at the right end of the short, overhanging section of rock surmounted by Route 11. Keeping left of a long, right-facing flake, climb steep rock to a bolt. Continue up somewhat easier ground to another bolt, head up left along a faint ramp to a third bolt, then go for the 2-bolt anchor directly above.
13. **Think Big** (5.10a R) Begin as for *Think Big Variation,* but instead of following the bolts, head up right and follow a flake crack as you work up the face. From the top of the crack, sidle up left to the third bolt on *Think Big Variation* and finish on that route. Take some small stoppers and TCUs to ¾" for the crack.
14. **Shit Kebobs** (5.11a) Look for another, similar overhang close to the ground and about 20' right of the overhanging section of the wall that marks the starts of Routes 11–13. Begin this local classic approximately midway between the two overhangs. Using 3 protection bolts, ascend the center of the face to a 2-bolt anchor.
15. **Unknown** (5.10d TR) Beginning 4' right of *Shit Kebobs,* climb onto a sloping shelf down and right of Route 14's first bolt. Head directly up the wall to a right-facing flake, then, from its top, move up to a small overlap. Angle up right to a flake, then follow it up left until you can reach the anchor atop *Shit Kebobs.*
16. **Unknown** (5.11a) Begin about 5' right of Route 15. Climb onto a sloping shelf under the prominent overhang, then work up an indistinct, zigzag groove that leads directly up the wall to the *Shit Kebobs* anchor.

17. **Implements Under Destruction, a.k.a. IUD** (5.9) Begin at the right end of the wall, near a short arete that curves up and right. Climb up and slightly right to a bolt, then head up right past 2 more to a tree at the top of the wall. Be sure to use sling material around the tree for your rappel anchor—do not subject the tree to the stress of rope friction.

## HOUDA POINT

The access stairway to the beach at Houda Point passes directly below an impressive, vertical wall of black greenstone. To date, nobody has tried to establish routes on this wall—probably because of the difficulty of placing anchors without excessive "gardening." At the foot of the stairs, walk toward the surfline, then bear left to reach the boulders.

1. **Houdini** (5.10d/5.11a) About 50' beyond the end of the stairs, duck under the severely undercut wall on the left to find this route: a gruesome-looking roof crack. Jam the crack to the lip of the roof, then drop off.

The remaining routes all lie on the northwest side of a prominent, juggy, flat-topped block that has fallen onto other boulders.

2. **Unnamed** (5.10d) Climb the far-left end of the short, wide northwest face.
3. **Unnamed** (5.11a) Begin 6' right of Route 2. Pull up on good handholds, then power up the overhanging face above.
4. **She's Got Jugs** (5.11a) Start this, the Houda Point testpiece, under the roof beneath the right side of the northwest face. Traverse up left under the roof on jugs that require some intricate combination moves, pop out onto the center of the northwest face and head up left to the top.

## MOONSTONE BEACH AND ELEPHANT ROCK

In one of the great contrasts that seem to be so common in California's landscape, the rocks of Moonstone Beach and Elephant Rock could scarcely be more different in character and setting, yet they lie less than a half-mile apart, separated only by U.S. Highway 101. Moonstone's rocks are sunny beachgoers, springing out of the gold-gray sands of Humboldt County's most popular beach, while secretive Elephant Rock sulks among the trees and bushes, aloof from the crowds. Moonstone's climbing consists of bouldering and toprope climbing, while the routes on Elephant Rock are one- and two-pitch sport climbs. Both, fortunately, are comparable in quality, although the salt air of the beach has curbed the growth of on-crag vegetation, while Elephant Rock

# MOONSTONE BEACH AND ELEPHANT ROCK

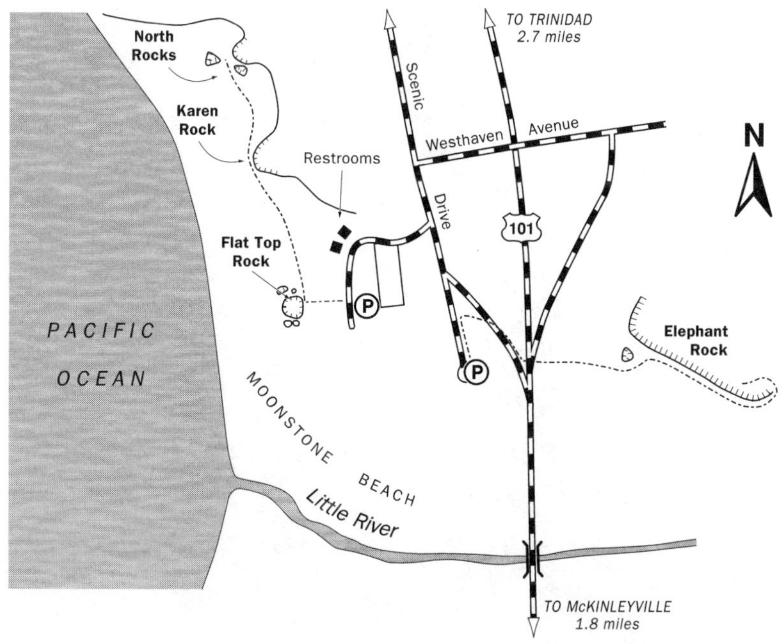


is festooned with succulents, seedlings, and mosses of every persuasion—but only on surfaces gentle enough to hold a bit of soil. The rock in both settings is Franciscan sandstone, a brownish gray, moderately hard variety that can be either heavily fractured, as on Karen Rock, or more compact as Elephant Rock shows.

No matter which crag is chosen for a day's climbing, climbers are sure to enjoy the range of challenges presented. Climbs at Moonstone range from easy fifth class to 5.12, while Elephant Rock presents greater challenges—most of its routes are 5.10a or harder. Any climber passing through the area should make time to stop and sample the climbing here; it might just call for a layover day.

**Climbing history:** The bouldering at Moonstone Beach was probably the first technical rock climbing done on California's north coast. Climbers attending Humboldt State University during the 1950s and 1960s often trained on these rocks to stay in shape for summer routes elsewhere. On the larger formations, most climbing activity focused on "practice" aid climbing. Records of these climbers and their exploits are scant at best. It was not until the late 1970s that local rock climbers began to explore the free climbing possibilities these crags offer. Concentrating initially on toproped climbs, the

*How it's done: starting* Buckhorn Bulge *(5.12a), Karen Rock.*

climbers soon cast their eyes on nearby Elephant Rock, and early ascents of the routes on the small pinnacle alongside the highway served as preparation for an eventual ascent of the central trough on the cliff, which later became *The Green Burrito* (5.9). Unfortunately, the names of this first ascent party remain unknown.

As on other North Coast crags, the 1980s and 1990s marked the golden age of climbing development at Moonstone and Elephant Rock. Area climbers came to see these local rocks as a worthy destination, instead of mere practice. Soon, the toprope anchors on Karen Rock were used to safeguard ascents of such testpieces as *Skyhook* (5.11a), *Groveling Gibsters* (5.11b), and *Nemesis* (5.12a). Across the highway, sport climbers enjoyed a heyday, putting up such gems as *Snuffalapigus* (5.11a), *This Bolt's for You* (5.10c R), *Lichen Ninjas* (5.11d), *Pachydermatitis* (5.12b), and *Raging Bull* (5.12d/.13a).

The continued popularity of the climbs at Moonstone Beach and Elephant Rock is perhaps the best testimonial to both the quality of the climbing and the vision of area pioneers who were willing to see these rocks for their own intrinsic value instead of as mere training ground for "real" climbing.

**Rack:** Take a modest rack for most routes, as the majority are still toproped. Because of the soft and sometimes brittle nature of the rock, you should bring plenty of runners and several cams to 2½ inches for gear-protected climbs, while eight to ten quickdraws will suffice for most sport climbs. Some of the most recent routes, such as *Elephant Man* (5.12a) were established using removable bolts; if you want to climb these, take 8–10 RBs.

**Descent:** You can scramble down from the tops of most of these formations. However, loose rock or vegetation near the tops may make lowering off or rappelling more feasible, especially if there are several people in the group. Because of the number of crags described, specific descent and approach directions accompany the description of each rock.

## TRIP PLANNING INFORMATION

**Area description:** Rocks at Moonstone Beach consist of groups of boulders, and large outcrops to 70'. Elephant Rock is a single, south-facing wall 150'–175' high. Both are composed of sandstone and some calcite-veined greenstone. Rocks at Moonstone Beach rise directly from the sandy beach, while Elephant Rock's base is vegetated and tree-shaded.

**Location:** On or near California's North Coast, at the south edge of the community of Westhaven, 10 miles north of the junction of U.S. Highway 101 and California Highway 299.

**Camping:** Because of the region's long history as a tourist destination, camping and other lodging facilities abound. The nearest public campground is the 123-space campground at Patricks Point State Park, located 6 miles north of Trinidad. The campground offers flush toilets, showers, picnic tables, and fire rings. Because of its popularity, reservations are required. These can be made by calling DESTINET (800-444-7275). In addition to Patricks Point State Park, there are many private campgrounds, RV parks, and motels along US 101 from Eureka to Crescent City, including several in Trinidad, McKinleyville, and northern Arcata.

**Climbing season:** All year, although long rainy periods from late October through April and foggy mornings from June through August limit activity; best in May and September, although a warm, dry spell makes for enjoyable climbing at any time.

**Restrictions and access issues:** The crags at Moonstone Beach are easy to access at any time and present no difficulties or restrictions. Elephant Rock, on the other hand, technically lies within the right-of-way of US 101, which means that climbers should take care to avoid any actions that could create a visual or physical disturbance to passing motorists. In addition, climbers should be aware that the land immediately adjacent to the summit area is private. Therefore, good manners and a low profile are called for.

The climate and comparatively sheltered microenvironment of the nooks and crannies in the rocks fosters a luxuriant growth of plants on and atop these crags. Some of these have supported a healthy growth of poison oak, so climbers should beware and avoid the urge to "garden." In wet conditions, the rock can be soft or brittle, and it should be given adequate time to dry out before yanking on thin flakes or small edges. The softness of the rock and the corrosive nature of the marine environment combine to gradually weaken fixed anchors. Any anchor is thus potentially suspect. Any new or replacement bolts should be of stainless steel with stainless steel hangers.

As mentioned previously, Moonstone Beach is Humboldt County's most popular beach. Climbers will be sharing the setting with sunbathers, swimmers, kite flyers, Frisbee throwers, little kids, dogs, and beachcombers. Suffice it to say that socially responsible behavior—including litter cleanup—is the order of the day. Do not leave valuables or gear unattended, and remember that dogs are best kept leashed.

**Guidebook:** The two guidebooks for this area are Douglas W. LaFarge's self-published *Climbing Notes for the Humboldt County Coast* (1996), which includes numerous additional routes and variations not described in this guide, and *Sandstone Supplement—Topographic Maps of Rock Climbs on the North Coast* (1998), by Eric Chemello. Both are available at area outdoor shops. Paul Humphrey is currently compiling a comprehensive guide to the area.

**Nearby mountain shops, guide services, and gyms:** The nearest mountain shops are Northern Mountain Supply in Eureka, and Adventure's Edge in Arcata. There are no guide services available, but Center Activities, a student outing and recreation program at Humboldt State University in Arcata, offers climbing instruction. A small climbing wall has been installed at Humboldt State University. Visitors should contact the university's physical education department for more information.

**Services:** Elephant Rock offers no services at all. There is a portable restroom at the north end of the Moonstone Beach parking area, but there is no drinking water. Climbers should therefore bring whatever they plan to eat and drink. Lodging, food, and other supplies can be obtained in the nearby communities of Eureka, Arcata, McKinleyville, and Trinidad.

**Emergency services:** In the event of an emergency, call 911 to summon an ambulance or rescue personnel. The nearest hospitals are Sutter Coast Hospital in Crescent City, Mad River Community Hospital in Arcata, and General Hospital and Saint Joseph's Hospital in Eureka.

**Nearby climbing areas:** The excellent bouldering of Houda Point and the sport routes of Luffenholtz are only a few minutes north of Westhaven on Patricks Point Drive.

**Nearby attractions:** The rocky cliffs and seaside forest of Patricks Point State Park are well worth a visit. In addition, no visit to the area is complete without seeing the spectacular redwood forests of Prairie Creek Redwoods State Park and Redwoods National Park. Elsewhere along the coast one can enjoy black sand beaches; whale watching from several scenic overlooks; sea kayaking at Big Lagoon and Freshwater Lagoon; and fine dining and shopping in the Victorian towns of Eureka, Arcata, and Ferndale.

**Finding the crags:** From Arcata, drive north on US 101 for 10.2 miles to the Westhaven exit. Leave the freeway, and turn left at the stop sign. At a T-intersection with a frontage road on the west side of the highway, turn left. Proceed south for 0.2 mile, keeping right to avoid returning to the freeway. For Moonstone Beach, just before entering the parking lot for Merryman's Restaurant, bear right and follow a narrow road down to a lower parking area at the edge of the beach. Flat Top Rock lies just a few yards away on the beach. Walk north on the sand to reach the other formations.

For Elephant Rock, follow the above directions as though going to Moonstone Beach, but instead of turning right, continue straight ahead. Bear right to avoid getting back onto the freeway, and park along a short dead-end street. Walk back up to the freeway on-ramp and follow it to the edge of the highway. After making certain that the way is clear, *briskly* scoot across the 4-lane highway to the rock. Some stairs near a small pinnacle lead down to the climbers' path along the base of the rock.

## MOONSTONE BEACH

The numerous boulders and outcrops of Moonstone Beach, combined with its easy access and nearness to the cities of Arcata and Eureka, have made this one of the most popular and completely developed climbing areas in Northwest California. Most rocks too tall for safe bouldering have toprope anchors installed, and these can be reached by scrambling or fairly easy climbing.

EAST FACE, FLAT TOP ROCK

## FLAT TOP ROCK

Flat Top Rock is actually a cluster of boulders centered on the large block that gives the group its name. Perfect for a warmup or an end-of-the day session, these rocks provide considerable variety. Their only drawback lies in the fact that they also attract a large number of non-climbers. From the top of Flat Top Rock, scramble down the south end of the southwest face to return to the ground. Route descriptions are listed going clockwise, beginning with the northeast face (i.e., the face toward the parking area).

1. **East Arete** (5.9) Beginning on either side of the arete at the left end of the northeast face, follow the steep face climbing on the arete to the top.
2. **Southeast Face** (5.12b TR) Start just right of the blocks east of the rock. Using thin flakes, climb directly up the face and over a difficult bulge at the top. Because of a possible bad landing, do not attempt this climb without a toprope.
3. **Sputnik** (5.8) Climb the steep, concave face of the pointed boulder south of Flat Top Rock. If you avoid the tempting holds on the edges, you can up the rating to 5.9.
4. **Descent Route** (5.2) Beginning a couple of feet from the right edge of the southwest face, climb easy slabs, bearing left as you near the top.
5. **Diagonal Flake** (5.5) Start 6' left of *Descent Route*. Lieback a thin flake up right, then face-climb low-angle slabs to the top.

SOUTHWEST FACE, FLAT TOP ROCK

6. **Center Route** (5.5) Beginning 5' left of *Diagonal Flake,* wander up the face; there are many possible variations.
7. **Right Gullwing** (5.10a) Notice a pair of small roofs, shaped like inverted Vs, at the left end of the face. From a point directly below the right-hand roof, climb up to it, pull over at its widest point, then move up left to reach easier friction climbing to the top.
8. **Seagull** (5.9) Climb the narrow face between the "gullwings," joining Route 7 near the top of the face.
9. **The Wedge** (5.9) On the south face of the sharply triangular boulder west of Flat Top Rock, pull up fingery face climbing just left of a shallow buttress that shoots up to the top.
10. **Walk the Plank** (5.10d) From the top of the last boulder northeast of Flat Top Rock, step onto the face, then work up left a few feet before going for the top.

## KAREN ROCK

Karen Rock is the largest of the rock formations at Moonstone Beach, and it is the one most local climbers refer to when they speak of "climbing at Moonstone." The 70-foot cliff of gray and yellow sandstone stands at the end of a short ridge about 200 yards north of the parking area. Its jumbled appearance is misleading, for this fractured crag, which resembles a pile of dirty marshmallows, is actually quite sound and provides quality climbing.

15
16
17
11
12
13
14
15
WEST FACE, KAREN ROCK

The routes on Karen Rock are customarily toproped, and local climbers have equipped the summit with several sets of chain anchors. These can be reached via a short, though slippery, scramble up the slope north of the rock. Most climbers rappel or lower off, although scrambling down is only somewhat slower. The following routes are listed from left to right. Note that the routes listed are only a sampling; hundreds of linkups and variations are possible.

11. **North Arete** (5.10b TR) Beginning atop a triangular block, at the foot of the arete at the far-left edge of the rock, pull up on overhanging rock, then follow easier, though smoother climbing to a trio of bolts about two-thirds of the way up the arete.
12. **Unnamed** (5.10d TR) Begin 10' right of the triangular block, at the foot of the north arete. Climb a shallow, right-facing corner, pass over a brown-stained bulge, then surmount an overhang near its right side. Higher, either head up left to the bolts at the top of *North Arete,* or follow a 5.7 crack up right to finish via the final moves of *Standard Route.*
13. **Lizard Head** (5.10d TR) Find the start 10' right of the previous route. Make several powerful moves up the overhanging wall, working gradually left to join Route 12 below the large overhang halfway up the rock. Finish via either version of that route.
14. **Skyhook** (5.11a TR) Start at the foot of the rock's west buttress, and a few feet left of a prominent brown streak. After some tricky moves, dyno to a horn, then work up right to join *Standard Route* at the foot of a conspicuous white area. Lower off, or finish via that route.
15. **Standard Route** (5.8 TR) Begin a few feet right of the brown streak on the prow of the rock's west buttress. Face-climb up the right edge of the brow-streaked bulge to a sloping ledge, then jam a short crack that leads up right to the base of an area of white rock capped by a prominent roof that slants up and left. Climb the left side of the white area to the upper end of the roof, then swing up left in a hand crack to enter the shallow chimney that leads to the summit.
16. **Urchin** (5.10c/d TR) Climb *Standard Route* as far as a flake below the top of the slanting roof. Work up and right around the flake, then pass over the roof at a slight break. Ascend the steep wall above, finishing with another small overhang.
17. **Unnamed** (5.11a TR) Climb *Standard Route* to the base of the area of white rock. Follow a finger crack up right to the right end of the slanting roof. Dyno to a triangular hold, then ascend the southwest arete of the summit block.
18. **Unnamed** (5.9 TR) Begin around the corner to the right of *Standard Route,* about 6' left of an obvious, wide crack that slants up right from the foot of the rock. Climb the right edge of a rectangular flake, then jam

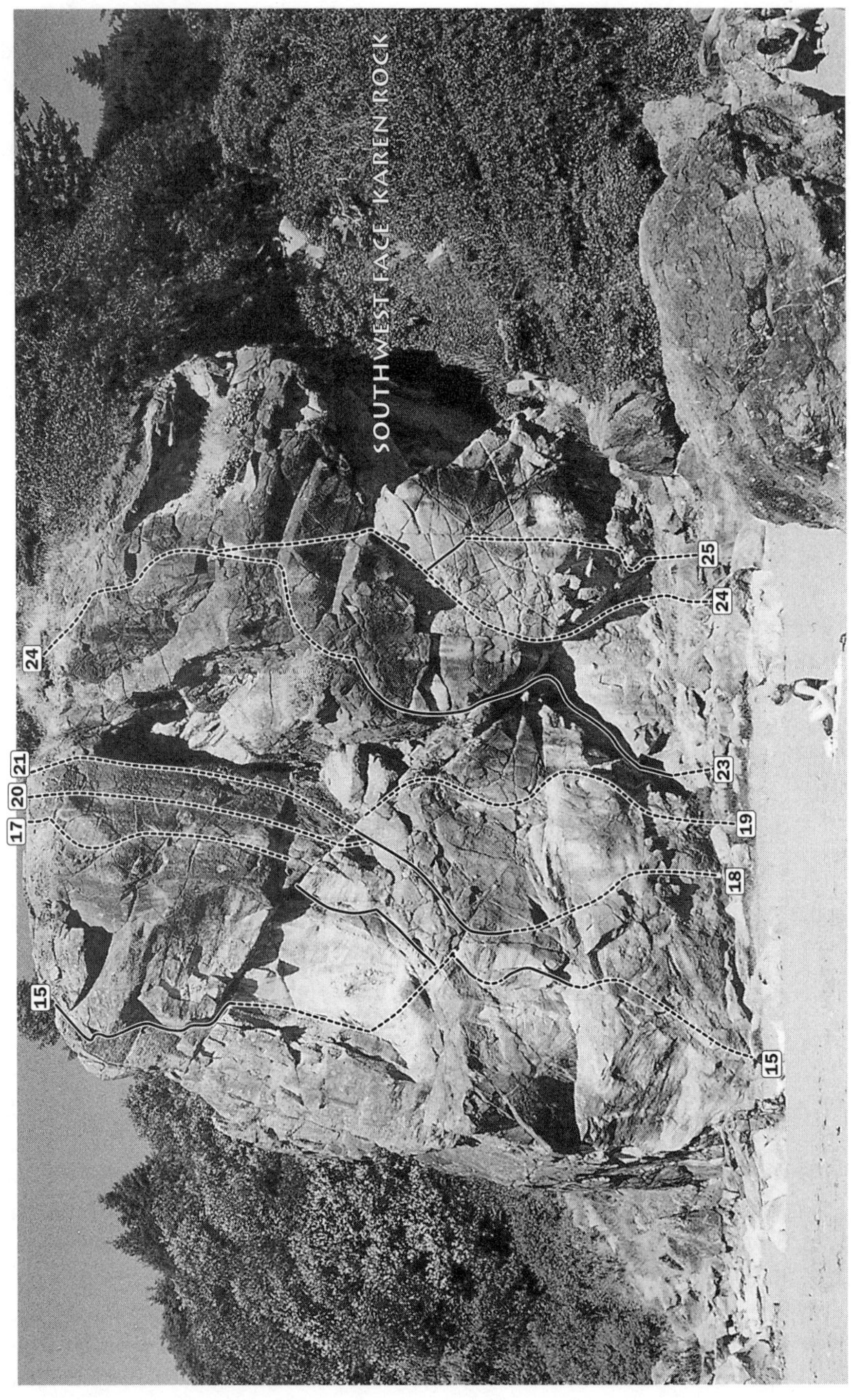
SOUTHWEST FACE KAREN ROCK
15
17
20
21
24
25
24
23
19
18
15

and hand-traverse up right along a finger crack to another crack system that slants up left, eventually becoming the slanting roof of the preceding several climbs. Either lower off, or hand-traverse up left along the crack and finish via *Standard Route* or one of its harder variations.

19. **Buckhorn Bulge** (5.12a TR) Start at the foot of a prominent, wide crack that slants up right. After an initial tricky sequence on overhanging rock, reach a sloping ledge. Climb the steep wall above to meet the top of the preceding route. Finish via one of the climbs that ascends the upper wall.
20. **Assembly Line** (5.11a TR) Climb either Route 18 or *Buckhorn Bulge,* then ascend the smooth, slightly overhanging south face of the summit block.
21. **Groveling Gibsters** (5.11a TR) Climb either Route 18 or *Buckhorn Bulge.* Follow a short, blocky ramp up right to the base of a deep cleft, then climb the striking arete on the left.
22. **Nemesis** (5.12a TR) Climb *Buckhorn Bulge,* then follow the slanting crack up left to join Route 17. Make the dynamic move, then move up left and finish via *Urchin.* (Not shown.)
23. **Curved Crack** (5.10a TR) Climb the wide crack that slants up right until it meets a long crack that slants up left and eventually becomes a slanting roof. Follow the left-slanting crack to a sloping area a few feet higher, then work up right, initially along a crack, then on face-holds. Finally, face-climb the outer face of a short, dome-like buttress to the top.
24. **Dream Theme** (5.11c TR) Beginning 18' right of *Curved Crack,* climb a short, left-leaning, left-facing dihedral, then work up and right along seams to a hole. Continue up right, then ascend steep rock, eventually meeting and finishing via *Curved Crack.*
25. **Don't Look Back** (5.12c TR) Start this bouldery route 6' right of *Dream Theme.* Climb directly up the face via a series of dynos. Follow a short crack up left, then finish via *Dream Theme.*

## NORTH BEACH ROCKS

At the north end of Moonstone Beach, the enclosing headland of the cove shelters a group of boulders and a small, though spectacular wall. These rocks tend to be far less crowded than those closer to the parking area, even though they require only a five-minute walk from the cars. The brushy tops of the rocks and the brush-filled gullies in between them are unappealing, but the climbing is quite good. It is possible to scramble to the tops of these rocks, and some toprope anchors are in place.

The following five routes ascend North Rock, the largest of the rocks in this group.

WEST FACE, NORTH ROCK

26. **Old Bolt Ladder** (5.11a) Begin around the corner to the left of the prominent west face of the rock. Watch for the old bolt ladder that marks this climb. Face-climb up to the line of bolts, then follow it until nearly to the top. Work up and around the corner to the right to the 2-bolt anchor at the top of *Launch Toast.*
27. **Launch Toast** (5.11d) Look for a pair of bolts under the roof at the top of the rock's west face. Climb partway up a short, right-curving arch, using 3 bolts for protection. Break out left and ascend the arete at the left edge of the face, using 3 more bolts on the climbing to 2-bolt anchor.
28. **Six Broken Ribs** (A1 or 5.12d/13a?) Begin as for *Launch Toast.* Follow the old ladder of 8 bolts to a 2-bolt anchor just below the summit roof.

You could climb the crack through the roof, but you would probably not enjoy it.

29. **North Crack** (5.10b) Jam the prominent finger crack that begins 6' right of Route 28.

30. **Halladay Traverse** (5.10a) Begin on the south side of the formation, in the gully separating North Rock from Wiffy Pillar, the smaller formation farther south. Climb up a few feet, then work up left across the southwest side of the rock, and climb to the top before reaching the deep, easy dihedral.

The next two routes lie on Wiffy Pillar, the satellite formation south of North Rock. Use the pair of bolts on top of the pillar to anchor a toprope.

31. **Unnamed** (5.12a TR) Climb the arete at the left edge of the narrow, triangular, overhanging buttress on the west side of the rock.

32. **Sticked Wiffy** (5.12b TR) Follow the right arete on the west side of the rock.

These routes ascend Pyramid Rock, the aptly named feature southwest of the other rocks in the group. There is a pair of bolts on top.

33. **Pyramid Rock—West Face** (5.4 TR) Wander at will up the low-angle, seaward-facing slab.

34. **Pyramid Rock—South Face** (5.9 TR) Climb the center of the steep face, employing an interesting mantle halfway up.

## ELEPHANT ROCK

Recently developed Elephant Rock is the nearest true sport climbing crag to the Arcata/Eureka area. Most of the routes, though difficult, are well-protected with bolts. Although most climbers opt for lowering off or rappelling, it is also possible to scramble down the east side of the rock. The anchors for climbs here are not safely accessible, limiting the scope for toproping.

## PEANUTS PINNACLE

This is the small pinnacle that stands between the main mass of Elephant Rock and the highway. Routes ascend its southeast and east faces.

1. **The Ear** (5.8) Starting practically from the edge of U.S. Highway 101, ascend the left edge of the pinnacle's slabby southeast face, using 2 bolts for protection. Lower off from a 2-bolt anchor on top.
2. **The Slug** (5.9+ R) Ascend the right side of the pinnacle's southeast face. Beware of the runout between the 2 protection bolts.
3. **Peanuts** (5.10c) Climb the narrow east face of the pinnacle; 3 bolts.

## MAIN WALL

The main wall of Elephant Rock faces west-northwest and southwest, and it offers climbs of one to two pitches. Only four of these top out; the rest require rappelling or lowering (using two ropes). Routes are listed from left to right.

4. **Elephant Man** (I 5.12a) You may have trouble locating this climb, as the protection for its first pitch is all removable bolts. Look for the first holes below and slightly right of a short, right-leaning, right-facing dihedral on the face behind Peanuts Pinnacle. **Pitch 1:** Face-climb up to the dihedral, follow it to its top, then gradually veer left as you head for a small overhang. Continue to a pair of belay bolts beneath a larger overhang. Rappel, or go on to **Pitch 2:** Surmount the overhang, then continue up much easier, though unprotected, terrain to a groove that slants right. Follow it to the top of the rock. Alternatively, friction-climb up left to a tree at the top of the rock. Take 8 ⅜-inch RBs for the first pitch.
5. **Raging Bull** (5.12d/.13a) Find the first bolt of this challenging route a few feet right of the leaning dihedral of *Elephant Man* (this is the first bolted line encountered at this end of the rock). Climb up to this first bolt, make a 5.11a move, pass over a small overhang to a second bolt, then pull a 5.12a section. Face-climb past 3 more bolts, pull down a small overhang, then head up left over another small overhang to a bolt beneath the overhang that marks the end of *Elephant Man*'s first pitch. Climb over the 5.12a roof, then move left to a bolt. From here, fire

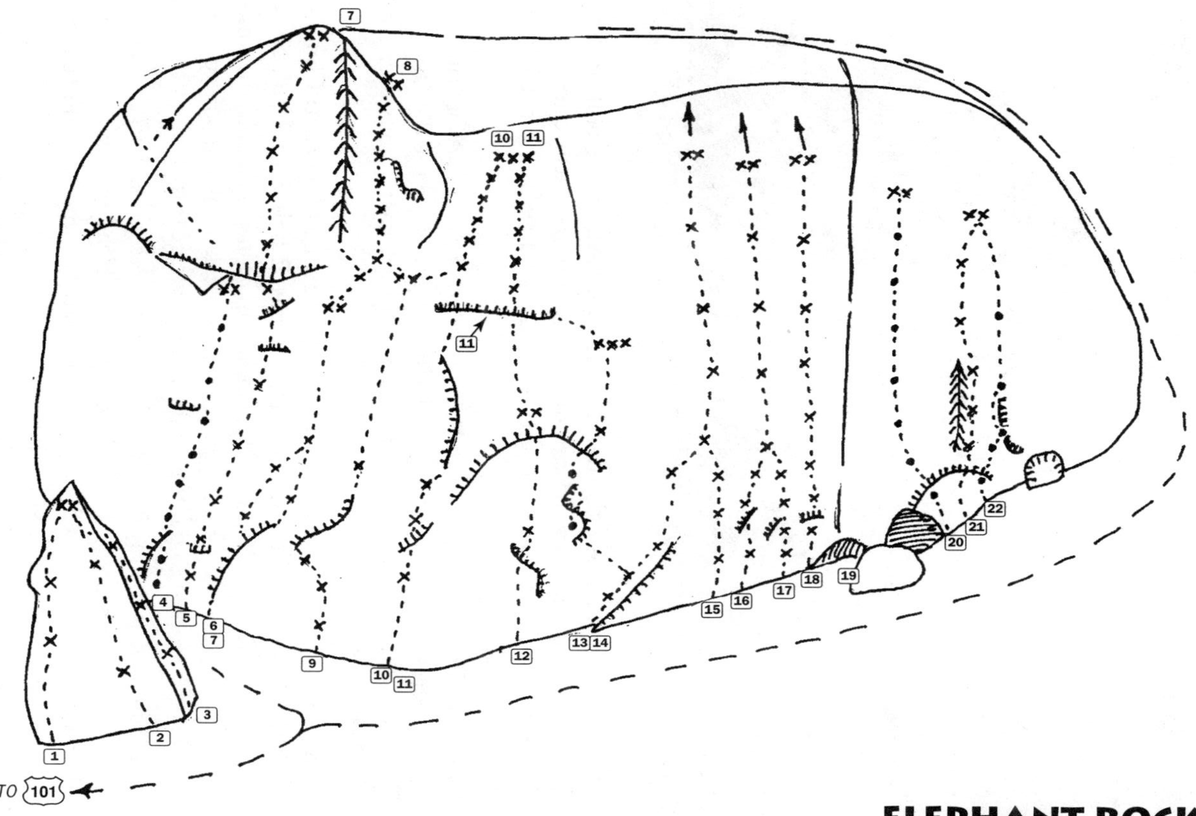


ELEPHANT ROCK

straight up the increasingly overhanging wall past 4 more bolts to the 2-bolt anchor at the top. Be careful: the route's technical crux lies just below the last bolt. Note that this route can be done as 2 pitches for the lower rating.

6. **Neighbor Packs a Load** (5.11a) Begin at a larger, right-curving, right-facing dihedral 8' right of *Raging Bull.* Climb halfway up the dihedral, then exit left onto the face above. Climb up and right past 3 bolts to a 2-bolt anchor.
7. **Five-Nine** (I 5.9) Start as for *Neighbor Packs a Load.* **Pitch 1:** Climb the dihedral to its top, then head directly up past 2 bolts to a 2-bolt anchor shared with Route 6. **Pitch 2:** Face-climb up right past a bolt, then move up left to the base of a huge, left-facing dihedral. Stem and jam your way up this 5.9 feature to the top of the rock. Take gear to 1½".
8. **Snuffalupigus** (I 5.11a) **Pitch 1:** Climb either *Neighbor Packs a Load* or *Five-Nine* to the first 2-bolt anchor. **Pitch 2:** Head up right past a bolt, then ascend the right wall of the huge dihedral, clipping another 7 bolts before reaching the 2-bolt anchor at the top.
9. **This Bolt's for You** (5.10c R) Begin 20' right of Route 7, and below a right-facing flake 35' up the face. Face-climb past 2 bolts, work up left past another, then make a run-out undercling of the crux flake. From its top, face-climb past another bolt, then run it out on easier ground to a

SOUTHWEST SIDE, ELEPHANT ROCK

pair of belay bolts. Either lower off or climb up left to join *Snuffalupigus* for a more exciting finish.

10. **Flying Dumbo** (5.12b) Start 15' right of Route 9. Note that the first bolt is high up and easy to miss. Stick-clip the first bolt, then face-climb up to and over a small overhang that slants up right. Clip another bolt, then make the crux move to reach a third bolt. Head up right, then lieback a right-facing flake. From its top, move up right to the left end of a horizontal roof. Once past the roof, head up the wall, chasing 5 more bolts and encountering 5.11 climbing before reaching the 3-bolt anchor. Take small cams and nuts to 1".
11. **Jiminy Cricket** (5.12b/c) Climb *Flying Dumbo* as far as the horizontal roof, then traverse right along the roof to its middle, haul over it, and climb the wall above past 5 bolts, eventually heading left to the anchor bolts on top of *Flying Dumbo*. Take small cams and nuts to 1".
12. **Spina Bifida** (5.12b/c R) Thirty-five feet right of the start of *Flying Dumbo,* look for a prominent arch on the wall below the horizontal roof of Routes 10 and 11. Begin below and slightly left of the high point of this arch. Climb up to and over a crescent-shaped flake to the route's sole protection bolt, then head up to and over the arch to a pair of bolts. From here, climb directly up to the horizontal roof and join *Jiminy Cricket.* Take small stoppers and cams to 1".

13. **Down Syndrome** (I 5.11b) Start at the foot of a right-slanting ramp 20' right of *Spina Bifida.* **Pitch 1:** Climb the ramp to the second bolt, then head up left to an S-shaped flake. Use 2 RBs here for protection. Pass over the right end of the arch of Route 12 to another bolt, then continue to a 3-bolt anchor. **Pitch 2:** Face-climb up left to the horizontal roof and finish via *Jiminy Cricket.* Take 2 RBs and a couple of small cams.
14. **Final Spank** (5.10c) Start as for *Down Syndrome.* Follow the ramp up right past 3 bolts, then continue up right past another to join *Lichen Ninjas* at its fourth bolt. Finish via that route.
15. **Lichen Ninjas** (5.11d) Begin 20' right of the ramp of *Final Spank.* Climb directly up the face past 7 bolts to a 2-bolt anchor, passing the crux just before the third bolt.
16. **Elephantitis** (5.12a) Locate the starting point below a right-facing flake 12' right of *Lichen Ninjas.* Face-climb past a bolt to a 5.11d move. Continue up and over the flake to another bolt, which protects the crux move up right to the third bolt. From here, keep right to another bolt, then head directly up past 2 more bolts to a 2-bolt anchor.
17. **Herd of Republicans** (5.10b) Start this easier version of *Elephantitis* 10' farther right and below a similar, right-facing flake. Climb past 2 bolts to the flake, make the crux move past its right side, then clip 2 more bolts before joining *Elephantitis* at its fourth bolt. Finish via that route.
18. **Reach for the Sky** (5.10b) Ascend the line of 7 bolts that starts 8' right of *Republicans* and lies between it and the prominent crack system of *Green Burrito.* Rappel from a 2-bolt anchor.
19. **Green Burrito** (5.9) Look for a crack system that rises to the top of the face, beginning at a conspicuous hole at the foot of the wall. Using stoppers and hexes to 1½", jam and face-climb the crack.
20. **Heffalump** (5.12c) Look for the initial hole on this Chemello/Humphrey, RBs-only route just right of a cave at the base of the rock, a few feet right of *Green Burrito.* Climb over the left end of an arch that curves up and right from the mouth of the cave, then follow a line of RB holes up left, then directly up the face to a 2-bolt anchor. Take 7 RBs for protection.
21. **Pachydermatitis** (5.12b) Just right of the hole at the base of *Green Burrito,* notice a cave at the base of the rock. Your route begins below an arch that curves right from the cave. Climb up to and over the arch to an arete. Pinch your way up the crux arete past 3 bolts, then face-climb past 2 more to reach the 2-bolt anchor.
22. **Jumbo Takes a Dump** (5.12b) Begin below the right end of the arch surmounted by the preceding 2 routes. Using RBs for protection, climb up to the arch, move left, then pass over. Head up right along a series of flakes, then face-climb up and gradually left to end at the anchors atop *Pachydermatitis.* Take 5 RBs.

# HONORABLE MENTION

## LOST ROCKS

Some of the North Coast's best bouldering can be found on a secluded beach a short distance south of the mouth of Klamath River, not far from the town of Klamath. Here, numerous black-stained rocks rise from a black sand beach practically at the edge of the Pacific and offer numerous interesting problems—not the least of which can be keeping your feet dry.

From the U.S. Highway 101/CA Highway 299 junction just north of Arcata, drive north on US 101 for 53 miles to a signed exit for Coastal Drive, just north of the Humboldt/Del Norte county line. Leave US 101 and follow Coastal Drive west, then south. This road can be rough after the initial half-mile, so drive slowly. Park in the High Bluffs parking lot, 2 miles from the start of the road; the boulders litter the beach from here northward for about a mile.

## HIGH BLUFFS

High Bluffs offers still more North Coast sea cliff climbing in a setting as wild and secluded as Promontory or Footsteps, but with a shorter approach. Routes of up to 150' can be found, and the difficulties range from about 5.8 to 5.10d.

Approach High Bluffs as for Lost Rocks. The climbs lie on the cliff below the parking area and can be reached via a short hike/scramble south, then west. Be careful—the top of the cliff is loose and vegetated.

# The Klamath Mountains

Among the most complex and interesting mountain regions in the country is the Klamath Mountains, a blanket term for a Gordian knot of small ranges and sub-ranges that twist and writhe across the land. This sparsely inhabited and generally little-known region lies east of the North Coast and west of the northern Sacramento Valley, and it extends from central Mendocino County northward through Trinity and Siskiyou Counties into southwestern Oregon: a region roughly the size of the state of Vermont. Only a handful of highways traverse this jumble of ridges and river canyons, and even today its climbing potential has scarcely been tapped. So little known are these mountains that even today most lack any official names, and it is still possible to claim first ascents of peaks.

The landscape is characterized by jagged, rocky peaks at the higher elevations, deep stream canyons, alpine lakes, forested ridges, and an abundance of outstanding rock. In general, the rock is of two types. At lower elevations, careful exploration reveals outcrops of excellent limestone comparable to the best found anywhere. Overhanging, pocketed walls, soaring aretes, and caves are typical, and most are solid enough to accept bolts or other protection. Because of the generally severe and often crackless nature of these formations, they are more likely to appeal to experienced sport climbers. Trinity Aretes, Natural Bridge, and Marble Caves are examples of these outstanding crags. Higher up, climbers and mountaineers can choose from among hundreds of granite crags. Although most require an approach of several miles, there are still many that lie close enough to the road for day use. These offer traditional climbs of up to Grade III–IV and about 1,200 feet long, and there are additional climbs in the backcountry that are probably Grade Vs. The granite is generally quite sound, and it is often quite smooth, providing enjoyable and challenging face climbing. Those whose tastes run to cracks will find all sizes here as well, although fingertips-to-thin-hands sizes are most common. Castle Crags, Babyface, Boulder Lake, and Ycatapom Peak represent only a sampling of the fine granite available in this area. This area offers California's greatest opportunity for new routes, comparable to that of Yosemite National Park during the early 1900s.

## TRINITY ARETES

Hidden among the tangled ridges and densely forested canyons rumored to harbor the mysterious, ape-like giant known as Bigfoot stands an equally mysterious—but very real—giant outcrop of superb limestone: Trinity Aretes. The rock rears abruptly out of the forest, rising to a height of over 220 feet in a series of three enormous, stark prows framed by trees, bushes, and the omnipresent mosses. One often reads of climbs that are "vertical," but here many routes begin at plumbline vertical and get steeper still, leaning out as much as 20 feet over their bases. As a result, the climbing tends toward battles of endurance as well as subtlety, and this is not the place to acquire basic skills. For the expert or nearly expert, however, Trinity Aretes offers a limestone climbing experience unsurpassed anywhere in California.

The climbs range in difficulty from 5.10a to 5.13a, with a few more beyond these limits. Most have been equipped with beefy, new ⅜-inch bolts and stout hangers. Note, however, that these provide protection only when no natural pro is available. Thus, even though this is primarily a sport crag, there is enough need for gear placement that it provides challenges to both sport and traditional climbers. The climbing consists of fingery and often very exposed face climbing on all the famous features of limestone: pockets, huecos, crimps, slopers, and tufas. In addition, the crag presents a number of exciting crack lines for variety.

**Climbing history:** For centuries, Trinity Aretes was known only to the Tsnungwe people, a local band of Native Americans. Though the crag was known to local ranchers as early as the 1870s, most visitors satisfied themselves with scrambling to the top, probably by what is now the descent route.

Considering the number of climbers active in nearby Humboldt County or passing through the area on California Highway 299, it is curious that serious exploration and development of the crag did not begin until the late 1990s. Unknown early climbers and rappellers had visited the crag prior to that time, but apart from a couple of abortive bolt ladders, no significant climbs had been established. Humboldt County climbers Paul Humphrey, Cedar Wright, and Eric Chemello made an exploratory visit to Trinity Aretes in the autumn of 1996, were pleased with what they found, and immediately began putting up routes. Some of these initial routes remain area favorites and include *The Gold Rush* (5.11a) and *Open Season* (5.10b). With various partners, such as Sharilyn Clark, Sean Leary, Travis Klawin, David Cressman, and David Manheimer, the three returned the following spring. Over the course of the summer, this group bolted and climbed nearly all the routes described in this section. The only exception was *On Safari* (5.9), which was added by Randy Adrian and Danya Parkinson that fall. With the exception of some particularly challenging projects, new route development has languished since

## TRINITY ARETES AREA MAP

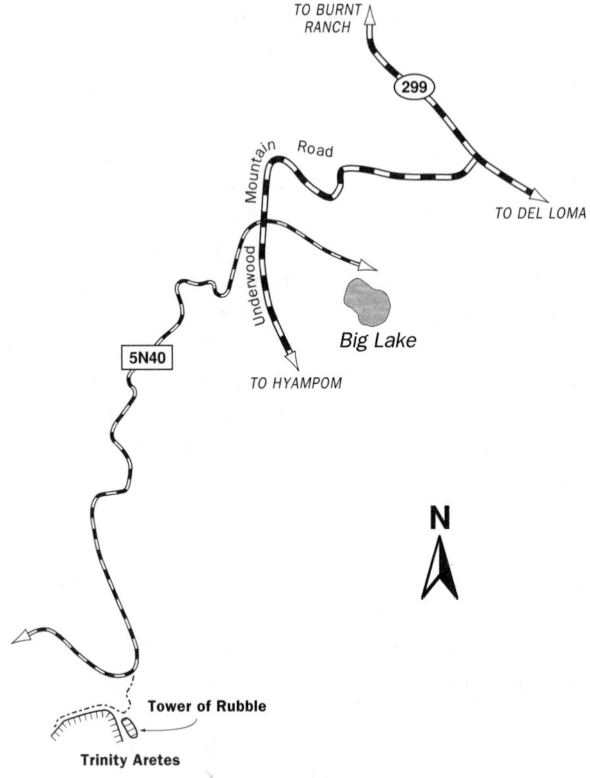


that outstanding season. The crag is far from climbed-out, however, and considerable potential remains, particularly for *really* difficult routes on Paisano Buttress and High Country Wall.

**Rack:** For the climbs on Trinity Aretes, plan to bring both traditional cragging and sport climbing gear selections. Several of the most difficult routes have "fixed" quickdraws, but most do not, so you need at least 14 of these. Bring a number of RPs, small tri-cams, at least one set of TCUs, and a set of larger cams from ¾ inch to 3 inches. One climb, *La Niña,* requires at least 8 removable bolts (RBs). These are long climbs by sport climbing standards—90 feet or better. If you plan to lower off, you need a 60-meter rope. Bring a second rope for rappelling. Last, and perhaps most important, bring and wear a helmet. The summit area of the crag, and especially the aptly named Shooting Gallery gully contain lots of loose rock.

**Descent:** From the top of the crag, scramble off to the west and circle down and right below the faces of Safari Wall and Paisano Buttress. Because most climbs stop well below the top to avoid loose material and slippery vegetation, the usual means of descent is rappelling or lowering off. Note that the length of some climbs necessitates the use of a 60-meter (200-foot) rope for lowering.

## TRIP PLANNING INFORMATION

**Area description:** Trinity Aretes is a north-facing, 220-foot limestone crag. The rock is pleasingly solid on the steeper faces, but fractured, loose, and vegetated on lower-angle portions. The crag offers a range of challenges, though the generally high level of skill required makes it appealing to more experienced sport climbers. Most climbs range in difficulty from 5.10a to 5.13b, although there are a few easier routes. All leaders should be skilled in finding and using gear placements.

**Location:** Southeast of the community of Burnt Ranch, at an elevation of about 4,000 feet in a side canyon high above the Trinity River/New River Gorge.

**Camping:** There are no camping facilities at or near the crag, but Shasta-Trinity and Six Rivers National Forests maintain campgrounds along nearby California Highway 299. Burnt Ranch Campground, located 3 miles northwest of the CA 299/Underwood Mountain Road junction and 0.5 mile northwest of the community of Burnt Ranch, is open all year and offers 15 campsites with piped-in water and vault toilets. There is a $2 per night camp fee. One mile farther west on CA 299, between Burnt Ranch and Hawkins Bar, lies Grays Falls Campground. Here, there are 33 tent campsites, piped-in water, and flush toilets. The campground is open from May through September and requires a $6 per night camp fee. The Hayden Flat Campground lies 8.5 miles east of the CA 299/Underwood Mountain Road junction and provides 35 campsites, piped-in water, and vault toilets for a $5 per night fee. The campground is open from June through October. Private campgrounds offering convenience stores, showers, flush toilets, laundry facilities, and water/electrical hookups can be found in the neighboring communities of Hawkins Bar, 6 miles northwest of the CA 299/Underwood Mountain Road junction, and Del Loma, 9 miles east of the junction.

**Climbing season:** Potentially all year, though the crag's elevation does result in some snow during winter. Summertime can be really hot, though the north-facing aspect of the cliffs makes for locally cooler climbing.

**Restrictions and access issues:** Trinity Aretes is located on public land administered by Shasta-Trinity National Forest. The site lies outside the nearby Trinity Alps Wilderness Area, so visitors are not required to secure wilderness permits. At present, there are no access issues, but climbers should note that this site is a cultural resource important to the Tsnungwe band of Native Americans. All visitors should treat the area with the respect it deserves.

This need for respect is particularly important because Trinity Aretes is a comparatively new climbing venue and the future of climbing access here and elsewhere in the extensive Shasta-Trinity National Forest depends on how well climbers can demonstrate care for the resource. This stewardship includes a strict rule of keeping to the newly established access trail, non-interference with logging traffic and other users, discreet use of bolts and bolting equipment (camoed hardware and appropriate placements, please), avoidance of disturbing plant or animal life (this includes over zealous "gardening"), and squeaky-clean housekeeping. Climbers should make a practice of taking home everything that did not originate here!

The crag has been equipped with fixed ropes in strategic spots by local climbers. These fixed ropes are intended to make the otherwise awkward approaches to climbs in The Shooting Gallery safer and more convenient. Until the access/descent trail is completed, additional fixed lines of retired climbing ropes line the base of the crag. Once the trail is completed, these can and should be removed. The often very technical starts to some of the routes has prompted some climbers to bring carpet scraps to stand on while putting on their climbing shoes, but these must be collected and taken home at the end of the day to avoid the buildup of rotting carpet at the base of the crag.

Climbers planning new routes should scope them out on rappel and toprope before drilling to be sure that the line is worth bolting, that the bolts are where they need to be to provide protection unavailable by other means, and that the proposed climb will not have an adverse effect on the climbing resource and its community of plant and animal life. No one should force the extension of an existing route that *nearly* tops out. Gaining another 15 or 20 feet of glory is not worth the impact to clifftop vegetation or the risk of dislodging choss onto belayers and bystanders.

**Guidebook:** Trinity Aretes is described, along with a number of other limestone outcrops and crags, in *Bigfoot Country Climbing: Guide to the Limestone of the Klamath Knot* by Paul Humphrey and Eric Chemello (M. Humphrey Publications, 1997). A condensed version of the Humphrey/Chemello guide also appeared in an article by Eric Chemello and Sharilyn Clark in Issue 94 (August 1999) of *Rock and Ice.*

**Nearby mountain shops, guide services, and gyms:** There are no mountain shops, guide services, or gyms in the immediate area. Adventure's Edge in Arcata and Northern Mountain Supply in Eureka are the best sources for local information. They offer full selections of gear, as do Sports Ltd. and Hermit's Hut, both in Redding.

**Services:** There are no services of any kind at the crag, so bring your own food and water. You can buy groceries, fast food, and fuel a few miles west of Burnt Ranch in the community of Hawkins Bar. While at the crag, be discreet in your personal sanitation, as there are no restrooms. Bury all human waste and carry out your toilet paper, as well as any litter you may find.

**Emergency services:** In the event of an emergency, return to CA 299 and head west to pay phones in the nearby communities of Burnt Ranch and Hawkins Bar. Call 911 to summon rescue or ambulance services. There are no hospitals nearby, although there is an out-patient clinic 14 miles west in Willow Creek for minor emergencies (Hoopa Health Association). For an ambulance, call either 911 or 707-625-4180.

**Nearby climbing areas:** There are several small walls and boulders in the immediate vicinity of Trinity Aretes, but no other nearby crags of any significance. The sea cliffs of the North Coast lie 1–2 hours west of here, and Natural Bridge and the granite crags of Trinity Alps are about the same distance east.

**Nearby attractions:** The greatest nearby attraction is the spectacular Trinity River Gorge and its confluence with New River. Grays Falls, located almost opposite Underwood Mountain Road, offers Class V–VI whitewater. For the more contemplative, the Trinity River offers many fine opportunities to fish for salmon and steelhead.

**Finding the crag:** If approaching from the coast, drive east from the U.S. Highway 101/California 299 junction, which is located just north of Arcata, for 55 miles to a signed junction with Underwood Mountain Road. From the east, drive 41 miles west from Weaverville to the Underwood Mountain Road junction. Turn onto paved Underwood Mountain Road and proceed for 4 miles, ignoring junctions with other signed roads. At 4 miles, where you encounter an obvious four-way intersection, turn right onto signed Forest

Road 5N40. Follow this lightly paved/gravel road past several unpaved spur roads for 1.8 miles. Here, you get your first view of Trinity Aretes. Where the road makes a sharp curve right, turn around and park on the downhill edge of the road. Note that this road serves the timber industry as well as climbers; park as far out of the traveled way as you can. For maximum car safety from big rigs, there is a small pullout 200 yards down the road from the turnaround point. From the apex of the sharp right curve, follow a footpath 200 yards to the foot of the crag, arriving in the vicinity of the mouth of the Shooting Gallery gully. Follow the steep climbers' trail up right for climbs right of The Shooting Gallery. Approach the climbs of Lower Shooting Gallery by scrambling up the gully (Beware of loose rock!). For Upper Shooting Gallery, either climb the gully, which involves some dangerously loose and unprotected 5.3, or take the faint left fork of the approach trail, which circles around the base of Tower of Rubble, then heads steeply up until you can access a ledge system halfway up the crag. Traverse right along the ledge and past a short bouldering wall to a narrow saddle with a large oak tree. From here, a fixed line eases access to the other routes of Upper Shooting Gallery.

Route descriptions appear in the order the climbs would be encountered during an approach to the rock and are listed from left to right.

## UPPER SHOOTING GALLERY

Left of Lower Shooting Gallery, and above and behind The Tower of Rubble stands Upper Shooting Gallery, a black-streaked face that begins halfway up the crag and extends to the summit area. The somewhat more moderate difficulty of Upper Shooting Gallery's routes makes this part of the crag fairly popular. Unfortunately, it is all but impossible to avoid knocking loose stuff down the Shooting Gallery gully, so climbers planning to do routes on this face should verify that nobody is already above them.

1. **Cedar's Dihedral** (5.10a) Begin this traditional, gear-protected route at the short bouldering wall on the approach to the Upper Shooting Gallery ledge. Ascend the obvious, right-facing dihedral for 100' of climbing to the crag's summit for a walk-off descent. Take pro to 2".
2. **Epic in a Bottle** (5.10a) Start 30' right of Route 1, at the chain anchor used to secure the south end of the Upper Shooting Gallery fixed line. Move up right a few feet, then follow 6 bolts to a 2-bolt anchor at 70'.
3. **Stumble in My Footsteps** (5.10c) Begin at the same spot as Route 2. Edge up right past a bolt, then proceed up the juggy wall, clipping 6 more bolts to the anchor. Lower off 70' to return.
4. **Limestone Cowboy** (5.10d) Starting 10' right of Route 3, face-climb past 6 bolts, then head up left past 2 more to the last protection bolt on

## UPPER AND LOWER SHOOTING GALLERY, EAST FACE (TOWER OF RUBBLE NOT SHOWN)

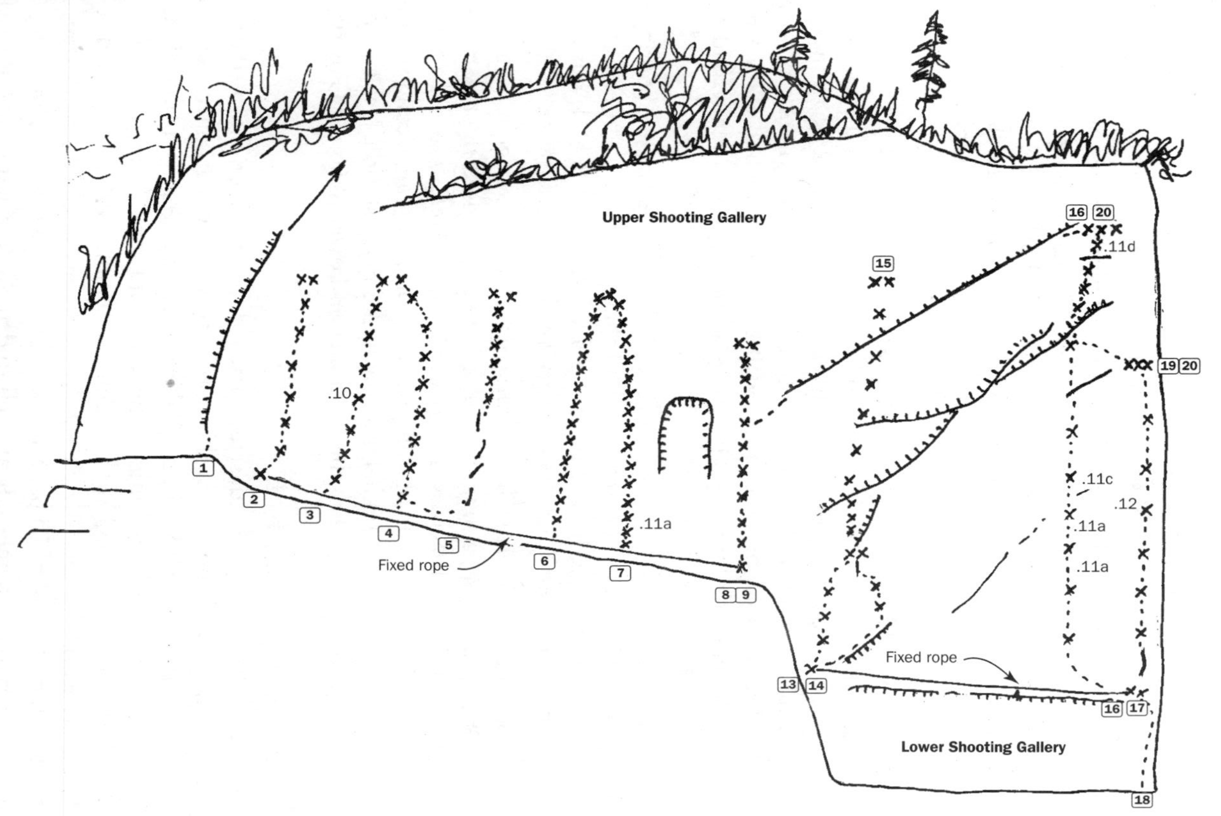

*Stumble in My Footsteps* and continue to that climb's 2-bolt belay anchor. Lower off 70' to return.

5. **Left for Dead** (5.10c) Start by climbing *Limestone Cowboy* as far as its first bolt, then move right, where you find a series of flakes and cracks. Climb these until you can clip a bolt about 35' up. Continue past 5 more protection bolts to a 2-bolt anchor. Lower off 80' to return. Take TCUs from ¾" to 1½" and several cams to 2", including an extra 1".
6. **Snakeshot** (5.10d) Take off on this technically easier but more sustained counterpart of *The Gold Rush* about 12' right of the previous route. Clip an even dozen bolts on your way to the 3-bolt anchor at the top of Route 7. With a 60-meter rope, you can lower off (barely)—otherwise, take your second rope and (after a well-deserved rest) rappel the 90' to the start.
7. **The Gold Rush** (5.11a) Begin this area classic just left of the chain anchor that secures the north (right) end of the fixed line at a spot overlooking Lower Shooting Gallery. Climb technical rock past 2 bolts, make a powerful move, then race fatigue up the wall, clipping a long procession of 12 more bolts on a beautiful wall to a 3-bolt anchor. With a 60-meter rope, you can lower off (barely)—otherwise, take your second rope and rappel the 90' to the start.
8. **Bambi Slayer** (5.10d) At the far-right end of the Upper Shooting Gallery ledge, anchor the belay to the bolt that secures the right end of the fixed line. From here, head directly up a white streak (Check out the big air under your feet!) past 9 bolts to a 2-bolt anchor. Lower off 70' to return.
9. **Side Effects** (5.11a) Climb *Bambi Slayer* to its sixth bolt, then launch out right, following a long, difficult, and very exposed right-slanting undercling/thin crack across the upper part of *Whiplash* to end at bolts atop *Blitzkrieg*. Take lots of thin pro, and consider your second when placing it; also, a 3-inch cam helps at the upper belay station. Use two ropes for the 120-foot rappel to the fixed line on Lower Shooting Gallery.

## TOWER OF RUBBLE

Tower of Rubble is a broad, semi-detached formation on the northeast side of the crag. Though not especially noteworthy from a distance, when viewed from the foot of The Shooting Gallery it can be seen as a thin blade whose architecture vaguely resembles the red sandstone formations of southern Utah. From certain angles, the summit resembles a dolphin's head. Descend by downclimbing the tower's east ridge, then rappelling from trees at and below the east end of Upper Shooting Gallery. Beware! The Shooting Gallery is not a frivolous name—always yell to determine whether any other climbers are active above you. If there are, climb elsewhere for a while to avoid the inevitable barrage of loose rocks.

10. **Chinese Puzzle** (5.6) From the lower end of the Shooting Gallery gully, head up left along a ramp, then climb a left-facing dihedral to a ledge below the sharp, overhanging prow of the tower. Traverse right into The Shooting Gallery to the Upper Shooting Gallery ledge. If you want to climb the tower itself, you could pass behind it to the large oak tree at the south end of the ledge, then climb the exposed but low-angle east ridge. Note that this (optional) pitch is exposed and not easily protected, and the descent is worse; most parties quit after the first lead. Take pro to 3" and several long runners.
11. **The Wright Stuff** (5.10 R/X) Begin by scrambling 20' up The Shooting Gallery, then enter and jam a wide, drafty crack that parallels the gully but keeps 8'–10' to the left, keeping right where the crack branches. If desired, you can belay on a ledge with a sapling at the top of the crack. Above, climb and traverse the top of a flake, where you find the route's only bolt, then tackle the virtually unprotected 5.10 face climbing up the face of the tower. Take pro to 3" and several long runners. The descent is tricky, with no fixed anchors—be careful!
12. **Gullible** (5.3 R/X) Climb the easy-looking but unprotected chimney that connects the lower and upper portions of The Shooting Gallery gully. For safety's sake, position the belayer around the corner to the right of the gully, and don't attempt this route without experience and a helmet.

## LOWER SHOOTING GALLERY

This awesome silvery-gray wall forms the right side of the Shooting Gallery gully. The exposure is immediate and constant, the difficulties unrelenting, and the whole climbing experience on this face is not to be missed. There is a good mix of fixed and natural protection, but Lower Shooting Gallery is no place for the inexperienced or faint of heart.

13. **Open Season** (5.10b) Begin at the bolt that anchors the gully end of the fixed line. Instead of following the ramp, edge directly up the wall past 3 bolts. From the upper bolt, angle up right to the anchor atop *Blew It Crack*. Supplement your rack with cams to 2". Lower off 40' to return.
14. **Blew It Crack** (5.10a) Scramble up The Shooting Gallery to the fixed line and rope up, then follow a narrow ramp up right. At its upper end, head directly up past 2 bolts, marveling at the numerous former bolt holes (remnants of the first ascent), then angle left to a tricky short crack, which leads to a 2-bolt anchor. Take pro to 3". Lower off 40' to return.
15. **Whiplash** (I 5.12b/c) Choose this Eric Chemello masterpiece for what may be the ultimate Trinity Aretes experience. **Pitch 1:** Climb either of the previous two routes. **Pitch 2:** Shake out arms and legs, then launch up the fabulous wall above, chasing a series of 9 more bolts past two

LOWER SHOOTING GALLERY
15
120'
120'
70'
8
9
40'
16
13
14
18
All starting points are hidden.
Protection bolts not shown.

diagonal overlaps to reach the 2-bolt anchor. After a rest, rappel 120' to the start. If you can hang on long enough to place it, take pro to 3", including a ½-inch cam.

16. **Blitzkrieg** (5.11d) Reach the start of this route by scrambling up The Shooting Gallery to the fixed line and follow it to belay bolts at the far-right end, just left of the spectacular arete at the right edge of the face. From the bolts, move back left along the fixed line, then follow a line of 6 bolts up the wall, cranking past several 5.11 moves. From the upper bolt, continue up and a bit left to a thin, diagonal crack (tiny TCUs here). Diagonal up left on very steep terrain, pass over a narrow roof, then face-climb past another 5 bolts and a 1-inch cam placement to arrive at a 3-bolt anchor. Look out! The crux lurks just below the anchors. Make a 120-foot rappel from here to return.
17. **Smack Daddy** (5.12a/b) Approach as for *Blitzkrieg,* sharing its initial belay bolts. Keeping just left of the arete, fight fatigue as you face-climb and occasionally lieback past 6 bolts to a 3-bolt anchor beneath a small roof. Lower off 70' to the starting point.

## VISIONS WALL

This impressive, dead-vertical, battleship-gray wall lies just right of Lower Shooting Gallery. The high-quality routes on Visions Wall are all difficult, and most require at least some use of nuts, cams, or other gear for protection. If you have doubts about your ability to select and set gear while in a sketchy position, don't try to learn here! Note that the hangers on these bolts have been camouflaged with gray paint; keep a sharp lookout.

18. **Flake Surfer** (5.10b TR) Locate this route, which is probably the best introduction to climbing at Trinity Aretes, immediately below the far-right end of the fixed rope used to access the Lower Shooting Gallery routes. Use the fixed rope anchor to run your toprope, then play on the variety of small holds leading up the lower part of the arete. Lower off 50' to the ground.
19. **Visions of Impalement** (5.12a) Begin immediately right of the left edge of the wall, just around the corner to the right of *Smack Daddy.* Climb past 4 closely spaced bolts, then continue to a short crack that accepts a 3-inch cam. Higher, follow 6 more bolts along the right side of the arete, working the crux above the fourth of these, and finally moving up left around the corner to a 3-bolt anchor beneath a small roof. (Note that this is the belay for *Smack Daddy.*) If you have a 60-meter rope, you can lower off to your starting point; otherwise, lower to the fixed line and bolt at the base of *Smack Daddy* and downclimb, or trail a second rope and rappel.

20. **Super Smack** (I 5.12b) If you want to prolong the experience on Route 19, here's your route. **Pitch 1:** Climb Route 18. **Pitch 2:** From the belay bolts under the roof, traverse left and slightly up to connect with *Whiplash* just above its small roof. Follow that climb past 4 bolts to its 3-bolt anchor. Rappel 120' to the fixed line in The Shooting Gallery. Take gear that includes a 3-inch cam.
21. **Indian Summer** (5.11b) Begin 25' right of Routes 19 and 20. After a slightly overhanging start protected by a bolt, head up past 4 more bolts to a horizontal crack, where you can place a 2" cam. Gradually veer up left past 5 more bolts, then follow a left-slanting crack to the belay bolts of Routes 19 and 20. Take pro to 2". Rappel with two ropes; even with a 60-meter line, you will not be able to lower off from here.
22. **Natural Selection** (5.11a R) As the name implies, if you are fumble-footed, you could be removed from the gene pool. Begin as for *Indian Summer* and follow that route to the third bolt above the horizontal crack. At this point, make a sweeping detour up right to a gear placement, then slink up left to a short crack. From its top, continue up and slightly right to another short crack that leads to a pair of belay bolts. Make a 2-rope rappel to return. Take gear to 2", including an extra 2-inch cam, a ¾-inch TCU, and a #8 hex.
23. **Survival of the Fittest** (5.11b) Find a large hueco 15' right of Route 22 and about 30' off the ground. Your route starts below this feature. Climb slightly overhanging 5.10 rock past 3 bolts to reach a cam placement in a crack in the back of the hueco. Power out the top to another bolt, continue up dubious, gear-protected terrain for 30', finesse the crux, then use 2 more bolts and another cam to reach the anchor bolts. With a 60-meter rope, you can lower off; otherwise, trail a second rope and rappel. Take #1 and #2 Camalots and #3 and #4 TCUs. You may be able to sneak in additional pro with small stuff.
24. **Gooseberry** (5.11c) Start behind the obvious dead tree near the middle of the wall. Climb straight up behind the tree past 7 bolts, then angle right past 2 more to a 3-bolt anchor. Lower off 80' to the ground.
25. **Karmakazi** (5.11a) About 15' right of the snag, climb slightly overhanging rock past 3 bolts (crux after the first) to a prominent, left-jutting flake. Use gear to protect the climbing around the flake's left side. From its top, clip 3 more bolts before reaching the anchor this climb shares with *Gooseberry.* Take pro to 2".
26. **420 Shadow** (5.11c) Move right 40' from the snag to find the start of this route. Climb the very blank face past 6 bolts, with the technical crux just beyond the fourth, then veer right to a right-leaning finger crack. Follow

it to the 2-bolt belay anchor. Lower off 70' to the ground. Take a ¾-inch cam for the finger crack.

27. **Chasing Vapors** (5.12b) Begin about 15' right of Route 26 and 10' left of Vision Wall's right edge. Face-climb up and gradually left on minuscule (a polite understatement) crimps and nubbins, following a line of 7 bolts. Above the last bolt, head up to the anchor on Route 26. Take a 2-inch cam to protect this last part.

## PAISANO BUTTRESS

Paisano Buttress is the bulging, nearly featureless wall right of Visions Wall, and it holds a collection of the most difficult climbs on the crag, some of which rank with the most challenging in California. Its lower half overhangs radically—nearly 20' in 90'! In fact, the rock overhangs so much that belayers can often better see the leader by facing *away from the rock* when they look up! Looking up, you can see that a number of bolts on this wall are already equipped with camouflaged quickdraws, but do not assume that they all are. You *must* have a 60-meter rope to do these routes, unless you are enough of an animal to lead 5.13 while trailing a second rope. For all climbs on Paisano Buttress, *make sure your belayer is well-anchored.*

28. **The Undiscovered Country** (5.11c R) You should have no trouble locating this route; it follows the corner crack between Visions Wall and

# VISIONS WALL, PAISANO BUTTRESS, HIGH COUNTRY HEADWALL, AND SAFARI WALL

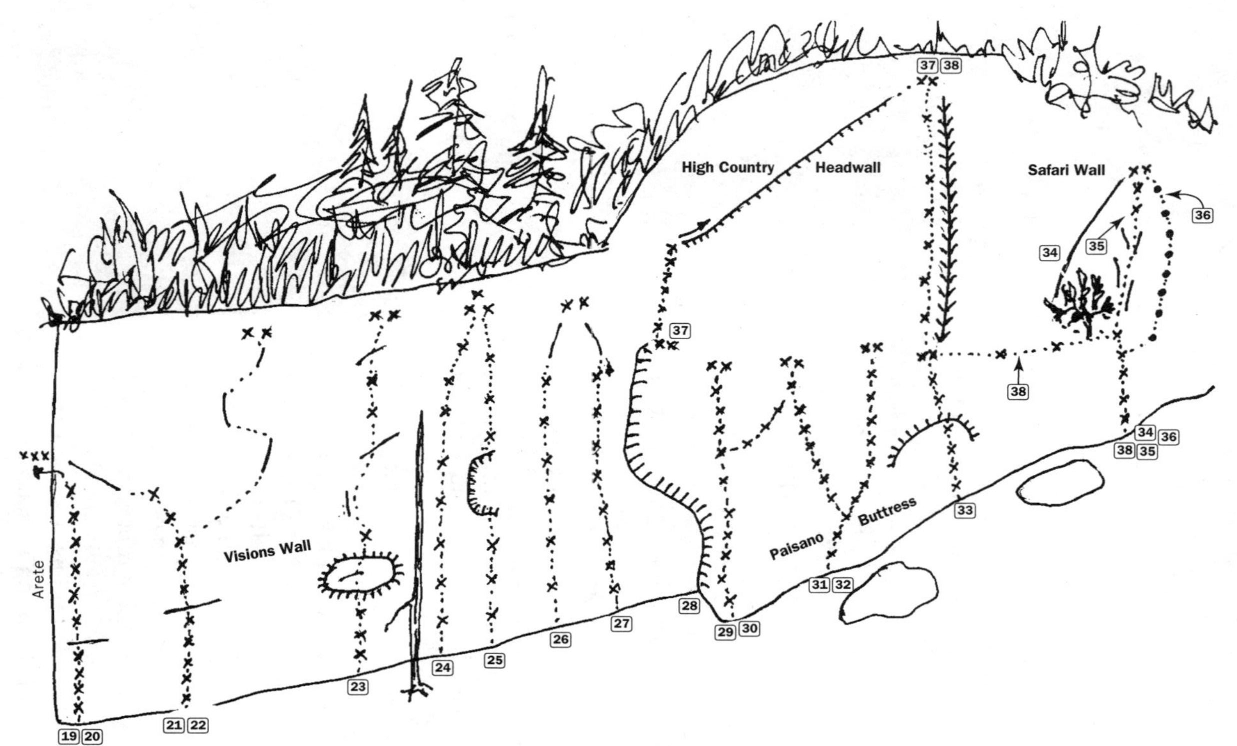

Paisano Buttress. Face-climb, jam, and lieback the thin, left-curving, and overhanging crack. Once past the curve, fist-jam the upper part of the crack, eventually curving back right to a 2-bolt anchor. Take plenty of gear up to 4", including doubles of all smaller cams and stoppers for the pocketed, lower crack.

29. **If** (5.13b/c) Start 8' right of Route 28. Climb the technical, improbable-looking, and overhanging wall right of the corner past 6 bolts. Above, where things really get lively, continue onward, clipping another 5 bolts before reaching the 2-bolt anchor. Lower off 90' to the ground. (Note that local climbers are working to produce a second pitch for this climb. Do not continue onward in the belief that the 2 bolts above the belay lead anywhere.)
30. **Spliff** (5.13b) Begin this harrowing variation of *If* by climbing Route 29 until you reach the seventh bolt. Head up right past 2 bolts, then collect yourself and make the crux dyno to reach another bolt. Continue up right to join *Mean Streak* at its final bolt, just below its 2-bolt anchor.
31. **Mean Streak** (Project) (5.14?) Start 30' up and right of *If*. (Note that starting by stepping across from the large boulders here is considered cheating.) Pull tiny crimps and pockets up right past 3 bolts on the overhanging wall. Break through the first major overhang by heading up left to another bolt. Now head up and more gradually left past 6 more bolts on a continuously overhanging wall to reach the 2-bolt anchor. Lower off 90' to the ground. You should probably use a shoulder-stand or clip stick to clip the first bolt or two.
32. **Paisano Direct** (5.12d) Start as for *Mean Streak*. Climb technical, overhanging rock past 3 bolts, then continue up right through a break past 2 more bolts. Proceed more directly up, clipping 5 more bolts to reach the 2-bolt anchor. Lower off 90' to the ground. Pre-clip the first bolt or two using a shoulder-stand or clip stick.
33. **Burnt Offering** (Project) (5.14?) Locate the start of this route 35' up and right of Route 32, where a prominent, shallow cave forms a roof about 40' up. Climb the overhanging, blank wall past 5 bolts to the roof. Surmount this feature, then head up left past 2 more bolts. Proceed more directly up to the belay bolts 80' off the deck. Either lower off, or continue to the top via *High Country.*

## SAFARI WALL

Safari Wall forms the west face of Trinity Aretes and lies up and right, around the corner from Paisano Buttress. Here, the rock is more featured and less steep, which also means that it is better terrain for harboring mosses and other vegetation. Climbs on Safari Wall are more moderate, but although still of good quality, they look pretty scruffy. More traffic will no doubt result in some change in vegetation patterns, perhaps revealing a new line or two. Visiting climbers should note, however, that deliberate gardening while prospecting for a new route is both selfish and destructive, and it could cause the Forest Service to consider restrictions on access.

34. **On Safari** (5.9) Start about 75' right of the cave of *Burnt Offering.* (Watch for the first bolt opposite a large, mossy boulder; it lies below a large oak tree.) Climb the face, clipping 5 bolts as you make for a large oak tree. Pass left around the oak, then climb up and gradually right to a 2-bolt anchor about 150' up. Either rappel, or carefully climb through moss and small trees to the summit, from which you can scramble down.
35. **El Niño** (5.9+ to 5.11a) Climb *On Safari* to the oak tree. From here, keep right of the oak, make a long reach up and ascend cracks and flakes for 50', then face-climb past 2 final bolts to reach the anchor atop Route 34. Note that the crux reach is very height-dependent, and shorter climbers get the higher difficulty rating.
36. **La Niña** (5.9+ to 5.11a) Climb *On Safari* as far as its fourth bolt, then make a long reach right, finding, as on *El Nino,* that the crux is height-dependent, with taller leaders having the advantage. Watch carefully as you face-climb the rest of the route, as the remaining distance to the anchor shared with Routes 34 and 35 is protected solely by using removable bolts. Take the standard rack and 8 RBs.

## HIGH COUNTRY HEADWALL

High Country Headwall lies left of Safari Wall and above Paisano Buttress. The best and safest means of access is via a traverse right from the top of *420 Shadow,* although ambitious parties could reach it by climbing one of the Paisano Buttress routes—in fact, linkups would provide some stunning multipitch climbs. If these "access routes" seem too troublesome, you could rappel from the summit, but that is a daunting and *dangerous* proposition, due to the abundance of loose rock on top.

37. **High Country** (5.10a) Begin by somehow getting to the anchor that marks the top of *The Undiscovered Country.* Surmount a mossy bulge, then switch to face climbing as you work upward past 6 bolts and some gear placements to the lower end of a long, right-slanting, fingertips crack. Follow the crack up right to the top of the crag. Take pro to 2", including numerous pieces for the slanting crack. Scramble down from the summit.
38. **Put Up or Shut Up** (I 5.10d) **Pitch 1:** Climb *On Safari* until you reach the fifth bolt, then traverse left past 2 bolts to a 2-bolt anchor atop *Mean Streak* and just left of an arete. **Pitch 2:** Ascend the arete, clipping 7 increasingly wide-spaced bolts interspersed with gear placements, to a 2-bolt anchor. Scramble down west from the top.

# MARBLE CAVES

One of the most pervasive characteristics of Marble Caves is the silence: no road noise, no blaring radios, no other climbers, just the wind and the intermittent cries of birds. Here, high on a ridge overlooking forested slopes and canyons stretching into the distance, it is easy to imagine being disconnected from the modern world altogether. Only the subtle glint of hangers and cold-shuts reveals the presence of man.

Marble Caves—an odd name, as the area has no real caves and only small, infrequent inclusions of marble—is a group of towering limestone crags. Virtually invisible from the east, from the west they present a formidable barrier of vertical stone rising over 100 feet from the steep, scree-covered hillside. The rock is a joy to behold, with cavities, pockets, overhangs, flutes, and blank sections all waiting to be experienced. The rock is hard, fine-textured, and generally pretty clean. The climbs here tend to be serious undertakings, with most ratings in the 5.11-and-up range, although additional exploration may disclose more moderate routes. In general, protection is adequate to very good, with well-placed, large, stainless-steel bolts and hangers, so leaders are free to concentrate on the actual business of climbing.

Marble Caves is made up of two major formations: Dream Wall, an impressive, ragged-topped face 150 feet high and nearly a quarter-mile long, and The Tower, a smaller, pale gray and orange formation just to the north and separated from Dream Wall by a brushy gully. A narrow ledge (The Catwalk) runs along much of the foot of Dream Wall, providing generally trouble-free access to most of the climbs. Route descriptions appear right-to-left, in the order they are encountered on the approach route.

**Climbing history:** Marble Caves was probably known to local Native Americans, who would have found these towering rock formations useful lookout points and landmarks. Early white settlers may have seen them while searching for strayed cattle, but actual exploration of the crags by climbers did not occur until the late 1990s.

Sometime in late 1997 or early 1998, an unknown sport climber visited, realized the crags' potential, and returned to bolt and climb *Mystery Route* (5.12a), a beautiful line up a golden, pocketed wall. Word of the area's potential eventually reached Paul Humphrey, the driving force behind most of the recent sport route development on the North Coast and at Trinity Aretes. Humphrey visited Dream Wall with Dave Cressman in March, 1998, liked what he saw, and put up *The 3rd Dream* (5.11d), the area's longest route. Hiko Ito established *Sunset Cruise* (5.11d) on June 20, and Humphrey climbed the challenging *Ascension Addiction Disorder* (5.12b) five days later. Two weeks after that, Humphrey discovered *The Poison Garden* (5.11d). The hot weather of summer brought a temporary halt to route development, but activity picked up again in the fall, with Ito's ascent of *Magic Kingdom*

## MARBLE CAVES AREA MAP

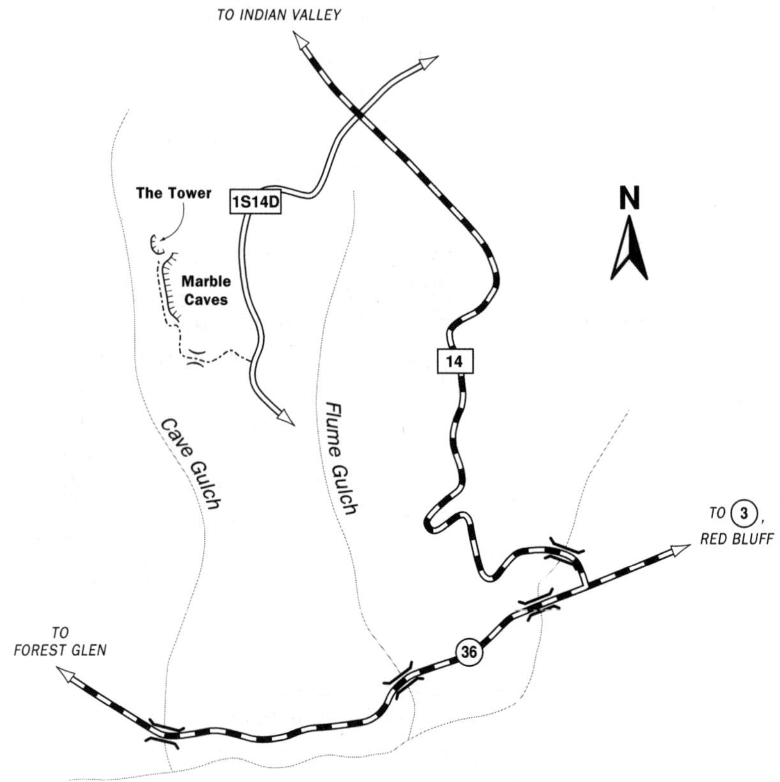


(5.12a) on October 18, and Humphrey's climb of *Son of a Preacher Man* (5.11d) the following week. Sean Leary put up *Broken Glass* (5.12c) on The Tower on Halloween, following with the elusive *Too Gripped to Whip* (5.11d) the next day.

Various projects have followed in the months since then, including Dan Yeager's *Hair for Humans,* Humphrey's *Sky Pilgrim* and *The Invisible Man.* The rather slim number of routes should not be taken as an indication that these crags are climbed out. Virtually hundreds of potential new routes, linkups, eliminates, and variations await those willing to explore and develop them. For sport climbing and, to a lesser degree, traditional climbing, the history of Marble Caves is only just being written.

**Rack:** Bring a selection of 12–15 quickdraws, runners, and cams from the smallest to 1½". Recent route developers have used Removable Bolts, so you should also bring 10–12 of these as well. Nearly all routes have been equipped with rappel/lowering anchors, but because of the length of the routes on Dream Wall, climbing with two ropes is mandatory unless you want to make a long scramble around the back in your climbing shoes.

**Descent:** From the top of Dream Wall, you can easily scramble east, then circle southward to return to the approach trail or the base of your climb. Most climbers prefer to rappel, however, as a number of climbs don't quite top out—this to avoid loose material on top. You can descend The Tower's summit by scrambling east to an oak tree, then rappelling 80' down the south side to the ground.

## TRIP PLANNING INFORMATION

**Area description:** Marble Caves is a group of very aesthetic limestone crags ranging in height from 40' to nearly 150'. Climbs are more likely to appeal to the expert, as most lie in the 5.11–5.12 range.

**Location:** On a west-facing ridge high above the community of Forest Glen in western Trinity County.

**Camping:** It is possible, though not pleasant, to camp in the vicinity of the parking area, but there is no reliable water or privacy. Camping at the crag is out of the question. The nearest Forest Service campground is Hell Gate, located just off California Highway 36 about a mile east of Forest Glen. The campground offers 18 sites, piped-in water, and vault toilets for $4.00 per night. It is open from May through November.

**Climbing season:** Potentially all year, though best from April to November. For portions of Dream Wall, the season is restricted to roughly late July to November, due to nesting peregrine falcons.

**Restrictions and access issues:** Marble Caves lies on land managed by Shasta-Trinity National Forest. The area lies outside any designated wilderness area, so there is no restriction—other than common sense and propriety—on bolting. The primary access issue for Marble Caves is the presence of nesting peregrine falcons on the crag. Molesting these birds by ignoring a voluntary, seasonal climbing closure of some of the routes on Dream Wall could result in a loss of climbing access for all. Marble Caves is a comparatively new climbing area, and local climbers are trying to keep good relations with area managers. To this end, locals have signed the restricted portion of the cliff, and they have worked to develop a decent access trail. All climbers are urged to observe any closures and to stay on the trail.

A good incentive to remain on the trail is the high-profile presence of poison oak on the slopes below the crags. Small colonies may be found along The Catwalk, but they can be avoided without much trouble. Below The Catwalk, however, the irritating shrub flourishes in murderous abundance. As a general precaution, immediately launder all clothing worn to the crag, and wash any exposed skin with detergent and cold water; using hot water opens epidermal pores, allowing the irritating plant oils to enter.

The presence of numerous small bits of limestone littering the ground below the crags demonstrates the fact that the upper portions of these formations contain loose material. Climbers should bring and wear helmets.

**Guidebook:** Paul Humphrey's *Bigfoot Country Climbing* (1998) describes climbs here and at other limestone crags in the Humboldt/Trinity County area.

**Nearby mountain shops, guide services, and gyms:** There are no climbing shops, guide services, or gyms in the immediate area. The nearest climbing shops are Adventure's Edge in Arcata, Northern Mountain Supply in Eureka, and Sports Ltd. and Hermit's Hut in Redding.

**Services:** Marble Caves offers no services. Visitors should plan to bring their own water and food. Any human waste should be carefully buried and the toilet paper carried out.

**Emergency services:** In the event of an emergency, return to CA 36 and drive west to Forest Glen to call 911. The nearest hospitals are Trinity General Hospital in Weaverville, and Saint Joseph Hospital and General Hospital, both in Eureka. Air ambulance service from Weaverville to either Redding Medical Center or Mercy Medical Center in Redding is available for cases Trinity General Hospital is not able to handle.

**Nearby climbing areas:** The nearest climbing area is Bowling Ball, a small crag under development, which lies a mile farther up Forest Highway 14, then 5–10 minutes south.

**Nearby attractions:** There are no nearby attractions. Interesting as this site is to climbers, for non-climbers, it may as well be the dark side of the moon.

**Finding the crag:** If approaching from the coast, proceed east 66.8 miles from U.S. Highway 101 on California 36 to the small community of Forest Glen, then continue another 2 miles to a signed intersection with Forest Highway 14, which branches off to the left just beyond a bridge over Rattlesnake Creek. If approaching from the north and east, reach this point by heading south on California Highway 3 from its junction with U.S. Highway 299 at Douglas City. Follow CA 3 south for 35.8 miles to a junction with CA 36, turn right, and continue west on CA 36 for 8.2 miles to the junction with FH 14. From the CA 36/FH 14 junction, follow the steep, narrow, paved road up a ridge, passing (and ignoring) unpaved spurs that branch off to either side. Where the pavement ends on a saddle at 3 miles, turn left onto Forest Road 1S14D. (Note that this road has numerous raised berms to channel water off the road; these may block access for those in low-clearance vehicles.) Head downhill on FR 1S14D for 0.8 mile to a couple of small parking spaces near a pair of log landings on the right. (In spring 2000, these still held noticeable piles of cull logs.) Keep in mind that this road is used for logging operations and park as far off the traveled way as possible. Locate a hard-to-spot trail that begins near the first landing, then follow it onto the flat clearing of the landing, and proceed west to an obvious, low saddle. From here,

follow the now more obvious trail right, then gradually downhill, reaching the south end of Dream Wall in about 15 minutes. To access the climbs, stay close to the wall, following a narrow ledge (The Catwalk) along the wall's base. Descending lower will land you in the midst of abundant poison oak.

## DREAM WALL

Dream Wall, the first formation reached by the access trail, is a beautiful, serrated wall of rock, striped with orange and black and banded with inclusions of marble and horizontal fractures. Dream Wall's west face soars upward nearly 150', making for long, pumpy pitches best climbed with two ropes. The shaded south side is much more broken and offers the possibility of easy-to-moderate routes up to about 60'. The Catwalk, a narrow ledge running along the foot of the southern half of the west face, provides access to many of the routes described here. The access path runs onto its southern end, traverses it, and continues for some distance beyond its lower north end.

1. **A Vise, Not an Addiction** (5.10a) Locate this easy-to-find route 30' right of the upper end of The Catwalk and a short distance above the trail. Struggle up the slightly overhanging, mossy offwidth between the main wall and a huge, detached block for 35' to its top. Bring Big Bros to span a 10- to 14-inch crack; otherwise, treat the climb as a toprope problem.
2. **Hair for Humans (Project)** (5.12?) Find this route by looking for the anchors at its top; they are the first you find on the approach. It is not fully bolted yet, so you may have to use the anchors for toproping. In general, follow the line leading to the anchors.
3. **The Poison Garden** (5.11d) As you start down The Catwalk, look for a hollow of pale orange rock, striped with dark gray. Begin at the foot of an arete at its left side. Follow a series of 11 bolts up the arete and onto the wall above, passing overhangs and an off-route bolt, and continuing up a steep, arm-burning wall to the 2-bolt anchor at the top. You can lower off (barely) with a 50-meter rope.
4. **Mystery Route** (5.12a) Locate this stunning route by walking left from Route 3, past a small oak, to the foot of a beautiful, gold wall. Follow the obvious line of 12 bolts up the pocketed wall to a pair of coldshuts at the top. Trail a rope for the rappel.
5. **Magic Kingdom** (5.12a) Begin at the same spot as *Mystery Route.* Instead of following the bolts, head up left along a steep, slabby corner

## MYSTERY ROUTE (5.12A) AND THE POISON GARDEN (5.11D), DREAM WALL (NOT ALL BOLTS ARE SHOWN)

that can be protected with very small cams. Watch for a bolt, clip it, then follow a procession of 11 more up the gently overhanging wall above. Rappel 110' to return. Take several cams smaller than ¾".

6. **Son of a Preacher Man** (5.11d) Start 40' left of *Magic Kingdom* and directly below the upper end of the ramp taken by that route. Look for the small bush growing out of the cliff; it marks the start. Climb shallow pockets up the wall, exiting onto the slab at the top of the corner. From here, follow the arete left of *Magic Kingdom* to the top of the wall. Rappel 110' from *Magic Kingdom's* anchors.

7. **Ascension Addiction Disorder** (5.12b) As you stand at the base of *Mystery Route,* this route follows the profile of the rock to your left. Begin 35' left of Route 6. Follow a seam and small, shallow pockets past 7 bolts on the overhanging arete. Take a ½-inch cam to protect the last bit to the anchors. Unlike most routes here, you can lower off this one.
8. **The 3rd Dream** (5.11d) From the arete of Route 7, walk north, heading for The Tower. About halfway along, watch for bolts and an unpromising-looking overlap. Begin below the overlap. Work up left on underclings to pass around the left side of a small roof. Clip bolts as you work up the face above to an easy, lower-angled section. (Check out the interesting bands of marble inclusions, the source of the area's name.) From the easy section, head up the orange headwall and some flutes to a large flake. Jam or lieback the flake to the 2-bolt anchor at the top; 16 bolts. Rappel 140' to return. Take cams to 4" for the final flake and a small one for additional pro on the wall lower down.
9. **The Invisible Man** (Project) (5.12?) If you have trouble finding this route, consider the name. Look for the start near a large oak tree growing near a small cave at the mouth of the gully separating Dream Wall from The Tower. Scan the rock for an RB hole to start, and repeat the process as you proceed upward. Plan to bring a dozen or more RBs.
10. **Sunset Cruise** (5.11d) Scramble up the gully behind The Tower to a large flake situated at the halfway point. Jam or lieback the flake, then climb past 7 bolts and additional traditional pro to a small roof. Surmount this to reach the anchors 120' up. Take pro—especially cams—to 3".

## THE TOWER

The Tower is a smaller companion formation to Dream Wall, located northwest of the larger formation. It offers clean, challenging climbing on beautiful gray and gold rock that appears somewhat more featured than that of Dream Wall. Due to the abundance of route possibilities on Dream Wall, The Tower has been rather neglected, which is a shame as it offers considerable potential for excellent routes.

11. **Broken Glass** (5.12c R) On the outside face of The Tower, look for a section of orange wall marked by a sequence of 12 bolts. (The first of these is pretty far off the deck, so look way up for it.) In general, follow the bolts to the anchors. Take some long runners to avoid rope drag. You may be able to utilize occasional additional pro, so take it with you. This climb is long, so definitely take two ropes to rappel the route.

# NATURAL BRIDGE AREA MAP

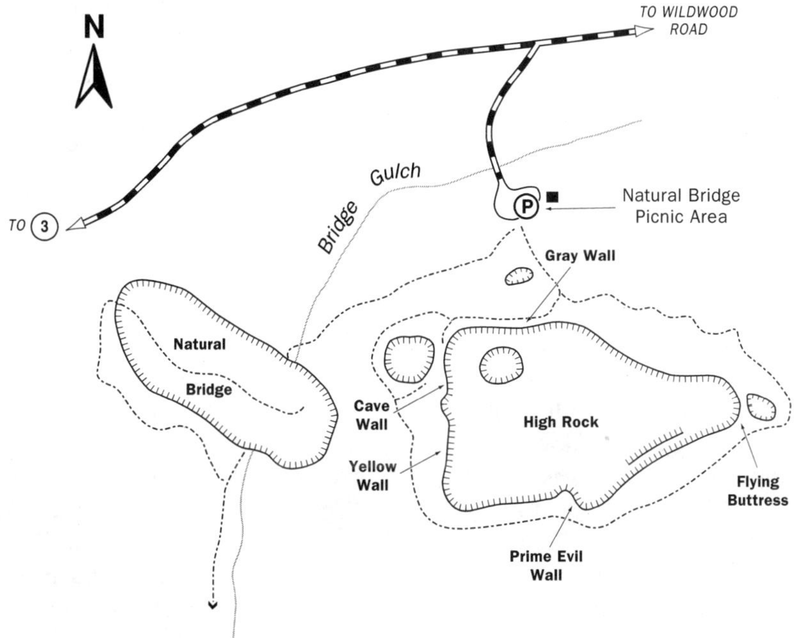


# NATURAL BRIDGE

In the hills southeast of the small town of Hayfork lurks what may prove to be California's largest climbing cave. Natural Bridge is an impressive 100-foot long tunnel through an 80-foot bulwark of rough-textured, gray limestone. If that were not enough to whet the appetite of any climber, Natural Bridge is the smaller companion of High Rock, a complex outcrop that offers both sport and traditional climbing spanning a wide range of difficulty.

Climbs on these formations range from 5.1 to projects that promise 5.14 climbing. Some of these "unfinished symphonies" may eventually prove to be among the hardest climbs in the state. In general, protection is adequate to good. The sport routes nearly all have new, beefy, stainless-steel bolts and hangers. The traditional routes require few long runouts.

All the limestone features near and dear to the hearts of sport climbers are here: huecos, pockets, tufa, grooves, slopers, thin crimps, and minuscule edges in abundance. In addition, traditional climbers find cracks from fingers to offwidth, as well as a few routes with exciting moves up very steep, gear-protected terrain. The rock is a Silurian limestone similar to that found at Trinity

Aretes, but it is far rougher, resembling sharkskin or coarse sandpaper. As a result, climbers should take care to avoid rope drag and to wear clothing that will stand up to abrasion.

**Climbing history:** The first individuals to ascend the rocks at Natural Bridge were undoubtedly the local native people, who, like those at Trinity Aretes, visited the summits during the course of spiritual ceremonies. The cave of Natural Bridge served as a temporary shelter for some during conflicts with white settlers, and, sadly, was also just downstream from the site of a massacre of Native Americans by whites during the 1870s.

Modern climbing was slow to develop at Natural Bridge, owing to its off-the-beaten-track location and the pervasive difficulty of most existing and potential routes. The Trinity County Sheriff's Search and Rescue personnel have used Natural Bridge as a training site for many years, but route development did not begin in earnest until the late 1990s, when Paul Humphrey, Eric Chemello, and other North Coast sport climbers discovered the crag's possibilities. The first routes put up were those on Yellow Wall, followed by the ambitious lines on Gray Wall and the fierce overhangs on Prime Evil Wall. The big plum routes of the area are, of course, those that ascend the awesome roof of the Natural Bridge formation itself. Currently, two do so on the downstream side of the rock, while another has reportedly been done at the upstream end of the tunnel. The area's obvious big project would be an eventual end-to-end traverse of Natural Bridge's tunnel. When finally redpointed, it would become not only one of California's most difficult routes, but possibly one of the most challenging in the world. New route development does not necessarily exclude the non-extreme, either, and local climbers have put up a number of more moderate, traditional climbs. The area is far from being climbed out, and many potential climbs of all grades remain to be done.

**Rack:** If your emphasis is sport climbing, take 12–15 quickdraws, as well as a few runners and extra carabiners. You may find a set of TCUs and some small wired stoppers useful as well. For the area's traditional climbs, take a rack of stoppers and hexes from small wires to 1½", cams from small TCUs to about 3", and a few runners. The newer bolts all have hangers.

**Descent:** Most climbers prefer to lower off from the bolts atop the sport routes. From the top of Natural Bridge, head west toward the hillside and scramble down to the trail that skirts the south side of the rock. If you top out on High Rock and prefer a walk-off descent, head east across the summit plateau. Make a short scramble down to the notch east of the rock, then follow the use trail back to the parking area.

## TRIP PLANNING INFORMATION

**Area description:** Natural Bridge and High Rock are outcrops of fine-grained limestone ranging from 30' to over 150' in height. Natural Bridge itself is a large bulwark penetrated by Bridge Gulch, a small stream that has carved an amphitheater-like tunnel nearly 100' long and having a ceiling height of 20' to 50'.

**Location:** In a stream canyon southeast of the town of Hayfork.

**Camping:** There are no opportunities for camping at the crag itself. The nearest Forest Service campground is Philpot, which offers 10 campsites, vault toilets, and piped-in water. Getting to the campground requires a return to California Highway 3, a short drive west to the town of Hayfork, a drive south from Hayfork on CA 3 to the community of Peanut, then a one-mile jaunt west to the campground. The facility is open from May to October. During summer months, it is also possible to camp at the Trinity County Fairgrounds in Hayfork, where there are showers, flush toilets, and nearby sources of supplies.

**Climbing season:** All year, though best from March through November. During and immediately following rain, the rock can be dangerously slippery. During winter months, Bridge Gulch can become too deep and swift to cross safely. Because of the "indoor" nature of the climbing inside the Natural Bridge cave, it is possible to climb in even the foulest weather.

**Restrictions and access issues:** Natural Bridge is located on land managed by Shasta-Trinity National Forest. The site lies outside designated wilderness, so there are no restrictions on access. Currently, there are no restrictions on climbing or the use of bolts. All visitors should keep in mind that this is a historic site. If anyone comes upon any sign of Native American or pioneer occupation, Forest Service personnel in the Hayfork Ranger District office in Hayfork should be notified. Because of concerns of the local Native American community regarding bolting and climbing on Natural Bridge, continued climbing access to this feature is in doubt. Contact Shasta-Trinity National Forest to verify access status. Climbers should remain aware that the area is commonly used by non-climbing visitors who may unintentionally dislodge debris from the clifftops or place themselves in target positions while trying to watch ascent parties. As at all high-use areas, locking the car is always a good idea.

**Guidebook:** This is the first guide to the area, although Paul Humphrey is compiling information for a forthcoming sport-climbing guide.

**Nearby mountain shops, guide services, and gyms:** There are no climbing shops, guide services, or gyms in the immediate area. The nearest climbing shops are Adventure's Edge in Arcata, Northern Mountain Supply in Eureka, and Sports Ltd. and Hermit's Hut, both in Redding.

**Services:** There is a small picnic area adjacent to the parking area for Natural Bridge, and there are vault toilets. The area offers no piped water, however; visitors should plan to bring whatever they plan to drink.

**Emergency services:** In the event of an emergency, call 911. The nearest hospital is Trinity General Hospital in Weaverville. For cases that Trinity General is not equipped to handle, air ambulance service is available to Redding Medical Center or Mercy Medical Center, both in Redding.

**Nearby climbing areas:** Just east of, and across the road from Natural Bridge lies the as-yet-undeveloped limestone formation called The Rhinecastle. The quality limestone of Marble Caves lies to the southwest, about a half-hour drive away via CA 3 and California Highway 36. A large limestone boulder that promises some interesting work crouches right alongside CA 3 just west of its junction with CA 36.

**Nearby attractions:** If you visit the area during August or September, you will be in time for either the Trinity County Fair, an old-time country fair; or the Trinity Tribal Stomp, a colorful mélange of music, dancing, and food.

**Finding the crag:** From Weaverville, head southeast on California Highway 299 for 6.1 miles to Douglas City. Turn right where California 3 branches off to the right, and proceed toward the town of Hayfork for 17.6 miles to Wildwood Road. Turn left, following Wildwood Road for 5.4 miles to a dirt road on the right signed "Natural Bridge 1." Wind up this narrow road for a mere 0.4 mile, then turn downhill onto a spur road on the left and follow it across shallow Bridge Gulch to a parking area suitable for 6–8 vehicles. From the picnic area adjacent to the parking area, take the level trail on the right to reach the actual natural bridge. To reach most of the established climbs, take the left-hand path uphill from the picnic area, reaching High Rock near the foot of Gray Wall. Access the other faces of High Rock via a use trail that circles the formation.

## HIGH ROCK

High Rock, though not as spectacular as Natural Bridge, is much larger and offers quality climbing on a number of faces, with traditional and sport routes that average 70'. High Rock's walls face north, west, and south, providing climbers with considerable temperature control throughout the year. Take care wandering about on its summit plateau, as there is much loose rock hidden under abundant moss and occasional poison oak. Route descriptions are listed from left to right, beginning with those on Gray Wall, the first major wall encountered on the approach from the parking area.

## GRAY WALL

Gray Wall, the formation's north face, faces the parking area and is the first wall encountered on the climbers' trail. Its moderate-to-difficult sport routes offer much to please first-time or repeat visitors, and its north aspect guarantees cooler climbing—a decided plus during the summer. All routes on the wall are protected by bolts and a modicum of gear. Most parties lower off to avoid the unpleasant and potentially dangerous moss-covered terrain on top of the rock.

1. **Gray Day** (5.10c) Begin below a prominent, large hueco near the left side of the face, 15' left of a large Douglas-fir growing near the base of the wall. Climb up to the hueco, exit left along a string of small pockets to a bolt, then ascend the steeper wall past 2 more bolts. Diagonal up right to

*Scott Morris checks out the opening moves of* Dirt Surfer *(5.11c) on Gray Wall.*

## GRAY WALL

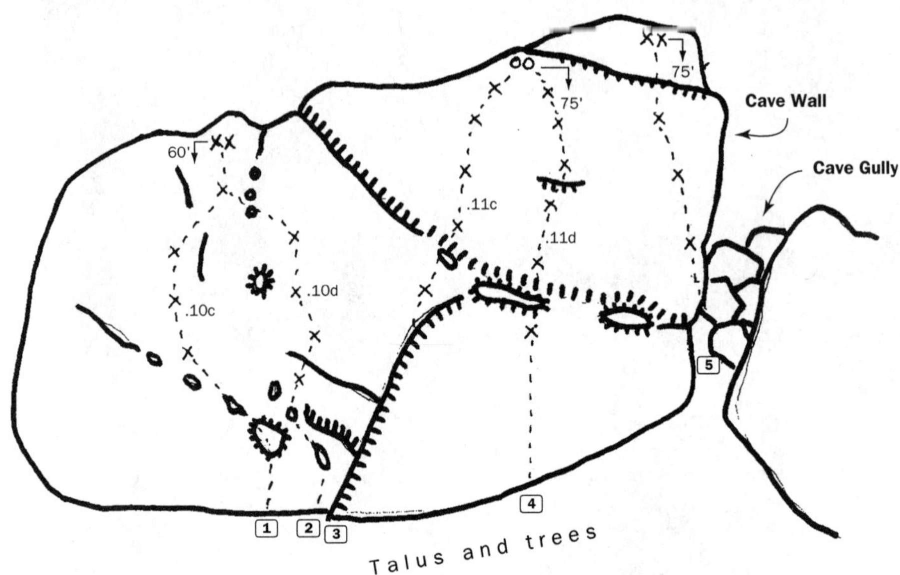


a fourth bolt, then charge up to a 2-bolt anchor. You may want to add a 2½-inch cam to your rack.

2. **Silver Lining** (5.10d) Start a few feet right of *Gray Day* and just left of a left-facing dihedral. Climb up to, and around the left side of a small overhang. Clip a bolt, then head up right to another. From here, work back left to a third bolt, then make the crux moves on the way to the fourth. Head up left to join *Gray Day* at its last bolt, and continue to the anchors. A couple of large tri-cams or SLCDs to 3" can be used in pockets for additional protection.
3. **Dirt Surfer** (5.11c) Climb the obvious, left-facing dihedral that extends halfway up the face to a long, upswept bulge. Leave the dihedral when it curves right and clip a bolt below the bulge. Pull past the bulge to a second bolt, then work up the steep wall above, past 3 more bolts, to a double-coldshut anchor.
4. **Unnamed** (5.11d/.12a) Look for a lone bolt just below a large hueco right of the *Dirt Surfer* dihedral, and begin directly below it. Ascend sketchy face climbing to the bolt, step into the hueco, clip another bolt just over the bulge above, then finesse your way onto the steep wall

above. Proceed up and eventually left past 4 more bolts to the coldshuts atop *Dirt Surfer.*

## CAVE WALL

The prominent, undercut arete that forms the right edge of Gray Wall marks the entrance to Cave Gully, a talus chute in which those with an adventurous streak can explore a well-hidden but remarkably large talus cave. The gently overhanging wall above the gully is Cave Wall. Although no routes currently ascend Cave Wall, it promises a good half-dozen climbs in the 5.11-and-up range. One project has been started near its left edge.

5. **Project** (5.12+?) Begin on boulders about 10' up from the mouth of Cave Gully. Move up left to the arete, make the crux step-around left to a bolt, then continue up and gradually left past 2 more before reaching the 2-bolt anchor above a small ledge. Considering the distance to the first bolt, you should consider using a clipstick.

## YELLOW WALL, A.K.A. MAIN WALL

Beyond the notch atop Cave Gully lies tiger-striped Yellow Wall, the largest face on the rock, overlooking Bridge Gulch. A steep, right-facing dihedral/gully separates the left side of Yellow Wall from Epitaph Buttress, a

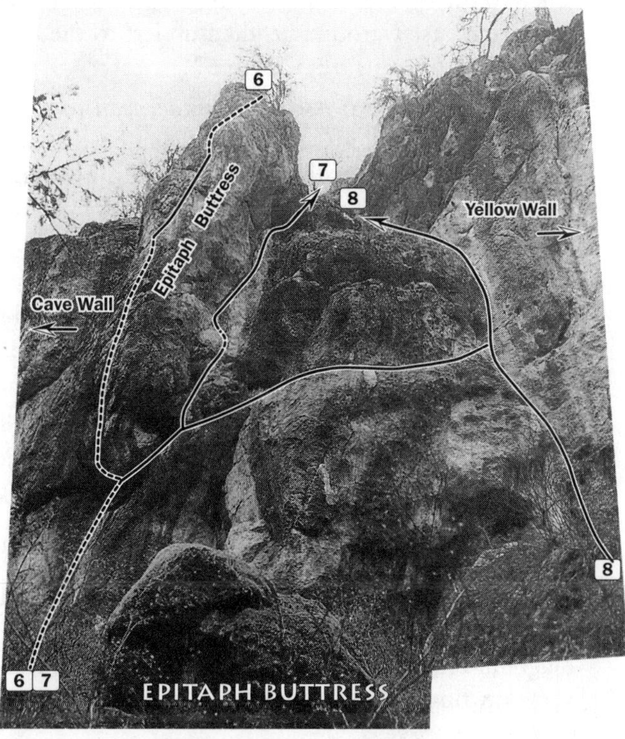

EPITAPH BUTTRESS

fierce-looking, undercut fin. The routes trace lines up the left end of the wall, but the attractive, tiger-striped right half of the wall promises future parties a number of excellent sport routes. Yellow Wall can be approached by climbing Cave Gully, by hiking through the tunnel of Natural Bridge and crossing Bridge Gulch, or by circling around the east end of High Rock.

6. **Elegy** (5.11d/5.12a X or TR) Begin at the base of a small, orange-and-black, right-facing corner that leads up to a rounded roof. Lieback the crack, then use awkward sidepulls to pull directly over. Climb small, vertical flakes, followed by a fingertip lieback on the prow of the buttress. Romp up easier ground to the top. If leading this route, take numerous stoppers, emphasizing smaller sizes, and cams to 3".
7. **Epitaph** (5.11a) Begin as for *Elegy,* but once you reach the roof, follow a flared crack right to an orange streak on the face above. Make a tricky exit from the crack, then follow a thin lieback crack up the right side of the buttress, eventually entering the top of the gully that separates Epitaph Buttress from Yellow Wall. Take 6–10 stoppers to 1", and cams to 3". If you do not like the looks of the upper lieback, you can follow the crack right, then mantle onto a ledge that leads right to *Thunderhead.*
8. **Thunderhead** (5.9) Scramble up boulders to the base of the gully that separates Epitaph Buttress from Yellow Wall. Climb a 5.8 hand-to-fist crack to the right end of a sloping ledge, then ascend a 5.9 offwidth until you reach easier ground heading up left to the top of the gully. Take an assortment of cams from 2" to 6".
9. **Thunderclap** (5.11a) Ascend *Thunderhead* to the top of an orange area near the end of its crux offwidth. From here, follow a thin (5.11a) crack up right across the wall right of the gully, heading for a large tree at the top of the crag. Carry the cams needed for Route 8, as well as several small TCUs for the crux finger crack.
10. **Tiger Bomb** (5.12b) Begin 8' right of Route 8, at the foot of a conspicuous orange stripe. Stay on the stripe as you ascend the often-vertical wall past 6 bolts to eventually top out at a large tree. If you take some small wired stoppers and RPs, you can coax some additional protection out of a thin flake crack on the upper-left edge of the stripe.
11. **Unknown** (5.11b TR?) Starting below the left end of a long, diagonal crack, face-climb parallel to *Tiger Bomb,* but keep to the gray-black rock 8'–10' to the right. (Note that the 7 bolts on the route appeared to be hangerless and/or chopped when the author visited in May 1999. If they have not been replaced, the climb will require a toprope.)
12. **Switchback** (5.11c/d R/X) Start as for Route 11. Once you reach the long, diagonal crack that snakes up and right, follow it for a long hand-traverse on fingers and jammed hands. Where the crack makes an abrupt

switchback left, make the transition and follow it up left to the top of the wall. Take lots of cams, from TCUs to 3-inch SLCDs, and don't be stingy in placing them; *this route has high "chop potential" for leader and second alike.*

## ORANGE WALL AND PRIME EVIL WALL

Farther around to the right of Yellow Wall is High Rock's south face. About 60 yards uphill and right of the right edge of Yellow Wall, a prominent gully splits this aspect of the rock. Just to its right lies Orange Wall, a cave-like face between the gully and a large roof 15' off the ground. The imposing face above the roof is Prime Evil Wall.

12. **Land that Time Forgot** (5.7) Beginning at the base of Orange Wall, head up left, following a conspicuous, left-leaning crack at the right edge of the gully. Take pro to 2½".
13. **Orange Wall a.k.a. Tangerine Dream** (5.11d) From the foot of Route 12, follow the crack a few feet, then exit right into a long, narrow, shallow, orange cave. Work up to the top of the cave via large, but awkwardly placed, holds protected by 3 bolts. Carefully pull over the razor-edged lip of the cave onto the steep gray wall above. Work up past one more bolt to the chains at the top.

PRIME EVIL WALL
14
15

14. **Prime Evil** (5.13a R) Locate the starting point for this difficult sport/trad route below the large, rounded roof right of Orange Wall. Stick-clip the first bolt, which lies about 10' off the deck, on a stepped section of the roof. Using powerful finger moves and sketchy footwork, head for the first bolt, then work up left to a second bolt perched just beyond the lip of the roof. From here, proceed up the vertical, black-striped wall, plugging cams into huecos to protect the 20-foot race against fatigue to reach the coldshuts at the top. Take cams and/or tri-cams to 3".
15. **Project** (5.13b/c?) Begin as for Route 14, but from the first bolt, head up right on overhanging rock to the second bolt, then up the initially overhanging wall above, past 3 more bolts, to coldshuts at the top.
16. **Project** (5.13b?) Beginning a few feet right of Route 15, head up and around the right side of the roof, then more or less straight up the wall, using 8 bolts.

## FLYING BUTTRESS

Just above the shallow notch east of High Rock, a small, shattered pillar leans against the main rock, forming a conspicuous "flying buttress." This small formation, with its abundant cracks and holds and its congenial angle, provides a friendly place for less experienced or less ambitious climbers to practice their skills.

17. **Flying Buttress** (5.4) Ascend the outside face of the formation, using any of numerous variations; all are about 5.4.
18. **Playing Hooky** (5.7 to 5.9) Begin 10' right of Route 17, then use a heel hook to pull over the overhanging right side of the Flying Buttress formation. The farther right you start, the harder the entry moves. Once past the initial overhang, the rest of the way up is easy.

## CRUMBLING LAND

West of the notch at the head of Cave Gully is the summit of Crumbling Land, a mossy, 150-foot pinnacle that forms the gully's right side. Historically, this formation has been used primarily as a rappelling site, but one fine traditional route has been done, and some decent other routes could be worked out with a bit of judicious cleaning. Care should be taken when setting toprope or rappel anchors, as the summit blocks are prone to looseness. Single anchors should definitely be avoided.

19. **Primordial Ooze** (5.9) Climb unpleasant, mossy rock to the foot of a much cleaner, left-facing dihedral. Lieback up the dihedral to its top, then follow the left-slanting crack that continues up out of the corner and across the steep, upper face of the Crumbling Land Pinnacle. Take pro to 2".

## NATURAL BRIDGE

Natural Bridge is a relict outcrop of limestone that in the far-distant past diverted the waters of Bridge Gulch through a narrow ravine separating Natural Bridge and High Rock. Earthquakes and freeze-thaw action eventually caused a large landslide that blocked the water's path, forcing it against the Natural Bridge formation until it had bored a tunnel completely through, creating the amazing natural tunnel that provides the region's most impressive roof and the possibility of all-weather climbing at the upper reaches of technical difficulty. The cave is a wonderful place to hang out in hot weather, so climbers should be aware of the possibility of having to share the formation with picnickers, hikers, and climber-watchers. The cave is also a natural wind tunnel, so climbers should bring sweaters or jackets, even in summer. In addition to the fantastically difficult routes in the cave, Natural Bridge also offers a wealth of possibilities for easy-to-moderate routes in its upstream face. Beware of abundant poison oak in the vicinity. Note that this formation is a cultural site important to the Wintu tribe. Confirm access status with the forest service before visiting; a partial or complete closure may be in effect.

20. **Futurama** (Project) (5.14b?) You may find the start of this ambitious and demanding route somewhere near the upstream end of the cave. It is not obvious. Watch for a lone bolt, then look for RB holes. Because this is a project, you may find additional holes and/or bolts. If you elect to give it a try, take along a minimum of 7 RBs and 2 cams (for supplemental protection).

21. **Bridge Route** (5.14a) It is easy to find this amazing cave route; you practically run into the lowest bolts as you cross the creek and enter the cave. Using 10 conveniently close-spaced protection bolts, work up left to the roof of the cave, then keep going, aiming for the apex of the roof, but stopping short at a pair of bolts equipped with lock links. Note that, at the time of this writing, the eighth bolt is bad (a quarter-inch "spinner"). Hopefully, it will be replaced in the near future. The crux, though probably not the most technically difficult move, involves an uncharacteristically long sequence along a thick flake just beyond the bad bolt.

22. **Unknown** (5.13c) Begin this overhanging, 8-bolt sport route about 10' right of the start of *Bridge Route*. Basically, head up and right on strenuous jugs, pockets, slopers, and crimps to a pair of coldshuts at the lip of the roof. Once you master this one, you will be ready for *Bridge Route*.

23. **Project** (5.14b?) Follow Route 22 as far as its seventh bolt, but instead of surmounting the roof and heading up to the anchors for that route, work left along a line of huecos. Clip 2 more bolts before reaching the left edge of another roof. Pull over onto a hanging slab, angle up left to another

## CAVE ROUTES, NATURAL BRIDGE

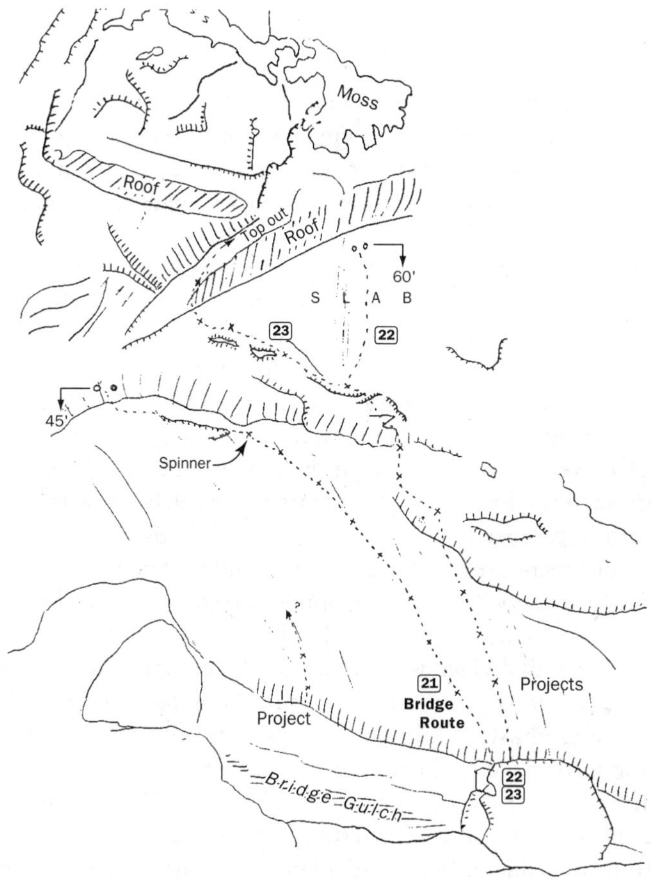


bolt beneath an even larger roof, then swing onto another hanging slab. Pass 3 more bolts to reach the last, positioned just beneath another (mossy) roof. One more strenuous pull puts you on easy but treacherous ground. *Do not unrope until you are on clean rock!* This route does not at present have lowering anchors, and its length mandates a 60-meter rope and plenty of runners to combat rope drag. You may be able to do this route as a second pitch to Route 22. An alternate strategy would be to climb with two 60-meter ropes. Use one for the first 7 clips, then switch to the other for the rest.

# BABYFACE, A.K.A. LITTLE SUICIDE

Granite Peak anchors a prominent corner of the Trinity Alps Wilderness Area and overlooks Trinity Lake, a large and popular waterskiing and fishing lake. From the lake, the south side of the mountain is a giant, forested pyramid studded with granite outcrops. Babyface is the most easily accessible of these, and it can be seen almost dead-center on the mountain's south side, near the bottom of a long, narrow, open area that resembles an avalanche chute. Its setting is well-nigh perfect, with a stunning view of the lake set against a backdrop of jagged peaks. A branch of Stoney Creek gurgles unseen a few yards to the west, and the sunny, south-facing dome dries quickly, providing nearly-all-year climbing.

Seen close-up, Babyface is a granite dome ranging in height from 40' to 150'. Ledges and crack systems have broken the dome into three progressively steeper (and progressively more challenging) slabs and walls. Babyface is an excellent place for less-experienced climbers to learn basics and practice their skills. At the same time, it offers enjoyable climbing for more polished practitioners. Ratings range from Class 4 to 5.12b, with the majority centered on the 5.8 to 5.10 level. Several routes can be led, and nearly all routes can be toproped, although the longer climbs require an upper belay with the belayer out of sight of the climber for much of the time. Climbs consist primarily of face climbing, but there are also short cracks, wild underclings, arches, and a flared chimney for variety. Route descriptions appear in right-to-left sequence, in the order the climbs are encountered by the visitor.

**Climbing history:** Babyface was discovered by climbers in the late 1990s. There is no first ascent record available, but it is safe to assume that most major lines were established early. The author and other local climbers are responsible for sorting out and defining the current routes.

**Rack:** Take a small rack of stoppers and hexes to 1", cams to 2", a few quickdraws, and several runners for setting toprope anchors. Loose rock does not appear to be a problem, but boulders in the vicinity often have bad landings, so you should use a spotter.

**Descent:** Descend most climbs by walking off and scrambling down from the top of the crag.

## TRIP PLANNING INFORMATION

**Area description:** Babyface is a small, south-facing granite dome. The 40- to 150-foot faces offer a collection of enjoyable slab and crack routes reminiscent of Southern California's Suicide Rock. Routes range from Class 4 to 5.12d.

**Location:** Halfway up the south face of Granite Peak in the Trinity Alps Wilderness Area, at an elevation of approximately 4,500 feet.

# BABYFACE, A.K.A. LITTLE SUICIDE

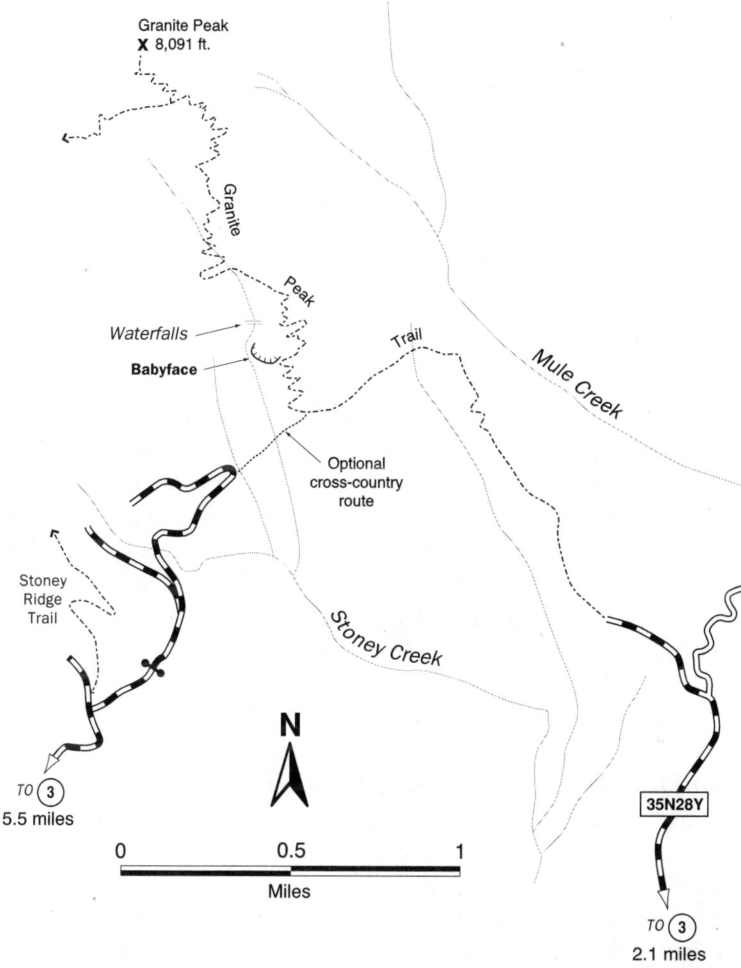


**Camping:** There are numerous opportunities to camp on Trinity Lake, and several Forest Service campgrounds are located in the vicinity. The Stoney Point campground lies across California Highway 3, a mere 0.2 mile west of the Stoney Ridge Trailhead access road. This all-year, walk-in campground offers 22 tent sites, piped-in water, and flush toilets for $8.00 per night. Another 0.3 mile west on CA 3, a spur road leads north through Trinity Alps Resort to Bridge Camp, which offers 10 sites for tents only and 8 more that can accommodate RVs. There are vault toilets and piped water. This site is $6.00 per night. The nearby waters of Stuart Fork offer a welcome opportunity to cool off on a hot day. The 21-site Minersville campground lies a short way down a spur road directly across CA 3 from the Granite Peak Trailhead access road. It offers flush toilets and piped-in water, as well as access to Trinity Lake, but it is currently closed due to a badly washed-out access road. Those seeking more civilized accommodations can stay at either Trinity Alps Resort or Cedar Stock Resort, which lies along CA 3, 1.4 miles east of the Stoney Ridge Trailhead access road. Additional camping is available at 74-site Pinewood Cove Resort 0.5 mile east of the Stoney Ridge Trailhead access road. The resort provides flush toilets, a recreation room, coin-operated laundry, and a small store. Primitive camping is also available at the parking area, though there is no water available.

**Climbing season:** Nearly year-round, limited only by snow and cold.

**Restrictions and access issues:** Babyface lies so close to the edge of the Trinity Alps Wilderness Area that there is some debate whether it is actually inside the wilderness. To be on the safe side, secure a Forest Service wilderness permit in Weaverville or Redding for your visit. The author checked with the wilderness managers for the Trinity Alps in 1999 to determine whether the within-wilderness bolt ban is in effect for this area and was told that the Forest Service had heard it was a problem elsewhere but not here. This cautious non-prohibition suggests a "wait-and-see" attitude on the part of wilderness managers that climbers would do well to respect. In short, if you must bolt, be very discreet. Make sure every bolt is justifiable, and make it worth the effort by installing modern ⅜-inch bolts, at least 2½" in length, with stainless-steel hangers. Do not leave webbing anywhere, and above all, pick up and carry out everything you find that did not originate on the site. By maintaining a low profile and a respectful attitude toward the rock and the countryside, you can ensure continued access to this and other crags.

**Guidebook:** This is the first guide to the crag.

**Nearby mountain shops, guide services, and gyms:** There are no mountain shops or gyms in the area. Guided climbing is available through Rush Creek Enterprises.

**Services:** There are no services available at the rock, although there is a small creek nearby for drinking water. Note that all water should be considered suspect and filtered or purified accordingly. Because of the absence of toilet facilities, all visitors should take care of business well away from the creek—preferably east of the trail—and should carry out all toilet paper in a plastic bag.

**Emergency services:** In the event of an accident, return to the car and proceed to one of the pay phones at either Mule Creek Ranger Station, located 0.5 mile north of the Granite Peak trailhead access road on CA 3; Cedar Stock

# BABYFACE

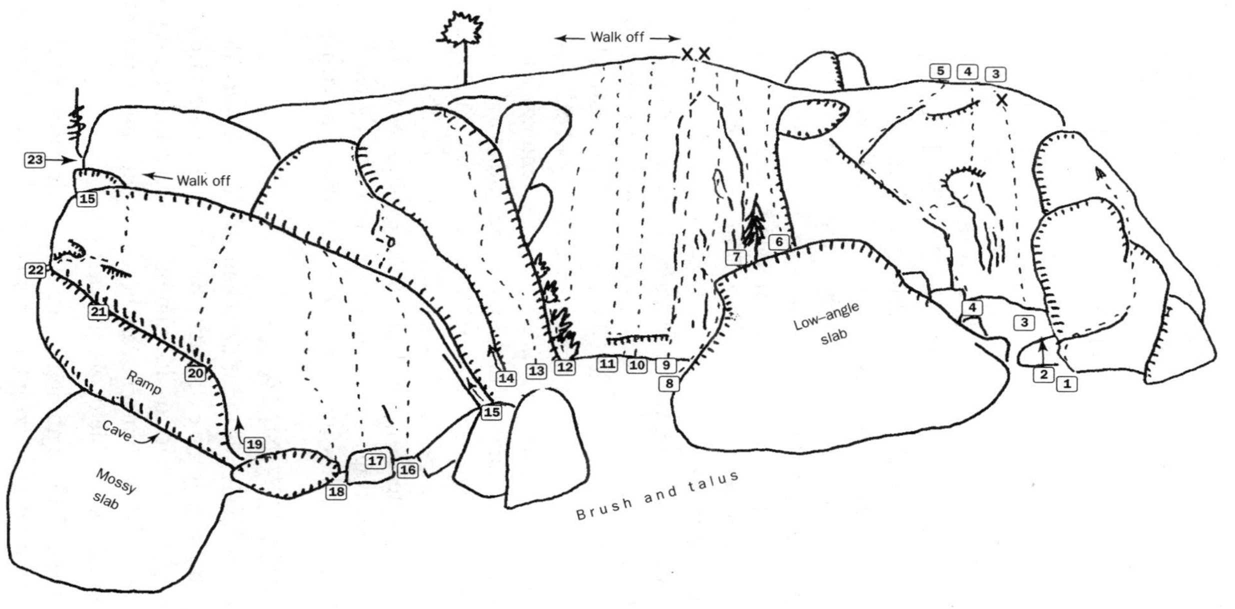

Walk off
Walk off
Low-angle slab
Ramp
Cave
Mossy slab
Brush and talus
1
2
3
3
4
4
5
6
7
8
9
10
11
12
13
14
15
15
16
17
18
19
20
21
22
23

Resort, located midway between the Stoney Ridge and Granite Peak trailhead access roads; or Trinity Alps Resort, located 2 miles up the signed road that heads north from the east end of the Stuarts Fork bridge, 1 mile west of the Stonewall Pass access road. Call 911 to summon an ambulance or the Trinity County Sheriff's Search and Rescue Posse. Trinity General Hospital is located in Weaverville, while Redding offers both Mercy Medical Center and Redding Medical Center. Both of the Redding hospitals have air ambulance service to and from Weaverville.

**Nearby climbing areas:** Rush Creek Spire, which provides opportunities for interesting alpine rock climbs, lies northwest of Weaverville and can be seen from Babyface. Farther north off CA 3 stands Ycatapom Peak, which offers the longest rock climbs in northwestern California.

**Nearby attractions:** For a rest day away from the rocks, the historic gold-mining town of Weaverville is worth a visit—especially its Joss House, a Taoist temple built by Chinese immigrants in 1874 and still in use today. Closer at hand, Trinity Lake offers swimming, sunbathing, boating, and fishing, while the surrounding Trinity Alps Wilderness Area boasts hundreds of peaks, lakes, and miles of trail.

**Finding the crag:** From the California Highway 299/CA 3 intersection in Weaverville, drive northeast on CA 3 for 16.7 miles to a signed junction with a Forest Road that leads to the Granite Peak Trailhead. (This junction lies about 5 miles past the highway bridge over Stuarts Fork.) Turn left here and drive 3 miles on the gravel surface to a large landing. Find the trail at the northwest end of the landing and follow the path for 1.5 steep miles to the Trinity Alps Wilderness Area boundary. Continue up the trail, zigzagging around granite boulders. Just beyond the third switchback that heads right, leave the trail and head up left through a few bushes to the east end of the crag. Climbs at the crag's west end may be most easily reached by hiking up and over the rock. Allow about 1½ hours for this approach.

## PUNCHBOWL PINNACLE

Punchbowl Pinnacle is a 40-foot detached slab whose left side forms a prominent flared chimney at the east end of Babyface. The formation's name comes from the large "birdbath" on its summit. Though lacking toprope anchors, climbs on Punchbowl Pinnacle can be done with an upper belay, and the descent is an easy scramble down the east side.

1. **Party Time** (5.6) Beginning at the lower left corner of the slab, follow a crack/ramp up right to intersect with a wide crack that angles up left. Follow it to a narrow ledge, traverse 6' right, then face-climb to the top of the formation. Take pro to 1½". For a greater challenge, begin 15' farther right and face-climb directly up to the upper ledge (5.9 R).

2. **Youth in Asia** (5.5 R or TR) Climb the deceptively difficult, low-angle squeeze chimney on the left side of Punchbowl Pinnacle. For an interesting time, try the 5.10d offwidth finger crack that leads up right from the base of the chimney and connects with *Party Time* about halfway up.

## BABYFACE

Immediately left of Punchbowl Pinnacle lies Babyface, a 70-foot, generally low-angle slab marked by several waterstreaks. This part of the crag offers a good environment for those learning face-climbing skills, and all routes can be toproped. There is a bolt anchor at the top of Route 3.

3. **High-heeled Sneakers** (5.6 R/X or TR) Starting 10' left of *Youth in Asia,* friction up the face to a small, semicircular, inverted flake. If leading, you can use a 2½-inch cam under the flake. Pass it on the right, making some interesting moves on steeper ground before reaching the anchor.
4. **Bongo Flake** (5.9) Begin 15' left of Route 3. Head up the open, low-angle face for 50' to a low-angle gray area. From the upper end of this gray area, make a few tricky face moves, then mantle onto the top of the "bongo flake," a hollow sheet of granite a couple of inches thick. If leading, take cams to 2". If you want a somewhat easier (i.e., 5.7) version of this route, move right a few feet from the "bongo flake," and proceed up less-steep rock to the anchor atop Route 3.
5. **Ricochet** (5.2) Climb a shallow groove near the left side of the face and a few feet right of a prominent, low-angle waterstreak, then work up left alongside the broad (and often active) waterstreak for a few feet before following a thin crack up right to the top of the rock.

## COUGAR TRACKS FACE

Cougar Tracks Face is the central feature of Babyface: a waterstreaked, featured slab about 80' high that offers the crag's most enjoyable easy-to-moderate face climbs. A pair of bolts atop *Cougar Tracks* provides a handy toprope anchor (note that these bolts require a short, easy, but exposed downclimb). Climbers can reach these routes by either traversing left from Babyface on a brushy ledge with a pine tree growing on it, or by scrambling up low-angle slabs from below. The descent is a walk-off.

6. **Luke Knobwalker** (4) Beginning near a small pine tree below the right edge of the face, ascend easy slabs to the top. You can use this route as a shortcut to reach the toprope anchors for other routes.
7. **Tree Route** (5.6 TR) From the larger of two small pine trees on the brushy ledge, climb interesting friction, then easier rock to the top of the face.

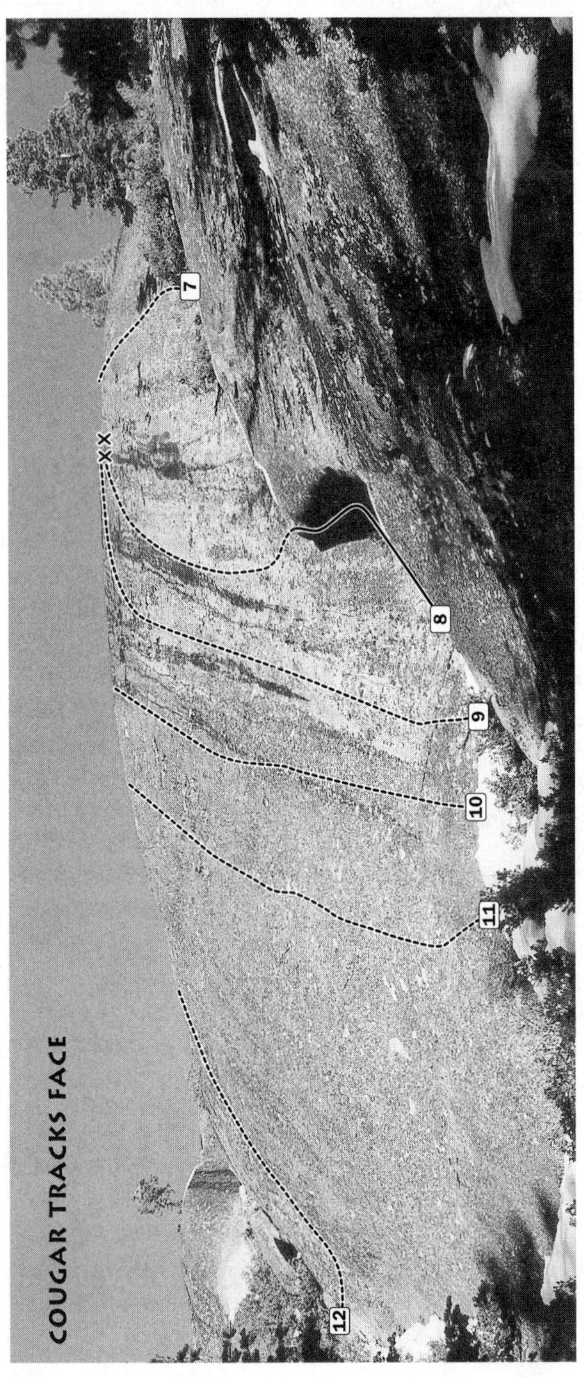
COUGAR TRACKS FACE
7
XX
8
9
10
11
12

8. **Giant Step** (5.7 TR) Start at the foot of a left-jutting flake that forms the left end of the brushy ledge. Lieback the flake, then move up left to knobs. Now head directly up the slab to the top, keeping right of *Cougar Tracks*.

9. **Cougar Tracks** (5.7 X or TR) Start by mantling onto a long, thin ledge a few feet off the ground and 6' left of the flake of *Giant Step*. From near its right end, climb knobs and ripples as you follow an obvious, white waterstreak.

10. **Ananova** (5.9 TR) Gain the long, thin ledge of *Cougar Tracks,* then head directly up from near its center, initially following a wide groove, then proceeding up the smoother face above.

11. **Millennium Falcon** (5.9 TR) Begin as for Route 10, then move to the left end of the long, thin ledge before climbing directly up the slab.

12. **Second Thoughts** (5.7 TR) Scramble about 15' up the brushy trough that forms the left edge of Cougar Tracks Face, then step right onto the slab, continue right about 6', and face-climb up the left side of the slab. Near the top, follow a thin, right-facing flake for the final 30'.

## RAINBOW ARCHES

Left of the brushy trough at the left edge of Cougar Tracks Face, the rock forms a prominent, left-curving arch flanked above and below by other, less well-formed arches. At present, these offer the longest gear-protected lead climbs on the crag. Because of their traversing nature and the architecture of the crag in this vicinity, these are serious undertakings and should only be attempted by experienced leaders who are well-versed in placing protection.

13. **Dolly Dimples** (5.6 X or TR) Start at the lower-right end of the largest of the arches. Face-climb up right, then head up the generally easy, knobby (but unprotected) face above.

14. **Over the Rainbow** (5.10a R) Start as for Route 13, but head left, following the thin crack that parallels the main arch. Protection is sketchy until you reach a knob at 45'. From here, either face-climb up right (5.3); follow a thin 5.7 crack up left, which eventually becomes a left-facing dihedral; or face-climb directly over a bulge to easier friction leading to the top. Take pro to 1½", emphasizing very thin wires and the smallest TCUs.

15. **Rainbow Bridge** (5.8 or 5.9+ R) Begin as for the previous two routes, then follow the main arch left, either hand-traversing the crack underneath or underclinging the arch itself. Once you reach an obvious gray knob above the arch, you can either continue to follow the arch (5.8) to a Class 4 scramble-off belay ledge, or you can make a wild 5.9+ mantle over the arch to finish via Route 14.

## RAINBOW WALL

Rainbow Wall, the face below and left of Rainbow Arches, is one of northwestern California's choicest granite walls. The rock is a beautiful, dappled gray and white, and it ranges from steep and featured to smooth and overhanging, offering routes to challenge the most ambitious. In addition, there is an interesting and convenient cave below the face, suitable for cooling off on a hot day or staying dry during the rare afternoon showers. Approach by either circling around from the top of the crag or scrambling down and left from Cougar Tracks Face. Descend by traversing off left (Class 4) from the ledge atop the face. Take several cams to 3" for setting a toprope anchor.

16. **Deliverance** (5.9+ X or TR) Begin about 6' left of the large, detached finger of granite at the right end of the face. Face-climb up rock that gets increasingly steep until you reach the arch of *Rainbow Bridge.* Mantle over at a prominent, gray knob and finish via Route 14.
17. **Under the Rainbow** (5.10b TR) Scramble onto a small pedestal at the base of the wall. From near its left end, head directly up the beautifully featured wall.
18. **Cultured Pearls** (5.11b TR) Begin as for Route 17, or for a greater challenge, start just left of the pedestal. Edge and crimp up very steep rock to ripples. Work up left a few feet, then proceed more directly up to the top.
19. **Shady Lane** (5.6) Follow the ramp that slants up left along the foot of the wall, providing access to the following climbs. Except for the initial few moves, you probably will not enjoy this route.
20. **Risky Business** (5.12d/.13a TR) Climb 15' up *Shady Lane* to the blunt prow that overhangs the ramp. After a very difficult move or two, gain vertical rock and continue to the top via tricky edging and friction.
21. **Lunge Hour** (5.12b TR) Locate an obvious shelf on the wall just right of the upper end of the ramp of *Shady Lane.* Dyno to this sloping shelf, mantle onto it, then make a few face moves to reach the ledge at the top.
22. **Shelf Life** (5.10a TR) Start at the upper-left end of the *Shady Lane* ramp (most easily reached from above). Undercling a mossy flake up and right until you can make a long move onto the shelf of *Lunge Hour.* Finish via that route. You can also reach the shelf by starting up the escape route to the ledge atop the face, then traversing right and making a long step right to the shelf.
23. **Lightning Bolt Crack** (I 5.8) Around the corner left of, and above the ledge atop Rainbow Wall, find a zigzag crack with a small tree growing out of it. **Pitch 1:** Beginning at the left end of the ledge that leads to the top of Rainbow Wall, hand-traverse up left along the crack to the tree. Follow the crack to a large belay ledge. **Pitch 2:** Ascend an easy friction

pitch to the top of the rock. Take pro to 2", including several pieces in the ¾" to 1" size.

24. **Thunderclap** (I 5.7) Begin below and slightly left of the tree growing out of *Lightning Bolt Crack*. **Pitch 1:** Climb a thin flake, then move right into *Lightning Bolt Crack*. Follow the crack past the pine tree and onto a belay ledge. **Pitch 2:** Finish via *Lightning Bolt Crack*.

25. **Saint Elmo's Fire** (5.9 TR) Locate this short climb 12' left of Route 24. Jam or lieback a short, steep flake/crack that gradually curves left and ends on the large ledge atop the first pitches of the preceding two routes.

# YCATAPOM PEAK

Ycatapom Peak rises abruptly from the edge of grass-carpeted Poison Canyon. Its impressive, 1,200-foot north and northwest faces host the longest climbs in the Trinity Alps, including Orion, the longest climb in northwestern California. The summit of the peak stands at the edge of the wilderness area, and the view extends many miles in all directions. The rock is granite, very solid despite its sometimes broken appearance. Most routes are easy to moderate in difficulty, but their length and intricacy make them serious undertakings. Although protection is adequate, long runouts are common, and cracks are frequently shallow or flared.

This area has been developed as a traditional (i.e., no bolted sport routes) climbing center, and all routes were established from the ground up, using nuts, cams, and runners for protection. The emphasis here is on free climbing; there are no aid routes. Most cracks encountered are one inch or thinner, which means smaller nuts and lighter racks—a godsend when carrying gear up the steep approach trail to the climbers' basecamp.

**Climbing history:** Ycatapom Peak was a well-known landmark to the local native people. The name of the mountain is a Wintu word which, loosely translated, means "Leaning Mountain (or Place)." It is entirely possible that a member of one of the tribes that routinely hunted in the area scrambled to the top.

The presence of USGS benchmarks on the summit rocks indicates that Ycatapom was climbed by government survey parties, who used the isolated summit as a triangulation point for area land surveys. Other ascents of the easier routes on the mountain's south face and west ridge were and are fairly routine occurrences.

In 1985, the earliest known technical climb was established on the peak's expansive north side. *The Old Goat* (Class 4) was climbed by Ken Kehoe, Mark Duden, and Steve Mackay. The party descended via what later became *The Keyhole* (II 5.1), when Mackay returned to climb it in 1987. Over the ensuing years, Mackay established several more routes, including *September* (II 5.4), *Six Pack Crack* (II 5.4), and *Tabby Road* (II 5.2). He added *Diagonal* (II 5.4) with Scott La Fein; *Sleepwalk* (II 5.5) with Don Bradbury, Paul York, and Nick Valenzuela, and the classic *Orion* (III 5.7) with Bruce Nyberg. Today, although several routes ascend the north and northwest faces, the peak's outstanding potential for new routes at all degrees of difficulty has scarcely been tapped.

**Rack:** Take a rack of 10–12 stoppers and hexes to 1½", emphasizing smaller pieces. In addition, take 3–4 runners and several cams in the 1" to 2½" size range. Because this is a wilderness crag—and a big one—you should also include a helmet, headlamp, and raingear.

# YCATAPOM PEAK AND BIG BOULDER LAKE AREA MAP

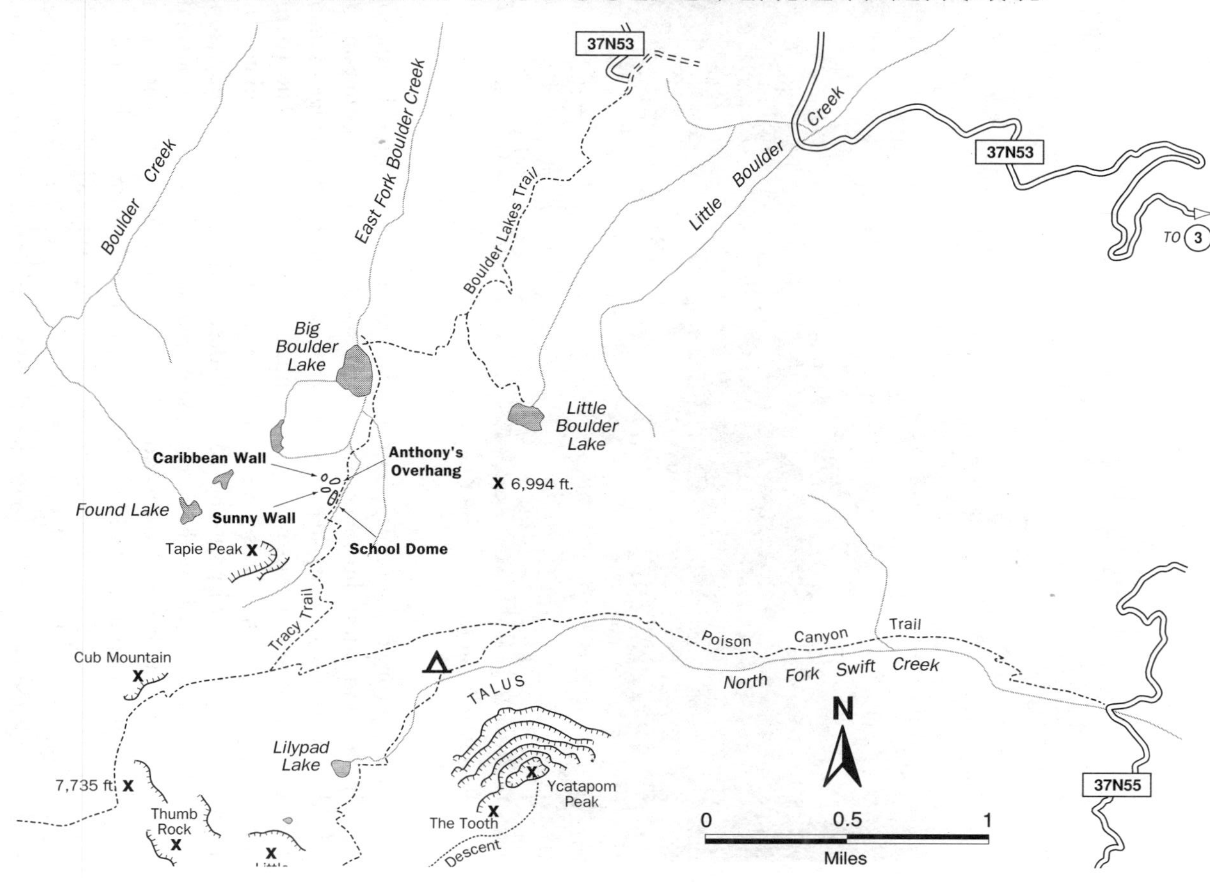

*Ycatapom Peak from Upper Poison Canyon.*

**Descent:** From the summit, you can take any of several ways down. For the simplest and safest, however, descend the south side of the mountain for 75', then work right (west), keeping below the crest of the west ridge. Regain the ridgecrest at an obvious notch between the main summit and The Tooth, a prominent gendarme. Cross over to the north side of the ridge and continue traversing west until past The Tooth. Proceed down a wide, sandy slope atop the ridge, then follow the north side of the ridge past a couple of small sub-peaks, and arrive at the meadow-covered pass west of the mountain. Follow the often faint Lilypad Lake Trail north into the canyon, then east to the climbers' camp. Those desiring a more direct approach (which should only be attempted with adequate daylight) can scramble down *The Old Goat.* (See descent information with the route description.) Either way, plan on 1½ to 2 hours to reach the floor of Poison Canyon.

*Don Bradbury races afternoon shadows on Ycatapom Peak.*

## TRIP PLANNING INFORMATION

**Area description:** The impressive, 1,200-foot north face of Ycatapom Peak towers over Poison Canyon, offering climbs ranging from a few pitches to all-day adventures. Although most routes are easy to moderate, their length and intricacy make them serious undertakings, even for experienced climbers.

**Location:** Northeastern part of Trinity Alps Wilderness Area, approximately 7 miles northwest of the town of Trinity Center.

**Camping:** To maximize time available for climbing, most parties hike to the climbers' base camp below the end of the talus slope below Ycatapom Peak's northwest face and approximately 0.5 mile below Lilypad Lake. Those who prefer to stay in campgrounds can choose from several operated by the Forest Service along California Highway 3, including several fairly near the trailhead. Preacher Meadow, 1.5 miles southwest of Trinity Center on CA 3, offers 45 sites with picnic tables, piped-in water, and vault toilets. Alpine View, which lies 6.6 miles southwest of Trinity Center on CA 3, then 2.5 miles south on County Road 160, provides 66 sites on Trinity Lake. There are no showers, but there are flush toilets and piped-in water. Trinity River, located 9.5 miles north of Trinity Center on CA 3, has only 7 spaces, but it offers piped-in water and vault toilets—and it is the only one of the three that is open all year. The communities of Trinity Center and Coffee Creek offer additional private campgrounds and guest cabins. The nearest of these is giant Wyntoon Resort in Trinity Center, which has over 100 spaces, as well as a store, gas, snack bar, showers, and boat ramp.

**Climbing season:** June through October, better later in the season. It is possible to extend this season in dry years, but the gated access road to the trailhead remains locked from October 30 to May 1 each year. The peak's north aspect and the depth of the canyon cause snow to remain well into summer most years. Some pitches run with water until late July. Although any route on Ycatapom can be climbed in a day, trailhead-to-trailhead, this becomes an iffy proposition after mid-September.

**Restrictions and access issues:** Ycatapom Peak lies within the Trinity Alps Wilderness Area, administered jointly by Shasta-Trinity, Six Rivers, and Klamath National Forests. There is no fee required at this time, but visitors are required to secure wilderness permits prior to entry. Note that, regardless of weather conditions, the Forest Service locks the gates across the unpaved access roads from October 30 through May 1. Currently, no bolts or other permanent anchors are permitted within the wilderness area. Although this policy has not been rigidly enforced, climbers should not test the warmth of their welcome by pushing the issue.

**Guidebook:** This is the first published guidebook to this area. The author compiled, but never published, a mountaineering guide to the Trinity Alps. Copies of the manuscript may be perused in some area outdoor stores and at the Weaverville Ranger Station.

**Nearby mountain shops, guide services, and gyms:** There are no mountain shops or gyms in the area. Guide services are available through Rush Creek Enterprises.

**Services:** There are no services on-site. Water availability is rarely a problem until late in the season, but the small creek near the climbers' camp often dries up by early August, forcing parties to fill up farther east or west along the trail. Although the area is no longer used for grazing, water should still be filtered or boiled prior to use. Visitors can obtain food, supplies, and lodging in the neighboring communities of Trinity Center and Coffee Creek.

**Emergency services:** In the event of an emergency, call 911. The nearest hospital is Trinity General Hospital in Weaverville. For cases that Trinity General is not equipped to handle, air ambulance service is available to Redding Medical Center or Mercy Medical Center, both in Redding.

**Nearby climbing areas:** Poison Canyon holds a number of crags suitable for climbing. Check out the north faces of The Tooth, the prominent gendarme just west of Ycatapom Peak, and Little Ycat, the impressive formation 0.5 mile farther west. A short hike over the ridge north of the canyon accesses the climbs on Tapie Peak and other crags near Boulder Lake.

**Nearby attractions:** The most obvious nearby attraction is large, scenic Trinity Lake, formerly known as Claire Engle Lake. Trinity Lake offers excellent fishing for trout and bass, as well as great swimming, boating, and water skiing. Climbers should not overlook the many opportunities for backpacking on the network of trails that accesses the Trinity Alps Wilderness Area.

NORTHWEST FACE, YCATAPOM PEAK

**Finding the crag:** From the town of Trinity Center, located 29.9 miles north of Weaverville on California Highway 3, turn west onto Swift Creek Road at a well-signed junction just north of the Swift Creek bridge. Proceed west 3 miles to a signed junction and turn right onto Forest Road 37N24, heading for Lake Eleanor and Poison Canyon Trailheads. Turn right again onto Forest Road 37N55 at another signed junction 0.5 mile later. Follow 37N55 for 5 miles, then keep right at a Y-intersection. At the next junction, make sharp left turn to remain on 37N55. Reach the inconspicuous trailhead on the left just beyond a bridge crossing of North Fork Swift Creek. Park on the right shoulder. Follow the often steep trail for 2 miles to a junction with the Thumb Rock Trail. Keep left on the Lilypad Lake Trail and continue for another 0.3 mile to the climbers' basecamp at a small meadow where the trail passes the foot of the talus field below Ycatapom's north face. If you prefer, you can continue to the campsites at Lilypad Lake 0.5 mile farther on. From the campsite, boulder-hop across the talus field, then trudge up an obvious scree fan to the base of the rock, arriving at the base of the huge dihedral of The Keyhole. Follow ledges up left or around the corner to the right to access other routes.

The following routes are listed from right to left, beginning at the huge, left-facing dihedral/gully above a scree and talus cone and just left of a prominent, dark buttress.

1. **The Keyhole** (II 5.1) Start at the foot of the obvious, left-facing dihedral at the top of a prominent talus cone near the right side of the northwest face. Scramble up the generally low-angle dihedral for several hundred feet until the way is barred by a large, precarious-looking block jammed across the dihedral. **Pitch 1:** Face-climb around the left side of the block (5.1), or tunnel underneath, then continue up the dihedral, exiting left near its top. Scramble up left, following Funky Broadway, a long system of sandy terraces and narrow ledges, for 500' to the top of a buttress that forms the right side of a wide gully leading toward the summit. Follow the gully upward to a 20-foot wall. **Pitch 2:** Ascend the wall by any of several routes (a hand crack around the corner to the left is 5.7; the chimney at the left edge of the wall is 5.1; the face of the wall is 5.5; and at its far-right side is a Class 3 trough). From the top of the wall, continue up the gully (Class 2–3), arriving on the summit ridge a few yards west of the highest point.
2. **Orion** (III 5.7) Begin 25' left of the huge, left-facing dihedral/gully of *The Keyhole.* **Pitch 1:** Climb a 5.4 slab to an overlap. Either surmount this directly (5.7) or via a short 5.5 detour right, up, then back left. Head up left to a sloping ledge at the base of a short, right-facing dihedral. **Pitch 2:** Climb the dihedral, friction up to a short wall, ascend a shallow 5.4 trough, then work up left past a ledge to a stance on an arete, which overlooks the steep slabs to the right. **Pitch 3:** Ascend stacked flakes

along the right side of the arete, then follow a short pour-off to a belay ledge. **Pitch 4:** Head up right to a spacious belay spot below stacked overhangs. **Pitch 5:** Climb to the foot of the lower overhang, then detour up left around its left side and traverse back right under the upper overhang, belaying at a crack. (You could also surmount the lower overhang directly at 5.7.) **Pitch 6:** Continue right under the overhang, then work up its right side to a large, sandy ledge. **Pitch 7:** Head up, then left, following a horizontal crack system above sandy ledges. Belay at the foot of a crack system 50' right of a prominent, right-facing dihedral. **Pitch 8:** Climb 5.4 cracks and a shallow trough to a belay ledge under an overhanging headwall. **Pitch 9:** Traverse left for 25', smear up a 5.4 face, then pull up steep flakes above to a sheltered belay spot amid blocks. **Pitch 10:** Traverse up left to the foot of a narrow gully. **Pitch 11:** Ascend the Class 4–5 face left of the gully. **Pitches 12–14:** Pass left of a small overhang in the gully, then, where the gully widens and branches, head up left, eventually reaching the top of the face at a point 75' west of the summit. Add a few RPs or thin pitons to the regular rack.

For a more interesting and challenging climb, try *Sasquatch* (5.8+), the prominent, right-facing dihedral left of Pitch 8.

3. **Sleepwalk** (II 5.5) Begin at the same spot as *Orion.* **Pitch 1:** Face-climb up left to a conspicuous block, passing over two right-slanting ribs. Climb a few feet up the block's left side, then diagonal 15' up left (5.5) to a good belay ledge with a small, broken tree under an overhang (the first belay ledge on *September*). **Pitch 2:** Move back right and follow an easy ramp to its end. Continue another 25', then surmount an overlap and belay on a comfortable ledge with a small incense-cedar tree. **Pitch 3:** Climb the 5.5 wall above the ledge to an arete, joining *Orion's* third pitch. Follow flakes and narrow ledges up the right side of the arete, then up right to a short pour-off. Belay 15' higher on a good ledge. **Pitch 4:** Leaving *Orion,* scramble up left on easy terrain, heading for a conspicuous tower on the skyline. **Pitch 5:** Continue scrambling left, following the rubbly ledges of Funky Broadway until they disappear temporarily at a slabby area. Cross the slabs to the base of Short Wall, a steep, 25-foot wall scored by several thin cracks. Climb a pillar near the wall's right edge, then climb a wide crack and shallow chimney (5.5) to a broad, sandy terrace just below and right of the tower. **Pitch 6:** Walk up left on the sandy terrace, then traverse left across a gully left of the tower to the conspicuous, low-angle slab called Green Slab. Ascend the easy trough up the right edge of the slab, then traverse left (5.2) to the foot of a shallow trough that descends from Green Slab's upper left corner. Follow the trough to the top of the slab. Unrope here and follow *The Keyhole* the rest of the way to a notch a few yards west of the summit.

*Bruce Nyberg samples the slabby face climbing low on Ycatapom Peak during the first ascent of* Orion *(III 5.7).*

For variety, climb one of the other cracks up Short Wall on the fifth pitch. They range in difficulty from 5.8 to 5.9+.

4. **September** (II 5.4) Notice 3 parallel troughs left of the slabs ascended by the first couple of pitches of *Orion.* Begin at the base of the right-hand trough, 40' left of *Orion.* **Pitch 1:** Use friction and a short 5.4 lieback to enter the tough, then proceed to a belay ledge on the right, marked by a broken tree growing under an overhang. **Pitch 2:** Re-enter the trough and follow it to a small stance on the left. **Pitch 3:** Continue up the trough until the way is blocked by a short, vertical wall above and right of a large, down-pointing horn. Traverse around the corner to the right, following a narrow ledge for 20', then join the two previous routes, ascending a short, shallow trough to a belay spot on Funky Broadway. Scramble up left along Funky Broadway for 400' to the mouth of a deep gully whose left side forms a low-angle slab (Green Slab). **Pitch 4:** Start up the gully, then make a 5.2 traverse left across the slab to a shallow trough. Follow the trough to a belay spot at the upper left edge of the slab. Join *The Keyhole* to continue to the summit. *September* is one of the crag's most popular routes, due to its scenic, easy climbing and minimal gear requirements: 8–10 nuts to 1½" will suffice.
5. **Six Pack Crack** (II 5.4) Begin 35' left of *September,* at the base of a trough blocked by a pair of large blocks. **Pitch 1:** Climb up to and over the blocks (5.4), then continue up the trough to a belay ledge. **Pitch 2:** Follow the trough up right to another belay ledge. **Pitch 3:** Continue up easy climbing to a belay spot just below Funky Broadway. Join *The Keyhole* or *September* to continue to summit.
6. **Diagonal** (II 5.4) Locate the starting point 50' up left of Route 5, where an obvious gully slants up right from near the highest point of the scree slope below the northwest face. **Pitch 1:** Instead of entering the gully, face-climb up left to enter a trough that parallels the gully. Follow it up right to a sandy belay ledge above a sprawling juniper bush. **Pitch 2:** Head up right on easy ground where the trough and gully merge. **Pitch 3:** Follow easy climbing up right along ledges and troughs to a belay along Funky Broadway. **Pitch 4:** Continue up right above Funky Broadway to a long, smooth ledge that slants up right. **Pitch 5:** From the upper end of the ledge, move right around an arete to the top of *Sasquatch* and the upper part of the exposed face climbed by *Orion.* Make a 5.2 traverse up right to join *Orion* at a belay spot. Note that the belay is not on the sloping stance below the left edge of the upper headwall, but 15' farther right. **Pitch 6:** Work back left, then climb 5.4 friction up left to the upper-left corner of the face. **Pitch 7:** Enter and follow an easy gully, keeping to its right side. **Pitch 8:** Move left into the center of the gully, then climb 5.2 rock up its left side, belaying just beyond a

small overhang in the gully. **Pitch 9:** Where the gully widens and splits, keep to the right branch. Climb easy, blocky stone to a stance not far from the top of the face. **Pitch 10:** Clamber over lichen-covered blocks, then up a narrow cleft to the summit ridge. Follow the south side of the ridge east to the summit

7. **Tabby Road** (II 5.2) Begin 20' left of *Diagonal,* where a deep trough and left-facing dihedral angle up left from near the highest point of the forested talus fan below the face. **Pitch 1:** Keeping left of the trough, ascend easy, low-angle slabs. **Pitch 2:** Continue easy face climbing to a sloping stance. **Pitch 3:** Work right into the dihedral and continue to a large belay ledge below a short, vertical wall. **Pitch 4:** Surmount the wall via a short, 5.2 chockstone chimney around the corner to the left. (You could attack the wall directly, but the difficulty jumps to 5.9+.) Proceed up easy rock to the east end of the Funky Broadway ledge system. **Pitch 5:** Either scramble up left to join Route 1, or follow Funky Broadway 70' down right to finish via *September.*
8. **The Old Goat** (I 4–5.7) To reach the starting point, follow the Poison Canyon trail 0.2 mile back down the canyon from the boulderfield access used by the preceding routes. Cross the creek, then hike up a low-angle ridge, aiming for a wide gully leading directly to the summit. **Pitch 1:** Where the gully steepens considerably and becomes slabby, follow a ramp up its left side, curving right to end at a short headwall. Climb a short (2-move) chimney to reach the east end of the Funky Broadway ledge system. Scramble up left several hundred feet to a 20-foot wall. **Pitch 2:** Take any of several ways up the wall: A hand crack around the corner to the left is 5.7; the chimney at the left edge of the wall is 5.1; the face of the wall is 5.5; and at its far-right side is a Class 3 trough). From the top of the wall, follow the Class 2–3 gully, arriving on the summit ridge a few yards west of the highest point. It is also possible to bypass this wall altogether by scrambling up left to the ridge east of the gully before you reach the wall and following the 3rd-class ridge to the top.

If you plan to use this route as a descent route, from the summit rocks head northeast down the ridgetop to a step in the ridge. Cut left and scramble down into the bed of the wide, tree-studded gully. Head down until the way is barred by a short dropoff above a slabby area. Walk left to the flat top of a buttress that forms the left side of the gully (as you look down). Descend a short chimney, then follow a narrow ramp down the right side of the gully. From its foot, head down and gradually left to avoid cliffs, eventually reaching the floor of Poison Canyon near the boulderfield below the northwest face. Beware of rockfall on this route, and don't try to descend it at night.

# BIG BOULDER LAKE

*(see Area Map on p. 125)*

Big Boulder Lake has long been one of the most popular destinations in the Trinity Alps for dayhikers and backpackers seeking quick access to a scenic wilderness lake. The meadow-fringed and tree-ringed lake occupies the floor of a basin surrounded by forested mountains whose flanks provide numerous opportunities for climbing, from bouldering to roped outcrop climbs.

Although visitors can enjoy interesting challenges close to the lake, the finest rocks lie southwest of the lake, right alongside the hiking trail that leads southwest to Poison Canyon. Here, at the foot of an open slope, lie a series of small walls and glaciated domes of beautifully sound granite. Climbs range from 10 to 60 feet in length, and they span a range of difficulty from easy scrambles to mid-5.10. For those learning to climb, or those wishing to improve their skills—all in a gloriously scenic setting—there is no finer classroom in the region.

**Climbing history:** Although School Dome, the largest formation in the area, was climbed long ago by sightseers, serious climbing exploration did not really begin until 1982, when the author and his wife first noticed the rock's climbing potential while working for the Forest Service. In the spring of 1990, they returned to the area with a troupe of students from Lewiston Elementary School and climbed a dozen or more routes. The most notable of these were *Slip-slidin' Away* (5.5), *Slider* (5.4), *Entrance Exam* (5.6), and *Stick to What* (5.7 R/X). Later visits with Scott La Fein, Neal Weiner, Tyler Crummett, Greg Poulton, Anthony Moyle, and Jorge Medina produced the climbs on Sunny Wall, Anthony's Overhang, and Caribbean Wall. Although this group of outcrops is pretty well developed, the lake basin and nearby mountainsides harbor a lifetime's worth of potential boulder problems.

**Rack:** Take a light-to-moderate rack of stoppers and hexes to 1½", emphasizing smaller pieces. In addition, take 3–4 runners and several cams in the 1" to 2½" size range.

**Descent:** Climbers can walk off or scramble down from the tops of any of the crags.

## TRIP PLANNING INFORMATION

**Area description:** A cluster of granite domes, ridges, and walls up to 50' high, surrounded by a multitude of other, unexplored outcrops and boulders that offer countless worthwhile bouldering opportunities. Longer routes can be led, although toproping is the norm. Difficulties of established routes range from Class 4 to 5.10b, although harder climbs are possible.

**Location:** Northeastern part of Trinity Alps Wilderness Area, approximately 7 miles northwest of the town of Trinity Center.

# BIG BOULDER LAKE CRAGS

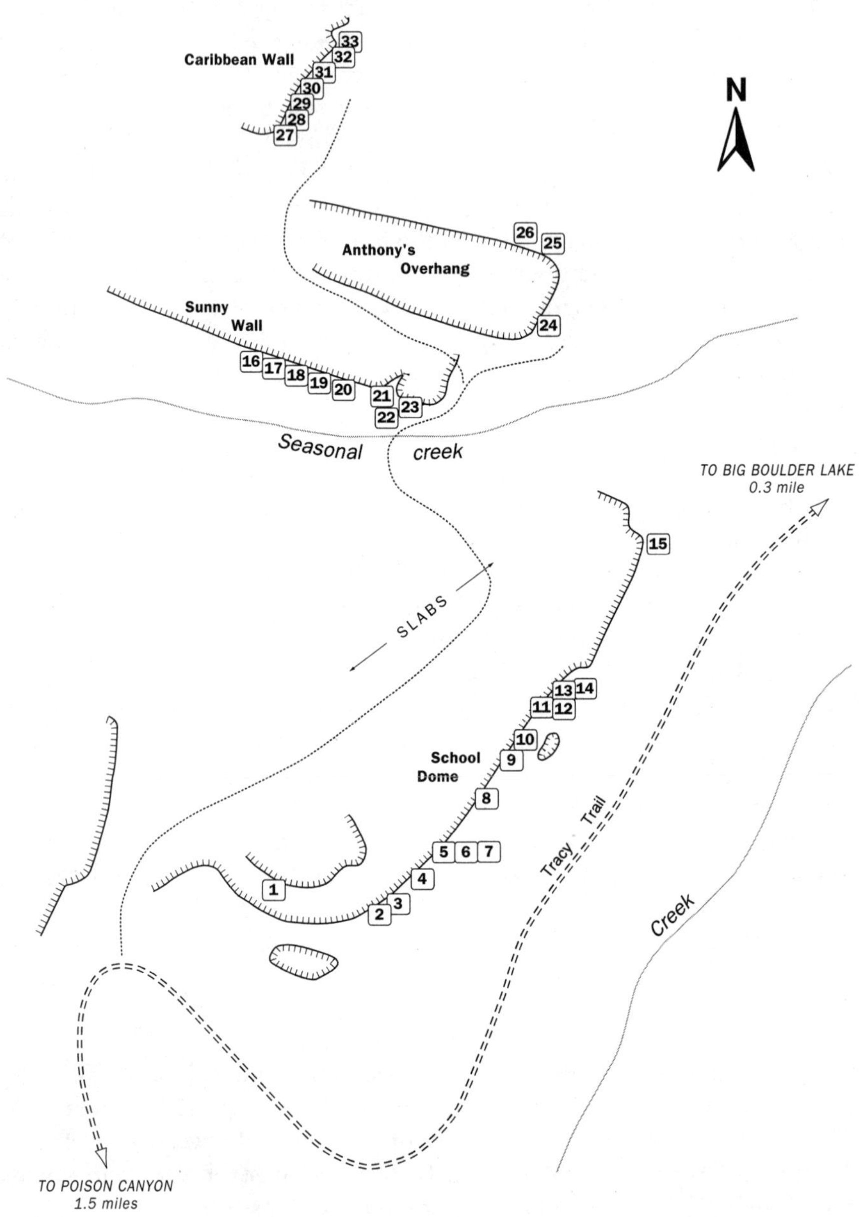

**Camping:** Most parties camp at Big Boulder Lake, where several comfortable campsites may be found. Those choosing to car-camp can stay in Forest Service campgrounds along California Highway 3. Preacher Meadow, 1.5 miles southwest of Trinity Center on CA 3, offers 45 sites with picnic tables, piped-in water, and vault toilets. Alpine View, which lies 6.6 miles southwest of Trinity Center on CA 3, then 2.5 miles south on County Road 160, provides 66 sites on Trinity Lake. There are no showers, but there are flush toilets and piped-in water. Trinity River, located 9.5 miles north of Trinity Center on CA 3, has only 7 spaces, but it offers piped-in water and vault toilets—and it is the only one of the three that is open all year. The communities of Trinity Center and Coffee Creek offer additional private campgrounds and guest cabins. The nearest of these is giant Wyntoon Resort in Trinity Center, which has over 100 spaces, as well as a store, gas, snack bar, showers, and boat ramp.

**Climbing season:** June through October or November, best mid-to-late season. It is possible to extend this season in dry years. Although the access road is not gated, it is also not maintained for winter travel, and snow essentially closes the area from December through April most years.

**Restrictions and access issues:** This area lies within the Trinity Alps Wilderness Area administered jointly by Shasta-Trinity and Klamath National Forests. There is no fee required at this time, but visitors are required to secure wilderness permits prior to entry. Currently, no bolts or other permanent anchors are permitted within the wilderness area. Although this policy has not been rigidly enforced, climbers should not test the warmth of their welcome by pushing the issue.

**Guidebook:** This is the first published guidebook to this area. The author compiled, but never published, a mountaineering guide to the Trinity Alps. Copies of the manuscript may be perused in some area outdoor stores and at the Weaverville Ranger Station.

**Nearby mountain shops, guide services, and gyms:** There are no mountain shops or gyms in the area. Guide services are available through Rush Creek Enterprises.

**Services:** There are no services on-site. Water availability is rarely a problem until late in the season. This is a popular area, so water should be filtered or boiled prior to use. Visitors can obtain food, supplies, and lodging in the neighboring communities of Trinity Center and Coffee Creek.

**Emergency services:** In the event of an emergency, call 911. The nearest hospital is Trinity General Hospital in Weaverville. For cases that Trinity General is not equipped to handle, air ambulance service is available to Redding Medical Center or Mercy Medical Center, both in Redding.

**Nearby climbing areas:** A short hike over the ridge south of the lake basin takes visitors to Ycatapom Peak and the crags in Poison Canyon, passing the impressive, craggy south side of Tapie Peak on the way.

**Nearby attractions:** The most obvious nearby attraction is large, scenic Trinity Lake, formerly known as Claire Engle Lake. Trinity Lake offers excellent fishing for trout and bass, as well as great swimming, boating, and water skiing. Climbers should not overlook the many opportunities for backpacking on the network of trails that accesses the Trinity Alps Wilderness Area.

**Finding the crags:** From the town of Trinity Center, located 32 miles north of Weaverville on California 3, continue north another 7.6 miles to a signed turnoff for Boulder Lakes Trailhead. Turn west onto Forest Road 37N52 and proceed 3.3 miles to a signed junction with Forest Road 37N53. Turn right onto this road and follow it 7 miles to the large, shaded trailhead parking area.

## SCHOOL DOME

School Dome, a glaciated, 45-foot granite mound, lies alongside the Tracy (Poison Canyon) Trail 0.3 mile southwest of Big Boulder Lake. As its name suggests, its friendly angle, generally easy routes, and easy access make it an ideal classroom for new climbers. Routes range from short bouldering problems to one-pitch climbs. The routes described represent only a few of the many potential ways up this very accessible rock. Descend by walking left off the back to return to the hiking trail. Protection ranging from thin wired stoppers to 2-inch cams suffices for all routes.

1. **Ball Four** (5.6) Begin near the midpoint of a broad ledge halfway up the southeast side of the formation. Climb the smooth face past two horizontal cracks.
2. **Double Play** (5.5) Begin at the low point of the smooth, low-angle apron below an alcove at the north end of the ledge used by Route 1. Diagonal up left along the margin of the apron to the left end of an overlap. Pass over, then angle up right to the ledge. Above, climb the rounded arete 8' left of the alcove.
3. **Stick to What** (5.7 R/X) Start as for *Double Play,* but head straight up the slab to a notch in the overlap. Pass over, follow a finger crack for a few moves, then step right and ascend the rib that forms the right side of a small alcove. Protection is hard to find or place.
4. **Warmup** (4) Climb the very easy, right-curving trough/crack that borders the right side of the slab ascended by the preceding two routes.
5. **Slider** (5.4) Start 15' right of *Warmup,* where the base of the dome suddenly drops several feet. Follow a long, thin crack up left, crossing the upper end of Route 4 and continuing to the top via an easy, flared crack.
6. **Dogleg** (5.0) Begin as for Route 5, but where the long crack intersects another crack, follow the latter up right to a small pine tree. Continue to the top on easy face climbing.

# SCHOOL DOME

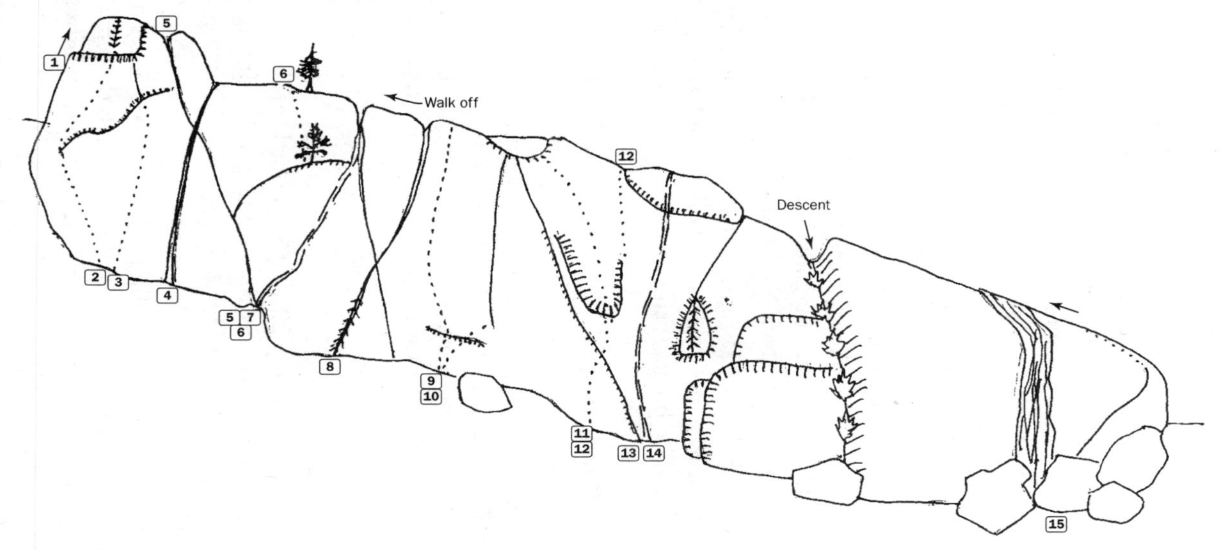

7. **The Foul Line** (4) Begin as for the preceding two routes. Follow the easy trough created by erosion of a prominent aplite dike.
8. **Entrance Exam** (5.6) Starting 8' right of *The Foul Line,* climb a wide crack that begins as a shallow, flared chimney.
9. **Playoff** (5.7 TR) Begin 10' right of Route 8. Mantle over a short, vertical wall, then switch to friction climbing up the slab above, avoiding the tempting holds offered by routes on either side.
10. **Slip-slidin' Away** (5.5) Beginning just right of Route 9, surmount the short, vertical wall, then follow a finger crack to a spacious ledge near the top of the rock.
11. **Fungo** (5.5) Start directly below a prominent, nose-like bulge visible halfway up the face. Climb directly up to the nose, surmount it directly, then proceed to the top on easier friction.
12. **Infield Fly** (5.4 or 5.6) Follow Route 11 as far as the nose-like bulge, then ascend its right side. Either diagonal up left to the top (5.4), or head up right and climb a short, steep 5.6 headwall.
13. **Line Drive** (5.0) Begin 15' right of Route 12, where the short, vertical wall is replaced by a low-angle slab. Follow a long, diagonal crack up left under the nose-like bulge, then continue to the ledge near the top of the rock.
14. **Ticket Line** (5.6) Begin as for *Line Drive,* but follow a thin quartz dike up right to the top of the rock.
15. **North Buttress** (4) Begin at blocks below a face bordered on the left by a prominent, black dike easily visible when first arriving from Big Boulder Lake. Ascend easy, broken rock to a smooth face. Follow a short, diagonal crack up right, then head back left on the crest of a short ridge.

## SUNNY WALL

Sunny Wall is the south-facing, 20-foot wall north of School Dome. It offers numerous short, enjoyable routes that make good morning warmups when other faces in the vicinity are still too cold for comfort. Descend by scrambling down the east end of the rock.

16. **Fun in the Sun** (5.10b TR) Begin at the foot of a pedestal below a right-facing dihedral positioned near mid-face. Climb the left side of the knobby pedestal to a small ledge. Step left, then jam an offwidth fingercrack to the top.
17. **Easy Way Out** (5.0) Climb either side of Route 16's pedestal, then ascend a short, right-facing dihedral to the top. For a slightly harder finish, use the crack right of the dihedral.

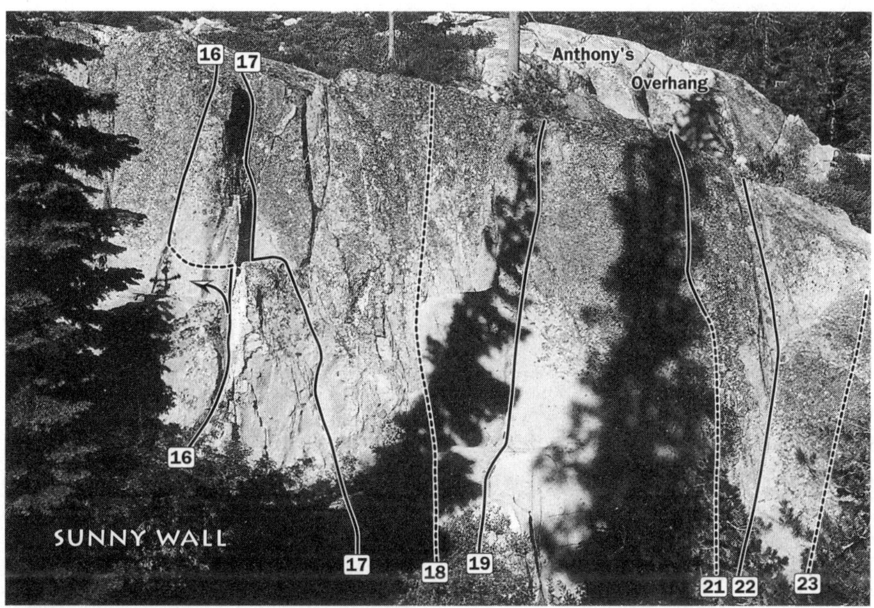


18. **Sunny Wall** (5.6 R or TR) Begin 6' right of Route 17. Ascend straight up the knobby wall, avoiding cracks on either side of face.
19. **Home Free** (5.0) Begin as for *Sunny Wall,* but climb a left-facing dihedral/trough.
20. **Easy Crack** (5.0) Start 10' right of *Home Free.* Jam and face-climb along an easy hand crack to the top.
21. **Morning Coffee** (5.8 TR) Locate the starting point at the foot of a left-facing, flared, shallow chimney. Avoiding the chimney, ascend edges and a thin crack to the top of the wall.
22. **Double Shot** (5.1) Starting as for Route 21, ascend the flared chimney, then continue up double cracks to the top.
23. **Latte** (5.4) Avoiding the arete on the left, ascend the short face immediately right of *Double Shot.*

## ANTHONY'S OVERHANG

Anthony's Overhang is a low, hogsback ridge situated just north of Sunny Wall. Most of the formation is rather uninteresting, but the northeast end of the rock forms a prominent, overhanging wall. The eastern end of the northwest face is high enough to provide interesting climbing. Approach the overhanging wall by scrambling down a gully along the southeast side of the rock; reach other routes by walking left along the northwest side. Descend by walking off the southwest end of the formation.

24. **Overhang Bypass** (5.1) Begin in a right-facing corner near the left side of the overhanging wall on the rock's downhill side. Climb up left over blocks to a ledge, then make an interesting move off the ledge to reach the top.
25. **Shady** (5.7 TR) Start below an undercut arete 10' left of Route 26. Climb the arete to the top.
26. **Bonsai Crack** (5.6) Ascend the obvious, left-slanting, thin-hands crack marked by a tiny tree partway up.

## CARIBBEAN WALL

Just west of the Anthony's Overhang formation lies Caribbean Wall, a striking, east-facing wall 20' high. Most climbs are fairly easy, but the steep, smooth slab near the wall's left side offers some of the area's most challenging face climbing. Descend by scrambling down left of Route 27.

27. **Left Margin** (5.3) Climb the right-hand of three closely spaced, thin cracks near the left edge of the face.
28. **Tropical Depressions** (5.10a) Beginning 6' right of Route 27, ascend the left side of a prominent, steep slab.
29. **International Incident** (5.10b) Locate the starting point 8' left of a left-curving flake/crack that forms a small, orange-stained corner close to the ground. Climb directly up the steep slab, keeping left of the crack. Take a ¼-inch stopper for a pocket in the crack.

30. **Trade Wind** (5.10a) Follow the left-curving flake/crack, which begins as a small, orange-stained dihedral. Take a 1/4-inch stopper.
31. **Bahama Mama** (5.5) Beginning 8' right of *Trade Wind,* follow a left-slanting crack nearly to *Trade Wind,* then ascend a thin crack that runs up right.
32. **Bermuda Shorts** (4) From the top of a low-angle ridge that abuts the base of the rock, ascend easy cracks to a ledge, then continue up a left-facing dihedral to the top.
33. **Oh Chute** (4) Climb the prominent, low-angle, straight-in corner near the middle of the face.

## CASTLE CRAGS

Known to early miners as "The Devil's Castle," Castle Crags, part of the 10,500-acre Castle Crags Wilderness Area/Castle Crags State Park complex, forms a picturesque jumble of granite spires, peaklets, and pinnacles overlooking the deep and scenic upper canyon of the Sacramento River about 60 miles south of the Oregon border. To the northeast, the snow slopes of giant Mount Shasta provide a stunning backdrop.

The formations of Castle Crags occupy an oval, roughly 2.5 miles by 3 miles, situated atop a spur ridge flung out southeast from the crest of the Trinity Mountains nearly to the Sacramento River. The summits of the crags themselves lie between 4,000 and just over 6,000 feet. Typically, the short,

CASTLE CRAGS FROM THE SOUTHEAST

# CASTLE CRAGS STATE PARK AREA MAP

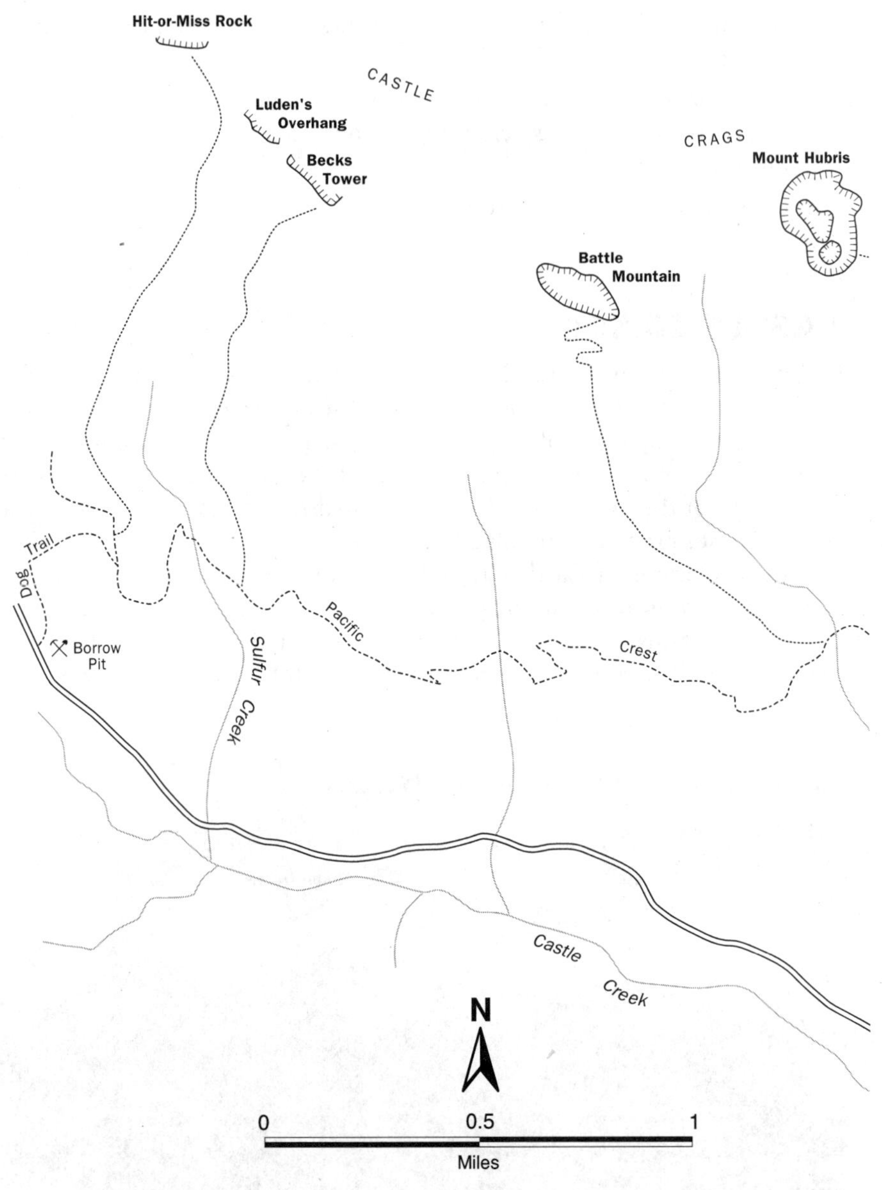

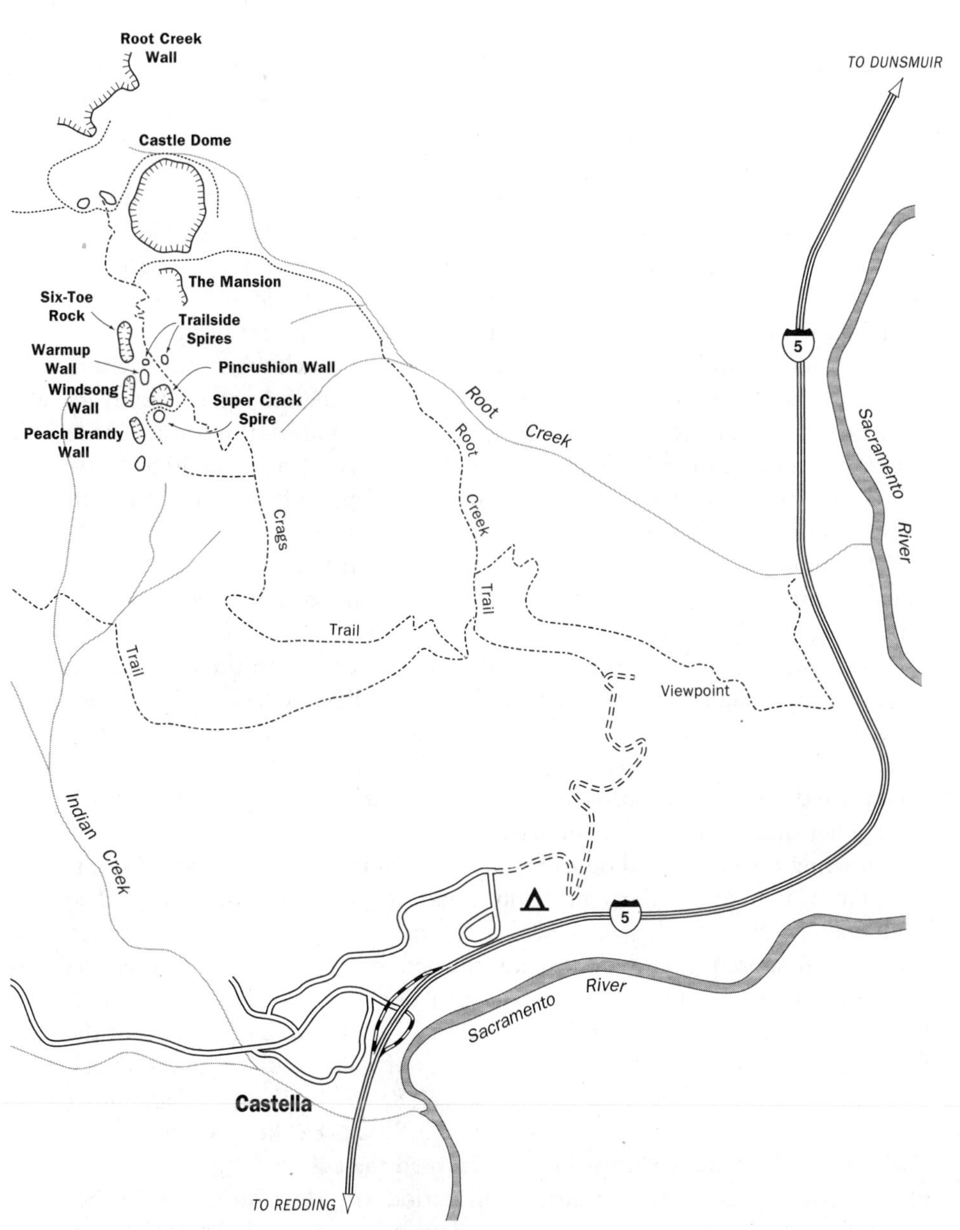

Root Creek Wall
Castle Dome
The Mansion
Six-Toe Rock
Trailside Spires
Warmup Wall
Pincushion Wall
Windsong Wall
Super Crack Spire
Peach Brandy Wall
Crags
Trail
Root Creek
Root Creek
Trail
Trail
Viewpoint
Indian Creek
TO DUNSMUIR
5
Sacramento River
5
Sacramento River
Castella
TO REDDING

steep approaches to the climbs begin at approximately 2,000 feet. Although Castle Crags offers an abundance of wild and lovely scenery, big, noisy Interstate 5 and the Southern Pacific tracks connecting northern California to Oregon thread the narrow canyon bottom just east of the state park. As a result, the traffic sounds infiltrate even some of the more remote-feeling sites.

The granite making up Castle Crags differs from the material at most other popular California climbing areas; its mineral composition leads to an abundance of rough, often crumbly, rock. The poorly hardened rock on some formations sometimes causes promising-looking holds to unexpectedly turn to sand. Therefore, climbs at Castle Crags often rely on bolted protection to avoid long runouts on suspect rock. Fortunately, formations with dangerously crumbly rock represent a minority. In many places, routes on excellent rock rival the quality of noteworthy climbs found elsewhere in the state. Generally speaking, the most reliable rock lies in or adjacent to waterchutes or grooves where the scouring action of rain or snowmelt removes the loose surface layer, along numerous dikes where recrystallization due to the heat of the liquified dike rock has occurred, and in zones of gold-colored rock where the mixture of minerals is slightly different. Regardless, wise climbers carefully test every hold before use and place protection whenever possible. Routes at Castle Crags span a range of difficulties from 5.6 to 5.11b and lengths of 50 to 1,000 feet. The labyrinth of rock formations at Castle Crags offers some of northwestern California's greatest new-route potential.

The climbs described here are concentrated into five primary areas. The Indian Springs area lies southeast of Castle Dome and a short distance above trail-accessed Indian Springs. The Castle Dome area consists of Castle Dome, Mount Hubris, and the formations immediately adjacent to the Crags Trail. North of, and slightly behind, Castle Dome lies Root Creek Wall. Farther west, on the south side of the ridge, lie Battle Mountain and the West Side area. Climbs have been grouped and described in roughly the order they are encountered during the approach, and they are listed from left to right unless some other order is necessary for clarity.

**Climbing history:** Based on cairns and rare slips of paper found on several summits, climbing activity probably began in earnest in the early 1930s. Undoubtedly, climbers first ascended many of the major formations during this era, but subsequent vandalism and the action of the elements caused the loss of most early summit records. The first documented climbing at Castle Crags occurred during the late 1940s and early 1950s, when members of the Stanford University Alpine Club made a series of visits. Club members Chuck Crush, Dave Harrah, Sherman Lehman, and John Harlin II climbed a number of trailside routes, including those on Bulldog Rock. Harlin's classic *Cosmic Wall* (II 5.6) on Mount Hubris in 1948 marked the culminating achievement of this early exploration. Also during this period, the Hoyt brothers, Fletcher and Bill, accompanied on occasion by pioneer Yosemite climber Al Steck, climbed many of the major spires along the south and west sides of the massif. Probably the most notable of these was Becks Tower at the head of Sulfur Creek. The discovery of Luden's Overhang during this same period provided the area with several memorable slab routes.

In the 1960s, rumors of an "undiscovered Yosemite" sent scores of hopefuls scrambling for routes. Visitors at this time included numerous climbers well known in other areas: Fred Beckey, Warren Harding, Chuck Pratt, Jeff Lowe, Nick Clinch, John Orenschall, and even British explorer and mountain personality Christian Bonington established or repeated routes at Castle Crags.

Activity at Castle Crags echoed the free-climbing push underway elsewhere in California during the 1970s and 1980s. Ardent free-climbers eliminated the aid from a few 1960s routes, launching the era of the 5.10. Gifted climbers such as Mike Zanger, Craig Ballenger, Mark Rodell, Byron Cross, Paul Gagner, and John Bald produced numerous landmark climbs, including *Castle Dome—East Face* (III 5.10d), *The Good Book* (II 5.10a), *The Plumb Line* (IV 5.10b) and *Hit Man* (5.11a).

Since the 1980s, climbing at Castle Crags lapsed into a comparative lull, largely due to a lack of route information and the extremely complex topography of the area. The most significant climb of this period is *Casino* (II 5.11a), an impressive route up The Mansion by Peter Chesko and Tim Loughlin. In the last few years, sport climbers have developed routes at Castle

*East Side of Battle Mountain, Castle Crags.*

Crags, albeit on a modest scale. Castle Crags awaits another boom in popularity; the scope for new routes of all degrees of difficulty remains essentially boundless.

**Rack:** Take a standard free-climbing rack of stoppers, hexes, and cams, emphasizing the smaller stuff. RPs are especially useful, as are smaller TCUs. Supplement this selection with 6–10 quickdraws and a half-dozen runners. It's probably a good idea to bring an extra bolt hanger or two, just in case.

**Descent:** Because of the number of different formations included in this chapter, descent information accompanies the various crag descriptions.

## TRIP PLANNING INFORMATION

**Area description:** Castle Crags offers a staggering array of granite crags, boulders, walls, and outcrops ranging from a few feet to over 900 feet in height. Climbs range in difficulty from short, third-class scrambles to all-day climbs exceeding 5.11. New-route potential is excellent.

**Location:** Atop a spur ridge overlooking the Sacramento River canyon just south of the town of Dunsmuir on Interstate 5.

**Camping:** Climbers and other park visitors typically stay at Castle Crags State Park Campground, located within the park, 0.5 mile from the park entrance, on the Vista Point road. The campground is open all year and offers piped-in water, flush toilets, and showers. There are interpretive programs during the summer. At the time of this writing, the cost to camp is $12.00-$14.00 per night; leashed pets are allowed for an additional $1.00 per night. Due to the high demand for campsites between Memorial Day and Labor Day, campsites must be reserved. Reservations may be made by mail by writing DESTINET (formerly MISTIX) at P.O. Box 85705, San Diego, CA 92186-5705; or by calling (800) 444-7275 or (800) 365-2267. Visitors desiring more "sophisticated" accommodations can choose from several motels in nearby Dunsmuir.

**Climbing season:** March through late October. However, since Castle Crags lies within Mount Shasta's zone of influence, storms from late fall through early spring often bring considerable snow, even at this comparatively low elevation. Mid-summer, on the other hand, often raises daytime temperatures to more than 100 degrees.

**Restrictions and access issues:** Hiking and climbing in Castle Crags State Park require no use permit, but the park charges a $5.00 per car day-use fee. Visitors may not take dogs on the Crags Trail or outside the campground. Use of campfires is restricted to the campgrounds only. Visitors must supply all their own firewood, as the park prohibits firewood gathering. The speed limit on the very narrow park roads is 15 miles per hour. Those visiting the adjoining Castle Crags Wilderness Area of Shasta-Trinity National Forest must secure a wilderness permit. For permits, maps, and information, visitors should contact the Forest Service at the Mt. Shasta Ranger District office in Mt. Shasta.

Here, as in all designated wilderness areas, the use of motorized drills is prohibited. Climbers planning to make new routes or replace bolts on existing routes should check with park rangers to verify whether park managers have placed any restrictions on the use of permanent anchors. Due to the steep, brushy, and rugged nature of the terrain, all visitors should take care to remain on trails as much as possible and to utilize game trails or natural clearings to avoid impacts on fragile plants and shallow soils in the area.

**Guidebook:** John Bald wrote and published *Castle Crags: A Climber's Guide* in 1989, but this first guidebook is now out of print. The current guide is *Classic Rock Climbs No. 18—Castle Crags California* by Laird Davis (1997).

**Nearby mountain shops, guide services, and gyms:** The nearest mountain shop is The Fifth Season in Mt. Shasta. Mike Zanger of Shasta Mountain Guides, also in Mt. Shasta, offers instruction and guided climbs of Castle Crags and Mount Shasta. There is no actual gym in the area, but Mt. Shasta Ski Park, located on California Highway 89 east of Mt. Shasta, offers an outdoor climbing wall during summer months.

**Services:** Although piped water and restrooms are available in the campground, these services are unavailable elsewhere in the park. Due to the general scarcity of water anywhere near the climbing area, climbers need to carry water on all outings. The few springs and streams should all be considered suspect, and any water from these sources requires filtration or disinfection before use. Visitors without bacteria-removing filters can use bleach, iodine, or boiling to kill bacteria. Groceries are available at Amiratti's Market, not far from the park entrance and adjacent to the freeway. Businesses in nearby Dunsmuir can provide most additional goods and services.

**Emergency services:** In the event of an emergency, contact park personnel or call 911 to summon assistance. The nearest hospitals are Mercy Medical Center in Mt. Shasta, and Mercy Medical Center and Redding Medical Center, both in Redding.

**Nearby climbing areas:** Castle Crags is essentially an isolated area. The nearest climbing centers are Gray Rocks and Cement Bluff.

**Nearby attractions:** If climbing is not on the day's agenda, visitors can busy themselves with numerous of other activities. A number of trails, ranging from short nature trails to a 10-mile segment of the Pacific Crest Trail, criss-cross Castle Crags Wilderness. The nearby Upper Sacramento River offers good angling for trout, while the entrance area of the park provides picnic facilities. A short drive north on U.S. Interstate 5, the picturesque town of Mt. Shasta, home of numerous local artisans, forms the jumping-off place for downhill and Nordic skiers or parties attempting to climb 14,162-foot Mount Shasta.

**Finding the crags:** To reach Castle Crags, either drive 46.2 miles north on Interstate 5 from Redding, or 6 miles south from the town of Dunsmuir to the exit marked for Castella and Castle Crags State Park. Head west for 0.3 mile to the state park entrance and turn right to the entry station. After checking in, follow the narrow paved road another 2.5 miles to the Vista Point parking area. From the day-use-only parking area, walk back down the road for 50 yards to the signed trailhead for the popular and heavily used, 2.7-mile Crags Trail. Directions to specific crags or groups of crags are given where appropriate.

## INDIAN SPRINGS AREA

This area consists of several formations up to 400 feet high along the west side, and at the head of, the narrow canyon that holds the source of Indian Creek. There are two routes commonly taken to reach climbs in the Indian Springs area: 1) Follow the Crags Trail for 1.6 miles to the junction with the spur trail to Indian Springs. Follow the Indian Springs Trail 0.25 mile to its end at the spring. Head up the brushy drainage to the crags. 2) Follow the Crags Trail for 0.4 mile past the junction with the Indian Springs Trail to a point at which it turns from dirt tread to stone "steps." Where the trail jogs abruptly right, leave it, heading left, and scramble up to a notch. From here, follow slanting "Newspaper Ledge" downward into the Indian Creek drainage, passing below Pincushion Wall and just above Super Crack Spire. Descent routes from the various formations accompany the descriptions of the climbs.

### PINCUSHION WALL

This ragged, 200-foot, southwest-facing crag hosts a variety of sporty, bolted face climbs, all of which can be easily reached from Newspaper Ledge. In most cases, descent is via 2-rope rappel, but those choosing to can top out and scramble or rappel down the formation's back side. Routes are listed from right to left.

1. **First Aid** (5.10a) Reach the foot of this route by scrambling down Newspaper Ledge to its lower end, then head east (left) to near the notch separating Super Crack Spire from Pincushion Wall. Watch for a single bolt on the wall below Newspaper Ledge. Face-climb past the bolt to a short jam crack, then follow it to the climb's end on Newspaper Ledge.
2. **Mild Steel** (5.10b) As you descend Newspaper Ledge, watch for a short jam crack that leads to a line of bolts up the face. Climb the crack, then head up the face, working left as you approach a small roof. Pass left of the roof, then head up to a 2-bolt anchor in an alcove.
3. **Whisper** (5.8) Starting 40' left of *Mild Steel,* follow a short ramp to a series of flakes. Ascend these to a leaning pillar, then pass below it, heading up right to the *Mild Steel* anchor.

## PINCUSHION WALL

4. **Psycho** (5.9) Begin 30' left of *Whisper* and below a deep gully in the upper part of the crag. Face-climb past 5 bolts to a belay at the mouth of the gully.
5. **Snag** (I 5.11c) Start 20' left of *Psycho*. **Pitch 1:** Jam a 5.9 crack up to and over a small overhang to a belay ledge. **Pitch 2:** Move left, then ascend thin 5.11c face climbing past 4 bolts to a good belay ledge up and left of the floor of the gully reached by *Psycho*.

### SUPER CRACK SPIRE

Super Crack Spire is a small, spectacular, leaning pinnacle that rises from the right side of the canyon above Indian Springs and looms over Newspaper Ledge. A telltale crack passing completely through the light-colored pinnacle identifies the crag. Parties usually approach by scrambling uphill from Indian Spring or by descending Newspaper Ledge to its lower end, then scrambling east to the pinnacle. A 50-foot rappel returns the summit party to the ground.

6. **South Arete** (I 5.6 R) Begin at the foot of the arete. **Pitch 1:** Face-climb up the crest of the arete to a small belay ledge. **Pitch 2:** Continue up the arete all the way to the summit.
7. **Super Crack** (I 5.9) Begin this clean and classic jam crack on a blocky ledge near the bottom of the spire's east side. **Pitch 1:** Climb to the ledge

EAST FACE, SUPER CRACK SPIRE

(Class 4). **Pitch 2:** Jam the short, left-facing 5.9 dihedral above, joining *South Arete* near the top of the spire.

8. **East Face** (5.6) Scramble up to, or down to, a small, blocky ledge 30' up and right of *Super Crack*. Ascend flakes and short cracks to the summit.

## WARMUP WALL

This rather small formation lies just west of the foot of Newspaper Ledge and faces east, toward Pincushion Wall and Super Crack Spire. The crag can be approached from either Newspaper Ledge or Indian Springs, and it can be descended by either rappelling Warmup Route or by scrambling off northward (i.e., toward the upper part of the canyon).

9. **Nameless** (5.7) Look for a small, triangular roof near the top of the formation to find this route. Begin below the right side of the roof and follow a line marked by several bolts and fixed pins that leads up to the right side of the roof. Pass around the right side and continue up to a belay alcove.
10. **Warmup Route** (5.6) Starting directly below the roof mentioned above, jam a great crack up to the roof, then work up and around its right side to a belay alcove higher up.

## WINDSONG WALL

Standing behind, and looming over Warmup Wall, Windsong Wall forms a two-tiered cliff with a steep, smooth face on its southeastern side. The lower tier sweeps up left to a small summit, while the pinnacle of the upper tier appears to have slid down and right a bit from the top of the lower tier. Climbs here are the longest in the Indian Springs area. Approach the first two routes by either heading uphill from Indian Springs or by following Newspaper Ledge down to its west end, then heading west to the foot of the crag. Descend from the lower-tier routes by scrambling down northward along the sloping skyline of the crag, then continuing north to a notch, beyond which lies the Crags Trail, or by scrambling down and left into the gully on the south side of the formation and following it to the ground. Descend the upper tier via a two-rope rappel, then follow the descent route for the lower tier.

11. **Rollercoaster** (II 5.10a R) Find the start of this route just right of the foot of a 30-foot pinnacle that leans against the face. **Pitch 1:** Scramble to the corner formed by the pinnacle's right side, then jam up the corner to the top of the pinnacle. From here, face-climb up left (5.9+) to a series of waterstreaks. Ascend difficult, run-out face climbing up these waterstreaks to a belay at a small pine tree. **Pitch 2:** Jam thin 5.10a cracks to

WINDSONG WALL

the top of the lower tier. Take pro to 2", including several finger-sized pieces.

12. **One Hand Scratching** (II 5.10c) Begin at the foot of the waterstreak right of *Rollercoaster.* **Pitch 1:** Ascend a 5.10c face past 5 protection bolts as you follow the waterstreak 85' to a bolted belay anchor. **Pitch 2:** Above the waterstreak, use 3 more bolts to protect 5.10a face climbing to a small but obvious shoulder on the upper right side of the pinnacle.
13. **Disappointment Dihedral** (5.6 or 5.7) Reach the start of this route by either scrambling up the lower tier descent routes, by traversing onto the rock from a notch along the Crags Trail, or by climbing a 5.7 pitch up the right side of the lower tier. Either way, begin on a ledge at the base of the prominent, right-facing dihedral. Ascend the dihedral by means of a chimney.

## PEACH BRANDY WALL

Across the canyon from the end of the Indian Springs Trail rises a row of two or three-tiered, 300- to 400-foot walls, each topped by a pinnacle. The second from the left, two-tiered Peach Brandy Wall, displays a prominent, right-facing openbook above a sharply cut roof on its upper tier. Approach this formation by either heading uphill and left from Indian Springs or downhill from Windsong Wall via the Newspaper Ledge approach. The normal descent route follows the brushy gully to the right of the rock.

14. **Peach Brandy Wall** (I 5.8) You have your choice of several initial pitches for this climb; simply pick the one that strikes your fancy. **Pitch 1:** From a point near the middle of the base of the crag's lower tier, head up the center of the wall via easy (5.1–5.4) cracks, or via 5.7 face climbing up the center of the wall. **Pitch 2:** Beginning somewhat left of a prominent, right-facing dihedral high on the face, gradually diagonal up right (5.8) to the dihedral. **Pitch 3:** Follow the 5.8 dihedral to the top of the rock.
15. **Peaches and Cream** (II 5.10a) Begin as for the previous route. **Pitch 1:** Ascend the first pitch of *Peach Brandy Wall.* **Pitch 2:** Head right on the terrace midway up the formation to a left-facing dihedral that leads to a sharply cut overhang about one-quarter of the way up the upper wall. Ascend the 5.10a dihedral, undercling the roof at its top past several fixed pins, then continue up the crack to its end. When the crack ends, face-climb up left to the upper dihedral of *Peach Brandy Wall.* **Pitch 3:** Follow the 5.8 dihedral to the top of the rock.

PEACH BRANDY WALL
.8
14
.8
15
.10a
14 15

CASTLE CRAGS FROM THE EAST

## CASTLE DOME AREA

The Castle Dome area is the most popular of the five primary climbing areas in the park, and for good reason: the crags are spectacular, the climbs are generally longer, and the approaches generally involve minimal bushwhacking. The area offers climbs of one to eight pitches, ranging in difficulty from 5.6 to 5.11a. The usual access route is the Crags Trail, which leads from the scenic viewpoint to an overlook just west of striking Castle Dome. Approach directions are the same as for the Indian Springs area but continue at the point where one leaves the trail for Newspaper Ledge.

### BULLDOG ROCK

Bulldog Rock, the first "real" rock wall visitors encounter as they huff up the Crags Trail, provides a number of toprope routes. By scrambling up the back, climbers can access several belay/rappel bolts on the top to protect routes ranging in difficulty from 5.6 to 5.9. Scrambling off the back provides an easy descent. In addition to these topropes, there are two lead climbs of note.

16. **The Bolt Route** (5.10a) Locate the start of this route by watching for the line of bolts as you skirt the foot of the rock. Make a tricky, bouldery move to reach the first bolt, avoiding an older, off-route bolt a few feet to the right. Keep to a light-colored streak as you chase the remaining 8 bolts to anchor chains at the top of the rock. Lower off 70', or scramble down the back.

17. **Far-right Crack** (5.10d R) Begin about 6' right of *The Bolt Route*. Make some tricky face moves to reach pockets leading up right to where the crack actually begins. Surmount a roof, then follow the severely right-leaning, thin-hand crack to a small notch down and right of the actual top of the rock. Scramble down the back. Take cams to 2½".

## TRAILSIDE SPIRES

After passing Bulldog Rock, the trail levels off briefly as it passes above the head of the narrow canyon of Indian Springs. A short distance farther on, it passes between two small spires: Spire #1 on the left, and Spire #2 on the right.

TRAILSIDE SPIRE 2

18. **Spire #1—South Arete** (5.7) Beginning at an oak tree growing near the foot of the arete, climb the tree until you can clip a shaky-looking bolt. Move onto the rock, pass the bolt, then climb onto the arete. Face-climb and lieback up the arete to the very small summit. Rappel the route to return to the ground. Be sure to take sling material for the rappel anchor.
19. **Spire #2—South Face** (5.6) From the base of the south face, which rises from the edge of the trail, climb a short, right-facing dihedral, then make an interesting hand traverse to the right. From here, climb past a small pine tree to the summit. Descend by rappelling the route. Take sling material for the anchor.
20. **Spire #2—Southeast Arete** (5.6) Begin 15' down and right of the previous route. Climb broken rock up the arete to meet the *South Face* route at the small tree.

### SIX-TOE ROCK

Just around the corner past Trailside Spires, Six-Toe Rock comes into view on the left. Although it at first appears to be a single pinnacle, Six-Toe Rock is actually the eastern-most of three pinnacles on a single formation. A long, clean flake-crack in the big, left-facing openbook that splits the rock easily identifies the main route. The best descent route is to rappel *Six-Toe Crack* from the small pine tree just left of the notch at its top. If you reach the actual high point of the formation, you can make a short rappel from a single bolt into the notch, then continue down the regular rappel route. If you have two ropes and feel particularly brave, you can make a 150-foot free rappel into the gully right of the pinnacle.

21. **Easy Street** (I 5.6) Begin 50' uphill and left of the dihedral of *Six-Toe Crack*. **Pitch 1:** Jam a clean, right-leaning crack to a small belay stance. **Pitch 2:** Continue up the crack to the cleft at the top of the dihedral. Take pro to 2½".
22. **Easy On** (I 5.7) Start 15' right of *Easy Street*, where another right-slanting crack begins. **Pitch 1:** Jam a long hand crack up right to join *Six-Toe Crack* at its second belay ledge. **Pitch 2:** Follow the 5.7 upper corner crack to the cleft at the top of the dihedral. Take pro to 2½".
23. **Six-Toe Crack** (I 5.8) Begin at the foot of the obvious, wide crack in a left-facing dihedral. **Pitch 1:** Jam the crack, passing the 5.8 crux early, then continue up the crack to a small belay ledge. **Pitches 2 and 3:** Continue up the corner via 5.6–5.7 jamming to the top of the formation. Take pro to 3½".
24. **Chocksucker** (I 5.9) Locate the starting point in the cleft behind a small, detached pillar 30' right of *Six-Toe Crack*. **Pitch 1:** Climb the pillar, then, keeping right of the main dihedral, ascend a hand-to-finger crack to the

SIX-TOE ROCK
21
22
23
24
25
26
27
.6
.7
.8
.9
.9+
.11a

second belay spot on *Six-Toe Crack*. **Pitch 2:** Again, keep right of *Six-Toe Crack* as you crank up a thin crack to a small roof, then work up left to the cleft at the top of the main dihedral.

25. **Purple Heart** (I 5.8) Begin by climbing the first pitch of *Chocksucker*. **Pitch 2:** Follow *Chocksucker*'s thin crack to the small roof, then head up right and follow the airy arete above to the summit of the formation.

Locate the following two routes on the north face of the westernmost, and highest, of the three summits of the crag. These are difficult to see from the vicinity of *Six-Toe Crack,* but are plainly visible from higher on the Crags Trail. Approach by hiking uphill for another 60 yards beyond the approach to *Six-Toe Crack,* then head up a steep, brushy gully and one easy pitch of Class 4–5 rock to the foot of an impressive, steep wall. Descend by down-climbing or rappelling from the top into the notch east of the summit, then scramble down brushy gullies to the trail, possibly making another short rappel partway down.

26. **Picture Perfect** (5.9+) Begin about 20' up left of a prominent, right-leaning, flared chimney. Jam a classic, right-leaning hand/fist crack, then ascend a short section of easy face climbing to the summit. Take extra pro to 3".
27. **No Mercy** (5.11a R/X) Using stemming, jamming, or whatever else works, climb the severely flared, right-leaning chimney. When it peters out after 50', switch to jamming and continue up a fist crack that curves up left to a small flake/ledge. Face-climb to the top from here (run-out).

## THE MANSION

On its way to Castle Dome, the trail passes the top of The Mansion, an impressive wall separated from Castle Dome by a steep, brushy gully, and having a distinctive, detached summit block the size of a small building. The rather unpleasant approach has limited the popularity of this fine crag. Follow the Crags Trail past Six-Toe Rock and continue up the steep, rocky tread until it reaches the obvious head of the gully. Leave the trail at this point, then head down and right along slabs to the brushy floor of the gully, and continue on down until you reach the foot of the crag. To return, walk southeast from the top of the crag and soon return to the Crags Trail.

28. **Casino** (II 5.11a) Use an obvious, cave-like formation near the base of the crag to locate the start of this challenging route. **Pitch 1:** After scrambling to the "cave," exit its right side on loose rock that quickly improves (5.9), then face-climb (5.9+) past 2 bolts to a 2-bolt anchor near a large, detached flake. **Pitch 2:** Face-climb and occasionally stem as you climb a shallow, left-facing corner past 5 bolts, encountering the 5.11a crux shortly before reaching the belay bolts at the foot of a dike. **Pitch 3:** Follow the 5.9 dike past 3 bolts to another bolted belay anchor. **Pitch 4:** Ascend easy face climbing to the summit.

29. **South Face** (5.7) You can work out several variations to climbing the south side of the summit block. All involve about 25' of interesting face climbing.

## CASTLE DOME

Castle Dome, the largest, most striking, and most easily identifiable of the Castle Crags, rises to an elevation of 4,966 feet and stands somewhat apart from the rest of the tangle of summits visible from the valley floor. At nearly 900 feet, the east face of Castle Dome forms one of the biggest granite walls north of Yosemite National Park. From the end of the Crags Trail, the exposed 400-foot rock scramble to the summit attracts hundreds of visitors each year. Approach the climbs on the east side by means of the approach used for The Mansion, or by departing early from the Crags Trail at its junction with the Root Creek Trail, following the latter to its end, then heading cross-country for the foot of the east face. Approach the remaining climbs by descending the gully below the observation point. Descend the dome via the *Regular Route.*

30. **The Good Book** (I 5.10a) Begin at the base of a prominent, left-curving, left-facing dihedral a few yards north of the bottom of the brushy, scramble-down gully between Castle Dome and The Mansion. **Pitch 1:** Climb the dihedral, or, if you prefer face climbing, slink up the face a few feet left of the dihedral. Negotiate a roof where the dihedral jogs left, then continue up the corner to a belay spot. **Pitch 2:** Keep going up the dihedral as it curves left and eventually becomes a roof. Belay below another leftward jog. **Pitch 3:** A pleasant surprise—instead of fighting left along the roof, drop down a few feet and ascend easy friction up left to the approach slabs to end the climb. If run-out face climbing is more your thing, you can climb directly up to the second belay stance in a single, long, essentially unprotected 5.10a/b pitch.
31. **East Face a.k.a. The Dike Route** (III 5.10d R) Use one of the following approaches to reach this climb: 1) From the base of *The Good Book,* continue down the gully for another 175' to the lower end of a conspicuous ramp that slants up and right across the dome's lower east face, or 2) About 0.5 mile up the Crags Trail, head right on the Root Creek Trail and follow it down and right 0.75 mile to its end at the edge of Root Creek, then head upstream, taking a left where the streambed forks, scrambling and bushwhacking up to the ramp. Either way, follow the ramp up right for approximately 500' to a detached pillar just right of a downward-pointing flake on the face. **Pitch 1:** From a point a few feet left of the pillar, face-climb up left (5.8), passing below the flake, to reach an amazing quartz dike that snakes all the way up the face. Clip a bolt a bit left of the dike (5.9), then follow the dike up right past another bolt

*East Face of Castle Dome.*

to a belay stance. **Pitch 2:** Leave the dike as you head directly up the face (5.8) to a bolt, then make an unprotected traverse back right to rejoin the dike. Continue up the dike to a belay spot below a long roof that crosses the entire east face. **Pitch 3:** Surmount the roof to a bolt, then follow the dike past 2 more bolts to a 2-bolt anchor under a small roof. **Pitch 4:** Detour right to a bolt, up to another, then back left to rejoin the dike again. Continue past 1 more bolt to a 2-bolt belay anchor. **Pitch 5:** Climb hard-to-protect, thin cracks and a groove to a bolt beneath another roof. Using a long sling to avoid rope drag, pull over the roof (5.10d) and continue up to another bolted belay stance. **Pitch 6:** Follow the 5.9+ dike past a single bolt to a belay spot. **Pitch 7:** Make another 5.9 run along the dike to a decent ledge, where the angle relents. **Pitch 8:** After a few moves of 5.6/5.7, romp up much easier climbing to the summit. Take a full selection of gear for this climb, including extras of thin wires and small cams, and at least 2 long runners. Because several pitches are 165' long, a second rope is essential if you are forced to retreat. Note that, in several places, this route requires long runouts on technical terrain—*do not attempt it unless you are very comfortable climbing at this level.*

32. **Regular Route** (3-4) Note that, because the route is not obvious and because getting off-route could put less-experienced climbers in a dangerous situation, more detail is given than otherwise. From the sandy saddle southwest of the dome, follow a faint path up right to a high point along the base of the south face. Pick out and follow ramp-like lines of pockets and thin ledges that zigzag up the face, eventually heading up left to the lower end of a prominent, wider, and occasionally brushy ramp that angles up right. Follow the ramp up right to a flat shoulder, then traverse farther right on ledges that lead out across the upper east face. Continue past a gully with a detached flake in it until you come to a deep slot that angles up left just left of where a fir tree grows out from under a large overhang. (Note that this spot would make a decent bivouac site in a pinch.) Scramble up the slot to its top, then face-climb up right on sloping holds to reach larger handholds and ledges that lead to the summit. Generally, if you diagonal up right after the short, tricky section, you will find the easiest going. Return the same way. Do not underestimate this climb—although it is routinely climbed without a rope, it is exposed in several places and can be treacherous in wet or snowy conditions.

33. **West Ridge** (II 5.8) Find the start of this route by descending the gully west of the dome until you reach a large Douglas-fir below the sandy saddle southwest of Castle Dome at the end of the Crags Trail. **Pitch 1:** From the vicinity of the tree, climb a narrow 5.8 dike on low-angle rock to a terrace with a small tree on the dome's north face. **Pitch 2:** Head up the

5.7 face until the rock steepens, then traverse right to a belay ledge. **Pitch 3:** Make a 5.2 traverse right to a belay spot on a large, brushy ledge beneath big, thin, crumbly "Potato Chip Flake." **Pitch 4:** Climb the flake, then continue upward to a belay ledge. **Pitch 5:** Move left into a trough, then follow it upward past two old and untrustworthy bolts to ledges on the crag's northwest buttress. **Pitch 6:** Head up left, then ascend an easy trough to the summit.

NORTH FACE AND WEST RIDGE OF CASTLE DOME

34. **North Face** (II 5.9 A0 or 5.10b) Begin this route as for *West Ridge*. **Pitch 1:** Climb the first lead of *West Ridge*. **Pitch 2:** Follow *West Ridge*'s second pitch until you reach a short, left-facing corner. Jam up (5.9) to a brushy ledge on the left. **Pitch 3:** Traverse left to the end of the ledge, then ascend a short 5.7 face to a belay spot on a higher ledge. **Pitch 4:** Follow the ledge back right to a right-leaning 5.7 crack and follow it up to a belay spot on the dome's northwest buttress. **Pitch 5:** Jam up a left-facing 5.9 dihedral, then make a short traverse left to a brushy ledge. **Pitch 6:** Climb the right side of a 25-foot pedestal, passing 2 bolts, then make a tricky 5.10b traverse or an easy pendulum left a ramp and follow it up right to its end at a small pine tree. **Pitch 7:** Climb a 5.9 dike and face to the summit of the dome.

## MOUNT HUBRIS, A.K.A. THE OGRE

The state park/Forest Service map of Castle Crags labels Mount Hubris, a jagged spire easily seen from the end of the trail, as peak 5,533. This crag, 0.25 mile southwest of Castle Dome, appears as a sharp-pointed peak with two pinnacles separated by a deep gash on its left side. The alternate name comes from a quirk of erosion—and a little imagination—that created a dour-looking "face" about one-third of the way up the crag and right of the big chimney. Mount Hubris can claim visits by a number of climbing luminaries, including Allen Steck, Warren Harding, Fred Beckey, and Jeff Lowe. *The Great Chimney* was first climbed by Chuck Pratt, while the late John Harlin put up the area's mega-classic *Cosmic Wall,* a route Christian Bonington declared was one of the best climbs he had done in this country. Although no maintained trail goes to Mount Hubris, several game trails through the surrounding brushfield provide comparatively easy access. The descent requires two rappels of 100' into the ravine on the crag's north side, so two ropes are mandatory.

35. **The Great Chimney** (I 5.8) Begin at the foot of the obvious, deep gash visible on the left side of Mount Hubris. **Pitch 1:** After a tricky 5.8 start, proceed up easier going to a belay spot. **Pitch 2:** Work up the 5.6–5.7 chimney 140' to a belay ledge. **Pitch 3:** Climb a long pitch of 5.6 chimneying to a large ledge. **Pitch 4:** Reach the top of the chimney via much easier climbing. Descend by scrambling left from the top of the chimney, or top out and rappel (using 2 ropes).

36. **Solar Wind** (II 5.10d) Start 175' right of *The Great Chimney.* **Pitch 1:** Ascend 200' by any of several routes, all of which require some 5.7 climbing and an intermediate belay. Belay at a long, narrow ledge just below "The Face." **Pitch 2:** Face-climb past a bolt, heading for The Ogre's "nose." Pull over the "nose" to another bolt, then continue up and over the 5.10d roof that forms The Ogre's right (your left) "eye." Clip a third bolt, then face-climb to a 2-bolt belay anchor. **Pitch 3:** Follow a 5.10a quartz dike, step right, and continue up whitish rock, eventually working up left to another bolted belay stance. **Pitch 4:** Climb up right past a bolt and a pine tree to join *Cosmic Wall* at a shallow chimney near the summit. **Pitch 5:** Climb the shallow 5.6 chimney to the top. Take a full selection of gear from RPs to 3½", including additional finger-sized cams.

37. **Faceted Dike** (II 5.10b) Begin this much more difficult variation of *Cosmic Wall* at the same point as that route. **Pitch 1:** Climb the first pitch of *Cosmic Wall.* **Pitch 2:** Instead of heading up right, proceed directly up a small, right-facing dihedral to The Ogre's lip, then up the indented 5.10b face alongside the right side of The Ogre's "nose," passing 3 bolts. Work up right to a belay at the left end of the roof that forms The Ogre's

MOUNT HUBRIS, A.K.A. THE OGRE

left (your right) "eye." **Pitch 3:** Pull over the 5.10a roof, then ascend the route's namesake faceted dike (5.9+), eventually working up and right to join *Cosmic Wall* at its fourth belay ledge.

38. **Cosmic Wall** (II 5.6) Begin at the lower right side of a semi-detached pinnacle low on the southeast side of the face and about 150' right of the start of *Solar Wind*. **Pitch 1:** Climb the right side of the pinnacle, then follow a diagonal weakness up and right to a system of ledges under a set of conspicuous overhangs about one-third of the way up the wall. Ascend several flakes on the face, then make an exposed step right to a small belay tree. **Pitch 2:** From the tree, climb directly up for a long pitch, stopping to belay at a bolt. **Pitch 3:** Continue upward for another short pitch to a belay ledge on the shoulder of the crag. **Pitch 4:** Climb a short dihedral above the ledge, move left into a groove, then follow it to a notch at the top of the wall. **Pitches 5 and 6:** Traverse left a short distance, then follow a 5.6 chimney to the summit.
39. **Golden Opportunity** (II 5.9 R) Begin at the lower-right end of a crack that curves up left to a large roof low on the face right of The Ogre. **Pitch 1:** Follow the crack up left to the right end of the roof, then head up the run-out 5.7 face and belay at a small tree. **Pitch 2:** Continue up the face (5.9) via several flakes, then make a long move left to another belay tree. **Pitch 3:** Head up left, joining *Cosmic Wall* at its fourth belay ledge. Finish via that route.

## ROOT CREEK WALL

Large and impressive Root Creek Wall is an east-facing wall that lies northwest of Castle Dome and overlooks upper Root Creek. It can be seen to good advantage from the vicinity of the Railroad Park Motel in Dunsmuir. The two routes here follow prominent buttresses at either end of the wall. If you do not mind the approach, these are pretty good climbs. The wall can be approached by following the Crags Trail 0.5 mile to a junction with the Root Creek Trail, then hiking down Root Creek Trail 0.75 mile to its end and following Root Creek northwest past Castle Dome, then southwest and uphill via substantial bushwhacking. An alternate route is to head cross-country west from the end of the Crags Trail, passing two small formations, then bushwhacking down to the foot of the wall. Descend by either heading southeast from the top of the wall and bushwhacking back up to the ridge west of the Crags Trail, or down its left edge to Root Creek.

40. **Dunsmuir Avenue** (II 5.10c) Begin on a tree-covered terrace at the foot of the left-hand buttress. **Pitch 1:** Follow a 5.8 dike to a belay bolt at the left edge of a roof on the prow of the buttress. **Pitch 2:** Climb a right-facing dihedral to a bolt-protected crux, then, a little higher, work left to ledges. Traverse left to the end of the ledges and belay. **Pitch 3:** Work up a 5.7

Walk off
40
ROOT CREEK WALL—SOUTH

Walk off
41
ROOT CREEK WALL—NORTH

chimney to a tree. **Pitch 4:** Climb a shallow 5.10b dihedral above the tree to a ledge. **Pitch 5:** Continue up much easier climbing to the top of the wall.

41. **Dike Hike** (II 5.8) Start from talus at the base of the right-hand buttress. **Pitch 1:** Climb a 5.4 pitch to a roof on the right side of the buttress. **Pitch 2:** Pass right of the roof (5.8), then continue up a dike to a belay ledge. **Pitch 3:** Climb easy rock to the top of the buttress.

## BATTLE MOUNTAIN

Battle Mountain, the fourth main climbing area in the park, boasts the largest rock wall visible from the road that passes the state park entrance. Climbers have established several routes up the enormous south face of this formation. The mountain derives its name from a fight between local native residents and miners near this site in 1855. The so-called "Battle of Castle Crags," the last major conflict in which the native people were armed solely with bows and arrows, began the prolonged regional conflict of the Modoc War. Reach the south face of Battle Mountain by heading left on the Pacific Crest Trail at its junction with the Crags Trail. Contour along the south side of the crags for about 2 miles. Shortly after the third stream crossing, where the trail rounds the end of a low ridge, leave the trail and hike cross-country along the crest of the ridge for another steep and sometimes brushy mile to the lower right corner of Battle Mountain's big south face. Head up left along the top of a terrace at the foot of the face to reach the starting points of the climbs. Descend Battle Mountain by downclimbing or rappelling its north side, crossing westward to a notch, then rappelling or downclimbing to the west base of the crag.

42. **Plumb Line** (IV 5.10a R) Begin about 25' right of a narrow, water-worn groove, which forms the right-hand terminus of a wall at the base of the crag's south face, and left of a prominent, white dike. **Pitch 1:** Face-climb up right past a flake and onward to a series of short, left-angling 5.9 cracks. From the last of these, move up past a couple of small trees to a belay spot at a loose flake. **Pitch 2:** Climb another short crack, then hand-traverse up left along a left-slanting 5.10a crack (several fixed pins). Enter the prominent groove, move up a few feet, then exit left to a belay at the foot of a dike on the face to the left. **Pitch 3:** Continue up the dike on runout 5.8–5.9 face climbing and stemming to the top of the wall. Move up right to re-enter the groove, and follow it to a belay ledge atop a small pedestal. **Pitch 4:** Pull crystals and tiptoe up the dike that forms the bed of the groove. **Pitch 5:** Move left out of the groove, ascend a series of short, discontinuous 5.9 cracks on the prow, then go back to

SOUTH FACE OF BATTLE MOUNTAIN

the groove and continue (5.8) to a belay at the second of two small trees growing out of the groove. **Pitch 6:** Finish the groove (5.7), which ends at a small notch. **Pitch 7:** Climb a short 5.8 offwidth or unprotected 5.9 face on the wall to the left of the notch. Higher, switch to scrambling as you run the rope out to a belay ledge. **Pitch 8:** Climb easy Class 5 rock on the crest of the summit ridge. **Pitch 9:** Climb 200' of Class 4 rock to the summit.

43. **South Face** (IV 5.10c) Note a prominent terrace that slants up left about one-third of the way up the face (*Plumb Line* begins near its right-hand side). Locate the starting point at the foot of a prominent, left-facing dihedral right of a very large tree and leading up to a notch in the terrace. **Pitch 1:** After a short crack, enter the dihedral and climb it to a small belay ledge. **Pitch 2:** Exit left, following a series of discontinuous, left-slanting, 5.10c cracks protected by fixed pins. Follow these up to the notch, clipping a bolt just below the terrace. **Pitch 3:** Traverse right along the terrace to a belay point in a hidden notch situated below the lower end of a left-slanting ramp/dihedral. **Pitch 4:** Face-climb up left to a crack and follow it until it becomes a smooth, right-facing dihedral. **Pitch 5:** Climb the 5.9+ dihedral, belaying at a small stance halfway up. **Pitch 6:** Continue to the top of the dihedral (5.8). **Pitch 7:** Leave the ramp/dihedral via short cracks along a dike. Follow these upward (5.9) to a belay at the lower end of a narrow ramp that slants up right. **Pitch 8:** Follow the 5.4 ramp up right to a ledge near the summit. **Pitch 9:** Finish with a short, Class 4 pitch up broken rock.

## WEST SIDE AREA

The West Side area of Castle Crags consists of several outstanding formations set far off the beaten track. Though these all involve rather lengthy and sometimes unpleasant approaches, they are well worth the effort, as the climbing is outstanding and the wilderness setting is delightful. The usual point of entry for west side crags is the Dog Trail. Find the Dog Trail by bypassing the state park entrance and driving 3.2 miles west up Castle Creek Canyon on the road that runs past the park entrance. When you spot a gravel-and-rock borrow pit through trees on the right, pull in and park at the edge of the clearing, near a couple of trash cans and a small trail marker. Directions to the various crags accompany their descriptions.

## BECKS TOWER

Becks Tower, named by Fletcher Hoyt to commemorate a climbing partner killed by lightning in British Columbia, is an impressive, flat-topped formation located at the head of Sulfur Creek. Although much of its face consists of decomposing rock, there are also several sections of sound stone that make for

## BECKS TOWER

some memorable climbing. Approach by following the Dog Trail 0.3 mile to the Pacific Crest Trail. Turn right on the Pacific Crest Trail and follow it to the ridge just east of Sulfur Creek, the first stream. Leave the PCT here, following a faint and sometimes overgrown climbers' trail to an open saddle. Keep going directly uphill until you are even with, and east of, the base of Becks Tower. Now, head left and return to the ravine containing Sulfur Creek. Take care crossing scree-covered slabs and climbing short, steep walls here and there on the approach. None of the routes described actually tops out, due to deteriorating rock higher up; descent routes are given for each route.

44. **South Face Dike** (III 5.10c R) Locate a left-curving arch low on the right side of Becks Tower's south face. Begin the route right of this arch. **Pitch 1:** Climb a short 5.10a crack, then face-climb up right past a bolt to a small belay stance. **Pitch 2:** Face-climb up left past 3 bolts to a short crack. Instead of climbing the crack, detour around it on the right, eventually working back left to belay at a fixed pin at its top. **Pitch 3:** Climb up right on 5.10a friction to a dike and follow it up the face (5.8 R) to a small ledge with a bolt. **Pitch 4:** From the left end of the ledge, face-climb up left, up, up right, then directly up (5.9) to a ledge with 2 bolts that marks the end of the climb. Rappel the route.

45. **West Buttress** (III 5.9) Begin at the foot of a right-facing dihedral 400' left of Route 44. **Pitch 1:** Ascend the 5.7 dihedral to a 3-bolt anchor. **Pitch 2:** Exit left to a slot left of a small roof. Climb the slot, then work up left, passing from one short 5.8 crack to another. Belay below a chimney. **Pitch 3:** Climb 5.9 cracks, move right into the chimney, then climb it to a bolted belay on a ledge. **Pitch 4:** Move to the right end of the ledge, then climb a 5.9 offwidth crack past a bolt. Chimney as the crack continues to widen, eventually climbing the left side of the chimney to a pedestal on the left. Scramble left from here to a point where you can make a 150-foot rappel into the brushy gully left of the tower.

## LUDEN'S OVERHANG

In marked contrast to the steep cracks and walls found elsewhere in Castle Crags, Luden's Overhang presents a handful of quality, moderate slab climbs. The crag's namesake overhang caps a long, broad, south-facing slab. You may find climbing here pretty hot going during the summer; the rock is at its best in spring and fall. Approach by driving to the rock-and-gravel borrow pit that marks the Dog Trailhead. Follow the Dog Trail to its junction with the Pacific Crest Trail. Turn left onto the Pacific Crest Trail and proceed 100 yards or so to the foot of a ridge that heads up and right. Leave the trail and follow the crest of the ridge a mile or so to the lower left corner of the crag.

46. **A Bridge Too Far** (5.9–5.11) Begin at the left end of a small, brush-and-tree-covered hill at the foot of the face. Face-climb up left to gain a flake. Clip a bolt on the face, then make a long reach up left to gain a crack. Jam to a ledge on the left at the top of the crack. Make some 5.7 moves as you head left along the ledge, eventually scrambling off left into a brushy gully. Note that the crux of this route is very height-dependent.
47. **Premeditated Leisure** (II 5.9 R) From the foot of Route 46, walk up right to the top of the little hill. Begin at a boulder just right of the high point. **Pitch 1:** Face-climb directly up past a bolt to a down-pointing flake. Undercling left, then traverse farther left to a 2-bolt belay at a small ledge. **Pitch 2:** Step left off the ledge, then pinch crystals up the 5.8 face, past a bolt, to a ledge equipped with 2 bolts. **Pitch 3:** Face-climb up to a left-curving arch, move right and up to a fixed pin (5.7), then head up to the brushy terrace under the overhang that gives the crag its name. Rappel the route; you will need 2 ropes. Take a couple of smaller TCUs.
48. **Guides Holiday** (III 5.10a) Begin near the middle of the slab, at the foot of the little hill's right side. **Pitch 1:** Mantle onto a shelf, face-climb to a bolt, then move right and ascend a finger of rock to its top. **Pitch 2:** From the finger, follow a 5.9 dike past 2 bolts to a ledge with a small tree. **Pitch 3:** Face-climb past 2 bolts (the second one is bad) to a fixed pin, then traverse left to a ledge with trees. **Pitch 4:** From the left end of the ledge, step

# LUDEN'S OVERHANG

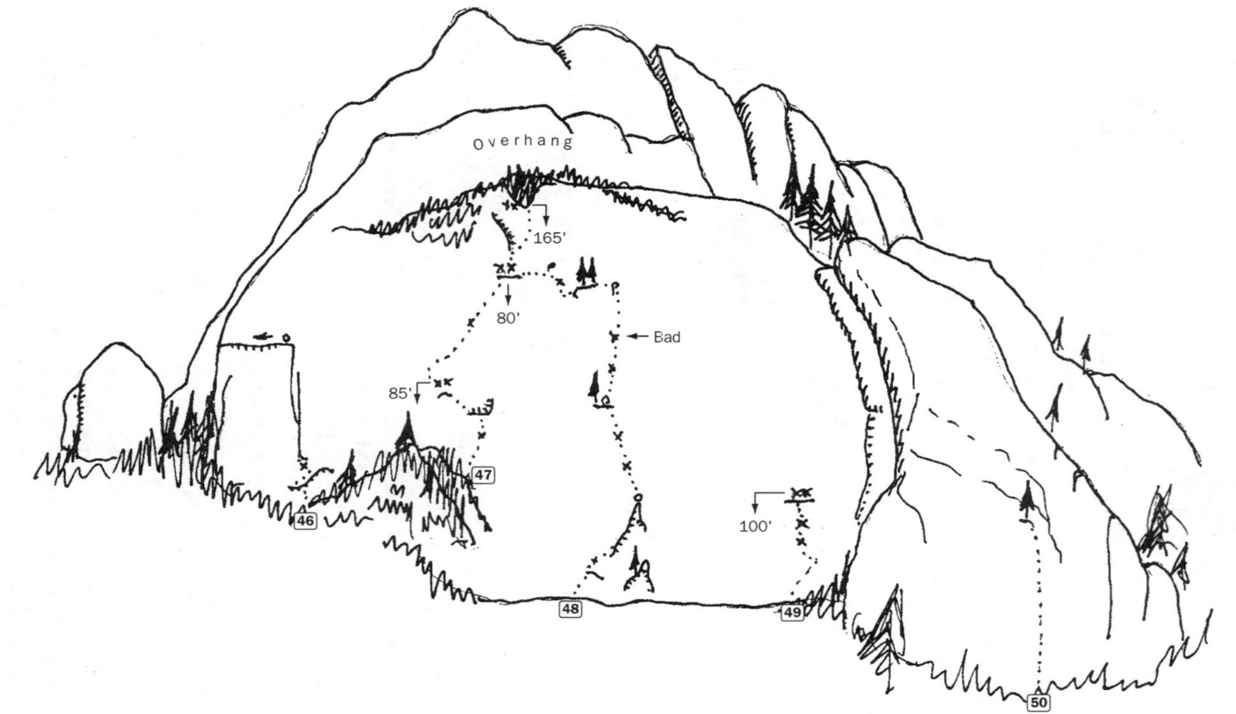

down, left, then up to a bolt. Traverse up left (5.8) past a fixed pin, then make a long runout up left to join Route 47 at its second belay ledge. **Pitch 5:** Finish via *Premeditated Leisure.*

49. **I've Been Framed** (5.9) Begin on the face below and left of the lower end of a prominent, left-curving, left-facing dihedral. Face-climb up right as though trying to reach the dihedral, then cut back left and head directly upward past 2 bolts to a 2-bolt anchor on a small ledge. Make a 2-rope rappel to return.
50. **Unnamed** (5.10b R) Start 100' right of the big, left-facing dihedral. Climb a crack, passing through a tunnel, then continuing up loose rock to a tree ledge. Make a 2-rope rappel to descend.

## HIT-OR-MISS ROCK

Hit-or-Miss Rock consists of a prominent, clean, white granite formation approximately 170 feet high, marked by a huge, left-facing, overhanging openbook on its southeast side. Several excellent short routes ascend this formation. Using the previously mentioned openbook as a starting landmark, the following routes appear in right-to-left order. Follow the Dog Trail uphill toward Castle Crags for one-third mile to the Pacific Crest Trail. Turn left and hike 100 yards or so until the trail rounds the crest of a ridge. Leave the trail and hike uphill, staying on the crest of the ridge for another mile to Luden's Overhang, then continue up and left for another 0.25 mile to the crag. Descend Hit-or-Miss Rock by rappelling from bolts on the rock's summit.

51. **Unfinished Business** (I 5.9) Locate the starting point several yards left of the foot of a small, left-facing dihedral, which becomes much larger higher up the rock. **Pitch 1:** Climb a short crack along the edge of a left-facing flake to a bolt, then diagonal up right past another bolt to enter the dihedral. Jam and lieback up the corner to a belay stance on a dike that roughly parallels the main corner but stays a short distance to the left. Face-climb along the dike to a double-bolt belay. **Pitch 2:** Continue up the dihedral to a 2-bolt anchor at the top of the face. Ascend a short bit of 5.9 friction to another double-bolt belay. Use two ropes to rappel to the ground from here.
52. **Bureaucratic Bullshit** (I 5.10a) Begin as for *Unfinished Business.* **Pitch 1:** Follow *Unfinished Business* to the foot of the large dihedral, where a conspicuous dike angles up left across the face. Follow the dike past 3 bolts to a small belay stance equipped with 2 bolts. **Pitch 2:** Continue to the end of the dike, clip a bolt, then friction up left, gradually working right to the 2-bolt anchor atop Route 51.

# HIT-OR-MISS ROCK

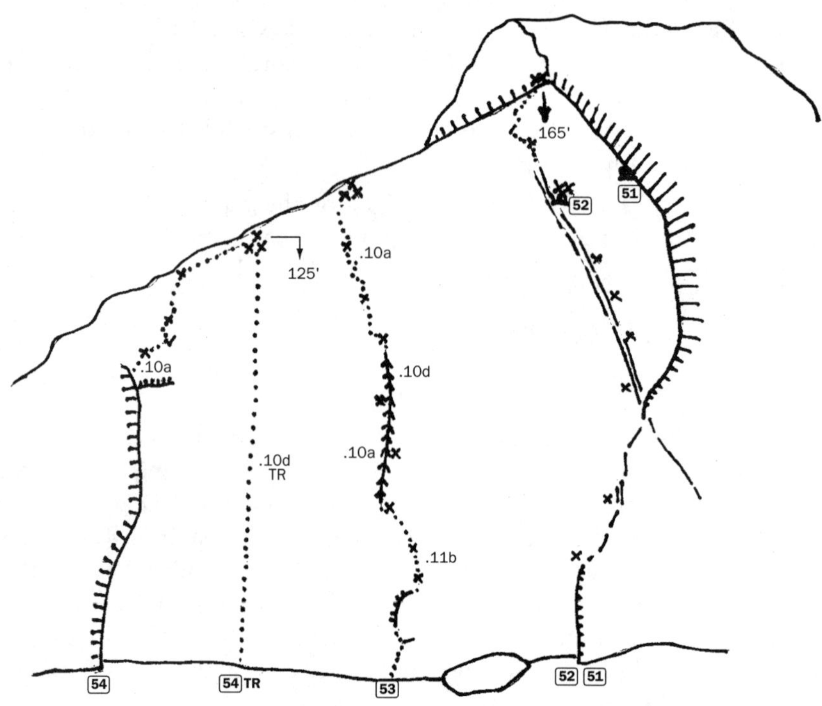


53. **Hit Man** (5.11b) Begin 15' left of a boulder, which rests against the wall about 10' left of the start of *Unfinished Business.* From the boulder, climb to a small arch that curves up and right. Undercling the arch, then face-climb (5.11b) past 2 bolts to a dike or small ridge on the face. Continue bolt-protected 5.10 climbing up the ridge to more 5.10 moves on the blank face above, then work up left to a trio of bolts at the top of the wall. Rappel the route.

54. **Hit or Miss** (5.10a) Start this, the original route on the rock, at the foot of an obvious crack left of the face ascended by the previous routes. Climb the 5.8 hand-and-foot crack, passing over a small overhang near the top of the crack. Face-climb past 3 bolts, then head up right on easier friction to a 3-bolt anchor. Rappel from here. For fun, you can also toprope the face right of this route, using the same 3-bolt anchor.

# HONORABLE MENTION

## THE SEVENTH VEIL

The Seventh Veil is a beautiful, waterstreaked slab that overlooks a meadow 0.25 mile northwest of Boulder Creek Lakes in the Canyon Creek drainage of the Trinity Alps Wilderness. This 400-foot granite slab, which is graced by a sheet-cascade waterfall on its southern end, offers the wilderness climber the opportunity to sample stunning, though run-out friction climbing ranging from 5.7 to 5.11d.

Approach by driving west from Weaverville on California Highway 299 for 8 miles to the community of Junction City. Head north on Canyon Creek Road 22 miles to its end at a large trailhead parking area. Follow the Canyon Creek Trail 4.5 miles to a junction on the left with the Boulder Creek Lakes Trail. Hike 2.5 miles up the Boulder Creek Lakes Trail to its terminus just north of the cirque that holds Boulder Creek Lakes. Head up right (west-northwest) via easy cross-country over granite slabs to reach The Seventh Veil.

## STONEHOUSE BUTTRESS

One of the premier landmarks in the Canyon Creek drainage is striking Stonehouse Buttress, an 800-foot granite crag on the west side of the canyon, approximately 6 miles up the Canyon Creek Trail from the trailhead. The impressive, giant dihedral on the southeast side has been climbed (IV 5.10d), as have several other lines on the crag's south and northeast sides.

Approach by driving west from Weaverville on California Highway 299 for 8 miles to the community of Junction City. Head north on Canyon Creek Road 22 miles to its end at a large trailhead parking area. Follow the Canyon Creek Trail 4.5 miles to a junction on the left with the Boulder Creek Lakes Trail. Continue up Canyon Creek, eventually reaching a suitable basecamp site in another 1.5 miles. Take any of several off-trail routes up left to the crag.

## RUSH CREEK SPIRE

Though all-but-hidden behind an intervening ridge when viewed from Weaverville, Rush Creek Spire can be seen as a ragged fin of dark granite, thrusting upward from a spur ridge northeast of Monument Peak. Rush Creek Spire forms the east side of the cirque that encloses the Rush Creek Lakes. Though currently more a technical mountaineering outing, the crag's west face promises numerous quality crack climbs in a series of large, parallel dihedrals.

Approach by heading west on California Highway 299 from the middle of Weaverville. Turn right onto Memorial Drive just west of the sheriff's office. Once the pavement ends, continue on Forest Road 33N38, heading for the Weaver Bally fire lookout. After about 11.5 miles, park on the shoulder at the signed East Weaver Lake Trailhead. Hike east, then north on the trail, cross the ridge, then drop to a bench just above East Weaver Lake. Continue north, then drop into a canyon and a trail junction at 2 miles. Turn left and follow the sometimes faint track to the saddle at the head of the canyon. From here, head north along an old firebreak on the ridgetop. When the slope becomes steep again, head up right on steep trail, topping out on the ridgetop east of Monument Peak, 4 miles from the car. Head east along the south side of the ridge for about 0.3 mile to a bald peak of decomposing granite. From here, you can inspect the spire. Descend northward to a narrow saddle, then turn left and drop down to reach the west face of the spire. For easier climbs, head down and right from the saddle to reach the east face. With care, you can scramble down the southeast side of the crag; otherwise, you will need to make a series of 4–5 rappels down the east face.

## LITTLE YCAT

Lying just west of Ycatapom Peak, Little Ycat is a fine-looking, nearly vertical granite cliff that overlooks a small tarn on a bench above the floor of Poison Canyon. Several challenging crack climbs can be found on the crag's north face, most in the 5.9–5.10c range. The descent entails nothing more than a short walk down the grassy south side, making the rock easily accessible for toprope climbing.

Approach as for Ycatapom Peak. From the basecamp site for Ycatapom Peak, continue another 0.5 mile to the east end of the meadow that houses Lilypad Lake. Continue up the abruptly steeper trail, which is marked by occasional ducks, for another 0.5 mile to the terrace that leads right to Little Ycat.

## TAPIE PEAK

Just a half-mile southwest of the small crags of Big Boulder Lake stands Tapie Peak, whose steep south and east faces provide numerous interesting, easy-to-moderate routes on generally sound rock. The gullies contain considerable loose rock, but the buttresses provide airy, fun climbing at about the 5.6–5.10a level, all in a delightful wilderness setting.

Approach as for the Big Boulder Lake crags, but continue up the hiking trail past them for another 0.5 mile, or until you can see the trees thin out and the slope on the right becomes more open. Leave the trail and hike southwest, eventually heading up left across an open slope of talus blocks to reach the south face of the peak.

## CEMENT BLUFF

This crag is one of the most unusual in California, consisting of a 120- to 300-foot cliff of natural concrete in which thousands of pebbles, cobbles, and small boulders are embedded. Its setting at the south end of Bluff Lake and within a stone's throw of the Pacific Crest Trail makes for delightful climbing. Few routes have been developed here, primarily due to its off-the-beaten-track location, but the crag promises a good three or four dozen routes in the 5.9–5.13 range on its gently overhanging north face for ambitious parties. Cement Bluff lies outside any designated wilderness area, so bolting—even with a motorized drill—is permitted.

Approach by driving north from Weaverville or south from Yreka on California Highway 3 to the signed junction with Parks Creek Road at the south base of the Scott Mountains. Drive northeast on Parks Creek Road (Forest Highway 17) for approximately 12.5 miles to a signed crossing of High Camp Creek at a sharp right turn. A hundred yards or so farther on, turn left onto a dirt-and-gravel road and proceed 1.5 miles to a ford of High Camp Creek. You can drive across late in the season if you have a high-clearance vehicle; otherwise, back up and park on the shoulder. Cross the creek and continue up the very rough dirt road to the northwest shore of Bluff Lake. Cement Bluff lies just across the lake from the campsites here. Descend the crag by walking west to the Pacific Crest Trail, follow it north for 200 yards, then descend a talus slope on the right to return to the lake.

# Lassen Volcanic National Park

Lassen Volcanic National Park contains the greatest collection of volcanic features in the contiguous United States, including shield volcanoes, cinder cones, lava flows, volcanic bombs, and the park's high point, Lassen Peak, the world's largest known plug dome volcano. The park's geothermal features display a variety comparable to that of similar features in better-known Yellowstone National Park. Park scenery includes not only the chaotic landscape born of volcanic activity, but also dense forest, sparkling lakes, idyllic mountain meadows, and plenty of rock for climbers. California Highway 89 traverses the park from north to south, providing easy access to park features and inspiring vistas. On clear days, the mountains of the Coast Range just north of San Francisco Bay can be seen, a distance of well over 100 miles.

The landscape seen today is a comparatively new one, geologically speaking. Most of the mountains in the western half of the park are the remains of ancient Mount Tehama, a huge volcano approximately the size of Mount Shasta. A powerful eruption, much like that of Mount Mazama, which created Oregon's Crater Lake, caused the mountain to collapse. Unlike Mount Mazama, however, Mount Tehama was more heavily fractured, and its eruption was more lop-sided, resulting in a series of jagged peaks around the newly-formed caldera, but no lake. Approximately 11,000 years ago, a mass of viscous magma welled up in a side vent of the former volcano. This molten mass pushed up a huge volume of material, creating Lassen Peak in a mere five years or so, but it did not erupt. Instead, the magma cooled in place, forming the giant dacite outcrops of Bellybutton and the summit rocks of the mountain. Similar circumstances formed nearby Eagle Peak and the rocks of Eagle Cliff.

The volcano, though quiet, was still active, and, beginning on May 30, 1914, it was rocked by a series of more than 150 steam explosions that lasted for nearly a year. On May 19, 1915, new lava filled the small summit crater, eventually spilling out through notches and flowing nearly 1,000 feet down the western flank of the volcano. To the east, the thick lava broke apart, melting snow and creating a huge mudslide that continued down the mountain and beyond for 18 miles. On May 23, the region was shaken by a huge explosion that sent debris into the air as high as 30,000 feet and created a

# LASSEN VOLCANIC NATIONAL PARK

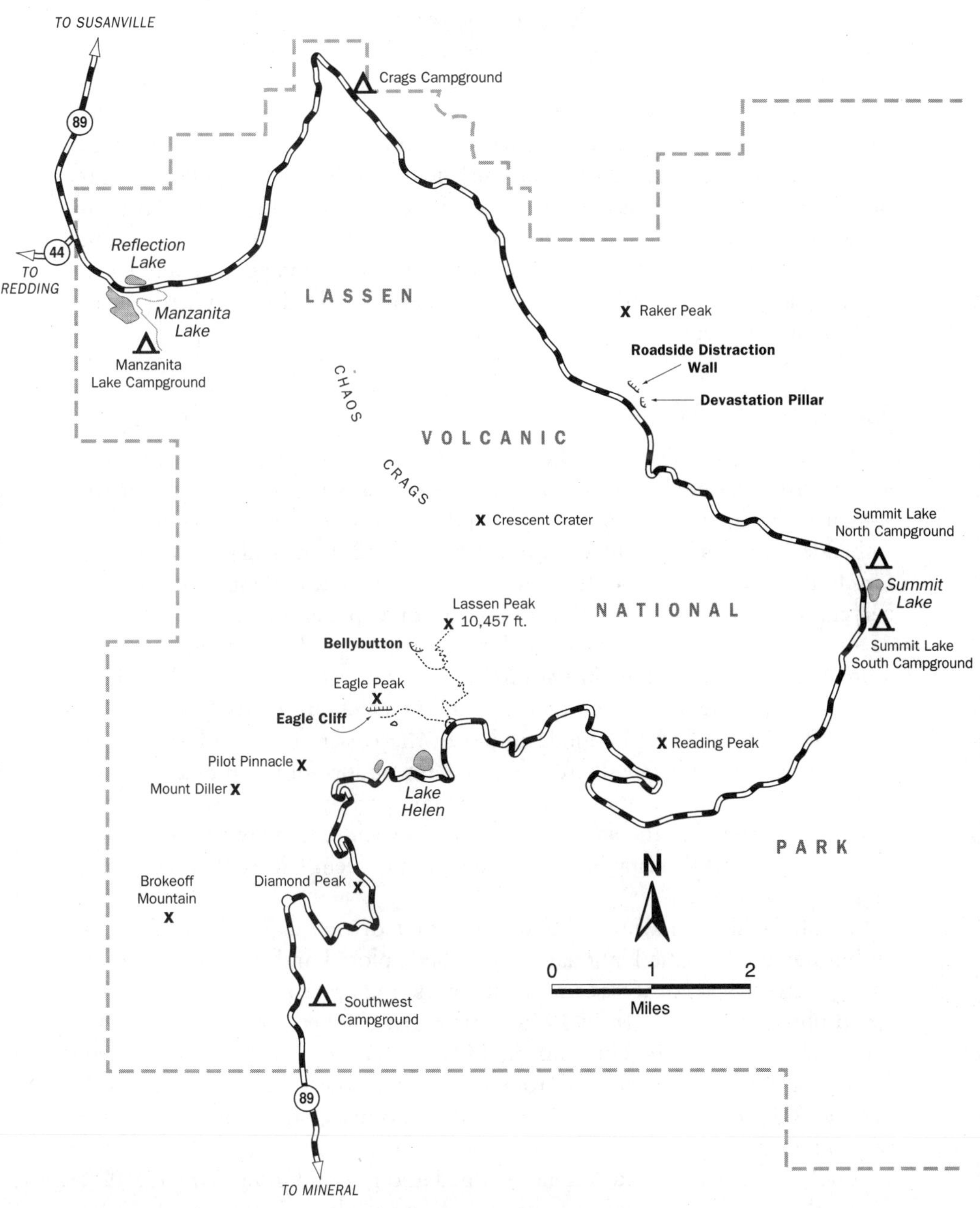

blast of ash and gases that swept down the path of the mudflow, creating the now-famous Devastated Area so easily visible from the climbs on Raker Peak. Residual steam jets in the summit crater did not subside until the 1940s.

Today, the land is quiet, but in recent years, climbers have discovered the joys of climbing on the park's accessible and aesthetic rock formations. The dacite rock that makes up most of the crags looks like a sort of artificial granite with a ceramic shine on freshly broken surfaces. Gases trapped when the rock was liquid have created numerous hueco-like pockets and cavities that frequently allow passage over otherwise unclimbable rock. In addition, occasional inclusions of cobbles and pebbles that became embedded in the lava but were not melted provide interesting holds. Glaciation has removed much—but not all—of the loose material on the steeper faces, providing generally clean and pleasant climbing. Add the striking scenery on all sides, and it is easy to understand this region's appeal for climbers.

## EAGLE CLIFF

Eagle Cliff is a prominent band of vertically jointed dacite that rises above a terrace overlooking beautiful Lake Helen in the southwestern portion of Lassen Volcanic National Park. The abundant crack systems, gas pockets, and embedded cobbles and pebbles have made Eagle Cliff particularly well-suited for climbing, and the crag offers over 50 quality routes ranging from beginner climbs to testpieces suitable for the most experienced. Climbs average 75'–100' in length, and each can be done in a single pitch, although a few can more conveniently be done in two. Most routes are traditional crack climbs, although there are a few high-quality bolted face climbs as well. Overhangs and overhanging cracks abound, and even the easier routes can be serious undertakings. Fortunately, there are abundant opportunities to place protection, and dangerously run-out sections are comparatively rare. First-time visitors should note that the nature of the rock is such that many climbs require both strength and delicacy in technique and may seem harder than their ratings would suggest.

**Climbing history:** Eagle Cliff was the first of the major climbing areas within Lassen Volcanic National Park to be explored and developed. Oddly enough, given the easy access and quality rock, the first routes were not established until the mid-1970s. In 1976, Chico-area climbers Eric Settlemire and Gary Adams visited the cliff and, in June of that year, they made the first ascents of the two *Bowling Ball* routes (5.6), the classic *Peapod* (5.8), *Mink Stink* (5.8), and *Lightning Crack* (5.9, A2). Curiously, no known new routes were added during the next several years.

In 1980, Settlemire and Adams returned and put up *Orangahang* (5.10b), one of the finest hand cracks on the crag. Word of the quality climbing to be found on Eagle Cliff apparently leaked out of the Chico scene, and 1982

*Eagle Cliff, Lassen Volcanic National Park.*

marked the arrival of the Redding-based contingent, led by Tahquitz/Suicide transplant John Bald. In 1982, Bald, with Randy Dewees and Jack Fisher, established *Stegosaurus* (5.10b). Bald's only real competition when it came to establishing new climbs at the cliff was Jim Yates. In 1983, while Bald climbed *Dogleg* (5.10b) with Wayne Schiff and *Nothing Special* (5.8) alone, Yates made the first ascents of *Skin a Cat* (5.7) and its 5.10a direct start, later teaming with Bald to fire off *Y-Not* (5.10a). While Bald and Yates were busy on the main cliff, Rick Boatwright made his mark with the first ascents of routes on the boulder that bears his name. New faces appeared in 1984 as Yates returned with Gabe Rodriguez to climb *Overhung* (5.10a), and Steve Lauderdale led *Peabody* (5.8). The next few years were a comparatively quiet period; Bald and Yates added *T-Too* (5.10a) in 1984, and Yates and Rodriguez climbed *Red Dawn* (5.10a) in 1985.

The latter half of the 1980s was surely the golden age of climbing at Eagle Cliff. In 1986, Yates and Rodriguez ticked *King Pin* (5.10a), and Bald and Mark Motes made climbs of *Slot* (5.10a) and *Top Gun* (5.10b). In 1988, a new contingent arrived, and remaining unclimbed lines fell in quick succession. Tim Loughlin, Todd Burrill, and Stan Miller climbed *Therapeutic Recreation* (5.9+), and the energetic Todd Swain soloed *Candlepins for Cash* (5.7), *Bowling Green* (5.7), *Lawn Bowling* (5.1), and *Peon U* (5.10d/.11a). The high points of the year were the first free ascent of *Lightning Crack* (5.10d/.11a) by Bald and Yates, and the ascent of *Eruption* (5.12a), the finest line on the cliff, by Bald and Travis Klawin.

In 1990, Rob Settlemire returned to establish the difficult and committing *Arms Control* (5.11a) with Dave Caunt and Stan Miller. Miller also soloed the unnamed 5.9+ route right of *Eruption* and completed the classic *Chips 'n' Salsa* (5.11a) with Tim Loughlin. In the years since, new route activity has continued, but records are sketchy. The remaining *Dog* and *Cat* climbs were made during this period, but the dates and first ascent parties of other routes are unknown. Although most of the cliff's lines have been climbed, there are still numerous opportunities for new routes, particularly at the ends of the cliff and on the plentiful boulders at its base.

**Rack:** Because Eagle Cliff is a traditional climbing area with only a handful of sport routes, plan on placing your own protection on most climbs. Most of the cracks tend to be finger-width or thinner, which means a lighter rack. You should bring a selection of 8 to 12 RPs, about the same number of stoppers to 1", and a set of cams to 3", emphasizing the smaller sizes. Tri-cams will help you utilize pockets for protection. Add a half-dozen quickdraws, a few runners—including a couple of double-length ones—and you are all set. One other thing: loose rock abounds on the terrace above the cliff; wear a helmet.

**Descent:** Descend Eagle Cliff by scrambling down from either end of the cliff. There are no established lowering or rappel anchors, but you can rappel from trees atop *King Pin* or from anchors at the top of *Peapod* using a single rope. There are rappel/toprope bolts on top of Rick's Boulder.

## TRIP PLANNING INFORMATION

**Area description:** Eagle Cliff is a south-facing cliff band of enjoyable, granite-like dacite situated high on the flank of 9,222-foot Eagle Peak. Climbs, which range from 35 to 90 feet in height, offer challenges primarily in the 5.8 to 5.12 range, although there are also several easier routes to entice the less ambitious.

**Location:** South flank of Eagle Peak, 1.2 miles west of Lassen Peak in Lassen Volcanic National Park.

**Camping:** There are numerous campgrounds located within a few minutes' drive from the trailhead. The following campgrounds are listed in order of proximity to the trailhead. Southwest campground, with 21 walk-in sites, lies 6.2 miles south on California Highway 89; the per-night fee is $12. Summit Lake South and Summit Lake North lie 10.5 miles east on CA 89. Summit Lake South offers 48 developed sites and costs $12 per night; Summit Lake North offers 46 developed sites and costs $14 per night. Crags, with 45 developed sites, lies 17.5 miles north on CA 89; the fee is a bargain $8 per night. Manzanita Lake, 20.5 miles north of the trailhead on CA 89, offers 179 developed sites adjacent to the lake for $14 per night.

**Climbing season:** June through October; earlier in dry years. Note that access depends on the amount of snow remaining after the preceding winter. In some heavy-snow years, the trailhead remains inaccessible to vehicles until late July. It is a good idea to call for road conditions before making the drive to the park early or late in the season.

**Restrictions and access issues:** All visitors entering Lassen Volcanic National Park must pay a $10 entry fee per vehicle. A Golden Eagle Pass, good for unlimited admissions for one year from date of purchase, can be obtained for $50—a bargain for frequent visitors.

Roughly two-thirds of the area within the park boundaries is designated wilderness area. The area along the highway, which includes the climbing areas covered in this book, lies outside the wilderness area, so a wilderness permit is not required; however, overnight camping is restricted to established campgrounds within this area. Eagle Cliff lies within an environmentally sensitive area where there could be access problems if climbers act irresponsibly. The access trail provides a low-impact means of getting to and from the rock, but extensive travel off-trail should be avoided. The many small whitebark pines growing on top of the cliff provide convenient rappel anchors, but these high-altitude trees are easily damaged. Care should be taken to rappel only from slings—never directly from the trees themselves. Other vegetation in all forms is protected by federal law, and climbers should resist the temptation to garden or excessively clean cracks. As always, every effort should be made to sensibly dispose of human waste, and to pick up and carry out all litter. There are currently no official restrictions on bolting, but climbers should use discretion when placing new bolts, determining first whether their installation will really produce a quality climb on this essentially traditionally-developed crag.

**Guidebook:** The only previous guidebook to this area is John Bald's self-published *Lassen Volcanic National Park: A Climbers Guide* (1989). Check with the personnel at area climbing shops for current route information.

**Nearby mountain shops, guide services, and gyms:** The nearest mountain shops include Hermit's Hut and Sports Ltd. in Redding and Mountain Sports, Overland Equipment, and Sports Ltd. in Chico. Guiding and instruction are available through Adventures Made Easy in Anderson and Shasta Mountain Guides in Mt. Shasta. The nearest climbing gyms are Ascent Climbing Gym/Outdoor Center in Grass Valley and Granite Arch in Rancho Cordova. California State University, Chico has a climbing gym on campus. It is open to non-students most evenings. Contact the university's outdoor center for more information.

**Services:** There are no services available at the crag, although there are vault toilets at the trailhead parking area. The nearest source for food and beverages is Lassen Chalet, located near the Southwest campground.

**Emergency services:** In an emergency, contact park rangers. There are ranger stations at both park entrances and at the Summit Lake North campground. Area hospitals are: Saint Elizabeth Community Hospital in Red Bluff and Mercy Medical Center and Redding Medical Center, both in Redding.

**Nearby climbing areas:** Bellybutton, with the park's longest and hardest climbs, stands high on the side of Lassen Peak and overlooks the approach to Eagle Cliff. Farther northeast, a pair of small formations on the southwest side of Raker Peak offer challenging sport and traditional climbs.

**Nearby attractions:** The most obvious nearby attraction is, of course, the giant slag-pile of Lassen Peak. For an unforgettable view, follow the 2.5-mile trail to the summit. South and west of the trailhead lies the park's famous hot springs area, with boiling mudpots, geysers, and fumaroles. To the east of the highway, the eastern half of the park offers backpacking in the Lassen Volcanic National Park Wilderness. The view from the top of Eagle Peak itself is also pretty nice.

**Finding the crag:** From Redding, drive 48 miles east on California Highway 44 to a junction with California Highway 89. Turn right and proceed to the park entrance. From the park entrance, follow CA 89 (known as Lassen Park Road inside the national park boundary) for 22 winding, scenic miles to the Lassen Peak Trailhead. If approaching from the south, head east on California Highway 36 from its intersection with Interstate 5 in Red Bluff. After 3 miles, proceed northeast on CA 36 at its junction with U.S. Highway 99. Follow CA 36 for 44 miles to a junction with CA 89. Turn left and drive 4.8 miles to the southwest entrance to the park. From the entrance, drive another 7 miles to the Lassen Peak Trailhead. From the trailhead, follow the broad, dusty Lassen Peak trail for 30 yards, then head left onto a narrow track that leads northwest up the floor of a small, narrow valley. After a few hundred yards, where the valley widens into a sheltered basin that holds a shallow pond early in the season, you can see the eastern end of Eagle Cliff just beyond the head of a steep, rocky ravine. Follow a ducked, zigzag trail up the ravine to the delightful terrace at its top. Follow the terrace to your choice of climbs. Climbs are described from right to left, in the order of their appearance.

1. **Red Dawn** (5.9 or 5.10a) Ascend the left-leaning, left-facing, red dihedral near the right end of the cliff. Stay in the dihedral for a 5.10a climb, or

make a short detour up right, then back left for an easier way through the red rock.

2. **Second Wind** (5.9) Begin as for *Red Dawn,* then follow a thin crack up left.
3. **Foxtrot** (5.10a) Follow Route 2 until the crack branches. Follow the left branch left across the face, then more directly up to the top.
4. **California Dreaming** (5.10a) Begin a few feet right of a detached block shaped like a map of California. Follow a crack that angles left initially, then shoots up to the left end of a small roof. Pull past, then follow the thin-hands crack to the top.
5. **A Porous Line** (5.11c TR) Ascend the smooth wall between Route 4 and the prominent overhang of *Overboard.*
6. **Overboard** (5.9+) Begin at the foot of a deep, jumbled, right-facing dihedral below a huge, overhanging block. Lieback, face-climb, and jam up to the block, then undercling right and lieback up its right side.
7. **Overhauled** (5.10d) Follow *Overboard* to the overhanging block, then ascend the offwidth up its left side.
8. **Top Gun** (5.10b) Follow the first major crack system left of Route 7. When the crack becomes a right-facing corner, jam the left side of the block that forms the final offwidth on Route 7.
9. **Top Dog** (5.10c) Beginning 20' left of *Top Gun,* climb a few feet up a left-facing dihedral, then jam a right-leaning crack. Where the crack system

branches, follow a thin crack farther right. Once this crack curves upward, follow it up a shallow V-groove on the face of the buttress to a small, triangular roof. You could go left here and finish via *Dogleg* or surmount the roof near its left side and proceed to the top on easier face climbing. Take extra RPs.

10. **Dogleg** (5.10b) Start as for *Top Dog.* Where the crack branches, take the left branch. Jam the prominent, right-leaning crack, keeping right where it branches again, and passing left of a small, triangular roof. Beware of a loose block on a ledge!
11. **Dog Days** (5.10c) Begin just left of the same left-facing dihedral as the previous two routes. Climb a thin crack in a groove left of the main dihedral. Pull past a small, left-curving arch just left of a bulging overhang, then continue up a short, left-facing corner that becomes a shallow groove before reaching the top. Take extra RPs and small TCUs.
12. **Cookies and Milk** (5.6) Start 10' left of *Dog Days,* just below and right of a pair of small pine trees growing on a sloping area about a third of the way up the face. Climb to a block right of the lower tree, then jam a crack to an alcove, and continue up its back to the top.
13. **Lawn Bowling** (5.1) Beginning left of the small trees that identify Route 12, ascend easy, broken rock to the upper tree, then head up left, cross a wide crack, and continue to the top, keeping between the crack and a small ledge on the left.

14. **Nameless** (5.4) Begin in a left-facing dihedral around the corner to the left of *Lawn Bowling*. Climb the dihedral, passing right of a left-slanting roof. Cross Route 13 at a sloping ledge, then follow a small, left-facing corner to the top.
15. **Bowling Ball—Right** (5.6) Climb a wide crack in the right-facing dihedral 15' left of *Nameless*.
16. **Bowling Green** (5.7 R) Climb the formidable-looking face of the buttress left of Route 15, veering left to bypass a small roof.
17. **Bowling Ball—Left** (5.6) Jam the wide crack in a shallow, right-facing dihedral that forms the left side of the buttress of *Bowling Green.*
18. **Candlepins for Cash** (5.7) Begin as for Route 17. Ascend the dihedral for 10', then exit left onto the face and face-climb to the top of the buttress left of the dihedral.
19. **Mink Stink** (5.8) Start 20' left of *Candlepins for Cash*. Hand-jam a short crack, then follow the left sides of large blocks past the right side of a large roof. Exit the face via a thinner crack in a short dihedral.
20. **Bump and Grind** (5.9) Ten feet left of the start of Route 19, climb a finger crack that becomes a small, right-facing corner. Where the crack ends under the large roof, work up right and finish via *Mink Stink*.
21. **Thumper** (5.11b X or TR) Climb Route 20 as far as the final dihedral on *Mink Stink*. Climb a few feet up the dihedral, then hand-traverse out left,

following a crack that starts out thin and improves as you go. Pass around the corner, then follow a wide, easy crack to the top.

22. **Buttocks Roof** (5.11c) Starting 8' left of *Thumper,* climb a dogleg crack system to broken ledges under the impressive roof avoided by the previous two climbs. The route ahead is obvious: climb the offwidth slot through the roof and follow it up a right-facing corner to the top. Take several larger cams to 5".
23. **Unnamed** (5.9+) Locate a trio of short cracks 50' left of the start of Route 22. Jam the right-hand of these to a small ledge on top of a block. Although many parties lower off from a 1/2" bolt here, you can continue to the top by following a right-curving crack into a trough.
24. **Locomotive Breath** (5.9+) Around the corner left of Route 23, find a sharply cut, left-facing dihedral blocked by a large, precarious-looking flake. Hand-jam past the flake, then lieback up a left-leaning corner that leads to easier climbing and the top of the rock.
25. **Eruption** (5.12a) Climb the beautiful, orange-tinted, curving arete left of Route 24, passing 6 bolts.
26. **Peapod** (5.8) Jam, stem and lieback up the left-facing dihedral that forms the left side of the *Eruption* arete.
27. **Peon U** (5.10d/.11a) Beginning 10' left of *Peapod,* ascend the steep, pocketed wall past 5 bolts.
28. **Peabody** (5.8) At the left edge of the wall ascended by *Peon U,* grunt up a squeeze chimney and wide crack.

29. **Porous Tactics** (5.11a/b) For this quality route, climb the narrow, orange-stained, overhanging left wall of the *Peabody* dihedral; 4 bolts.

30. **Therapeutic Recreation** (5.9+) Begin as for Route 29, but after clipping the first bolt, traverse left around the corner of the arete and climb the colorful face above past two more bolts.

31. **Arms Control** (5.11c) Locate the start of this memorable face climb by walking left from *Peabody* until you are about 8' right of the left edge of the impressive, undercut wall. (The route requires a cheater stump or rock to get started; if you can make the entry moves without, it would probably be 5.12.) Use two bolts to protect difficult moves up the overhanging lower portion of the wall. Follow a water groove past a third bolt, then head up right to a fourth. Use two more bolts to protect the sustained face climbing up a black waterstreak.

32. **Slot** (5.10a) Starting 8' left of *Arms Control,* climb a brushy hand crack to a sloping ledge, then continue up a cleaner fist crack in a left-facing dihedral.

33. **Funky Dung** (5.10c) Beginning 25' left of Route 32, jam up a deep, left-facing dihedral, pull over a small roof, and continue up easier going to the top.

34. **Orangahang** (5.10b) Begin this excellent hand crack at the same point as Route 33. Climb *Funky Dung* until you can exit left, following a vegetated crack that slants up left across the face, leading to a small stance at the base of an overhanging, left-facing dihedral. Hand-jam the dihedral to the top.

35. **T-Too** (5.10a) Start 30' left of *Orangahang,* at the base of an orange, pebble-studded wall. Work up left into a shallow, right-facing dihedral that forms the right side of a 45-foot pillar. Follow the dihedral as it becomes a crack and continues to the top of the cliff.

36. **Unnamed** (5.12a TR) Beginning 15' left of Route 35, pull cobbles and pebbles up the gently overhanging lower part of the face of a 45-foot pillar. Higher, edge and smear to a ledge atop the pillar. You can reach the anchors on the ledge by climbing partway up *T-Too* or by rappelling from the top of the cliff.

37. **Legends of the Fall** (5.9) Chimney and jam the dark, left-facing dihedral around the corner to the left of the pillar ascended by Route 36.

38. **King Pin** (5.10a) Starting 10' left of Route 37, face-climb to a bolt, work up right for 15', then head more directly upward to the top of the cliff. Take a #1 Tri-cam.

39. **King Pin Direct** (5.10c/d TR) Begin as for *King Pin,* going as far as the bolt. From here, continue straight up the face.

40. **Perineal Massage** (5.11a) Start 20' left of *King Pin*. Jam a hand crack to its end, then move left and head directly up a black waterstreak to the top; 5 bolts.
41. **Stegosaurus** (5.10b) Climb a groove line that forms the right side of a pillar left of Route 40.
42. **Chips 'n' Salsa** (5.11a) Starting 12' left of Route 41, just right of the pillars's left edge, face-climb up, then up right to a bolt on the centerline of the pillar. Continue past 4 more bolts, making a short detour right for the second of these.
43. **Nothing Special** (5.8) Access the hand crack that forms the upper left side of the pillar by climbing either a series of thin face moves left of the crack or a flared chimney below it.
44. **Slick** (5.10b) From Route 43, walk left up a gully to its end. Chimney and jam a flared crack in a right-facing dihedral at the head of the gully.
45. **Lightning Crack** (5.10d/.11a) Jam the prominent crack on the tiger-striped wall left of *Slick*. Take additional small wires.
46. **Overhung** (5.10a) Begin this route around the corner left of Route 45, below the left end of right-slanting overhang that lies just above a cobbly orange area. Pull cobbles past the overhang and continue to a similar right-curving overlap. Follow it up right, then pass over and face-climb to the top. Beware of loose holds on the lower part of the wall.

47. **Mix Master** (5.7) Begin just left of a small tree on a ledge left of the starting point of Route 46. Jam and chimney up an obvious trough that splits this otherwise rather uninteresting section of the cliff.
48. **Y-Not** (5.10a) Locate this climb just above flat-topped Rick's Boulder. Fist-jam the wide, often wet crack that forms the stem and right side of a distinctive, Y-shaped crack system. Bring larger pro to 4".
49. **Unnamed** (5.11d/.12a TR) Begin at the base of a right-slanting crease 10' left of the base of *Y-Not.* Ascend the crease for a few feet, then angle up left and follow the crest of the buttress to the top.
50. **Skin a Cat Direct** (5.10a) Walk left around the corner from Route 49. Jam a finger crack 15' to a junction with the broken crack system of *Skin a Cat.*
51. **Skin a Cat** (5.7) Starting 6' left of Route 50, follow a jumbled crack to the terrace atop the cliff.
52. **Copy Cat** (5.8) Begin 15' left of Route 51. Lieback past a block, then follow the crack above as it eventually curves left. Make an interesting move to reach easier climbing to the top.
53. **Polecat** (5.9) Head left 20' from *Copy Cat* to a crack and chimney system marked by a tree growing a few yards off the ground. From the tree, follow a thin crack to a flared chimney. Make an awkward exit up left from its top, then follow a left-curving crack to the top.

54. **Rats and Cats** (5.7) Locate a tree growing at the base of a crack system 20' left of Route 53. Climb a braided series of cracks that separates a smooth face on the right from more broken rock to the left.

The following routes ascend Rick's Boulder, the large, square-topped block just downhill from the left end of the cliff. There are anchors on top to facilitate descending or toproping.

55. **East Face** (5.10a TR) Climb the slender east face of the boulder.
56. **South Face—Right** (5.9+) Beginning a couple of feet left of the right edge of the boulder's south face, face-climb past 2 bolts to the top.
57. **South Face—Left** (5.9) Start this, the easiest route up the boulder, near the middle of the face, where a short, thin crack slants up left. Clip a bolt at the top of the crack, head up left to another bolt, then angle up right past a third before reaching the top.

## BELLYBUTTON

In a state renowned for its world-class rock and spectacular views, Bellybutton ranks with the best California has to offer, providing superb climbing in a setting that overlooks ranks of surrounding peaks and the distant farmland of the Sacramento Valley. At an elevation of nearly 10,000', Bellybutton is the highest, largest, and most impressive crag in Lassen Volcanic National Park. Like its parent volcano Lassen Peak, Bellybutton is the remains of a plug dome. It formed when a secondary magma conduit near the top of the mountain failed to reach the surface, allowing the trapped molten material near the surface to congeal before being pushed upward again. The result is a large rock formation high on the side of Lassen Peak. Later glaciation, exploiting the joints that formed in the dome, quarried away loose material, leaving a crag of hard, solid dacite. Climbs ascend the crag's classic cracks and corners and maneuver past gas pockets (the volcanic equivalent of huecos) to scale the smooth, bulging "belly," a curiously unjointed face marked by the giant indentation that gives the crag its name.

Bellybutton offers dozens of quality traditional and sport routes from 75' to 400' in length. There are few routes for novices; most climbs lie at or above the 5.9 level. Unlike nearby Eagle Cliff, the routes here are all serious undertakings that involve exposure, occasionally long runouts, and subtle use of passive protection.

**Climbing history:** Although it began a bit later, the development of Bellybutton roughly paralleled that of nearby Eagle Cliff and featured many of the same performers. On their initial visit to Eagle Cliff in 1976, Rob Settlemire and Gary Adams could not help seeing the much larger formation of Bellybutton and wondering about its climbing potential. They returned in 1977, made the trudge up to the crag, and climbed the impressive crack line of *Sporting Chance* (II 5.9) up the left side of an impressive pillar on the west end of the formation. They kept mum about their new discovery, and the next new route was not made until 1980, when the pair returned and put up *Tangerine Dream* (II 5.9+), a series of classic hand and fist cracks up the orange-stained wall left of their earlier route.

Word soon leaked out, however, and in 1984, new teams arrived to make their marks. John Yates, Travis Klawin, and Steve Lauderdale attacked the crag's longest face, producing *Regular Route* (II 5.8). John Bald and Andy Selters discovered and climbed *Trinity Crack—Left* (5.10a) and *Trinity Crack—Center* (5.10a), two of the three strenuous cracks that split Trinity Wall, the gently overhanging wall uphill from *Tangerine Dream.*

After a year of comparative quiet, which saw a single new route, *Wanderer* (5.8+) by Pat McGrane and Jim Yates, climbers again flocked to Bellybutton, starting a four-year blitz that produced the majority of the crag's routes. In 1986, John Bald and Mark Motes added a challenging 5.9 finish to *Regular Route* and climbed *Trinity Crack—Right* (I 5.11a), Bellybutton's first route at this grade. More important, they made the first serious exploration of the nearly crackless, bulging "belly," producing *Sympathetic Hygiene* (II 5.9+). Convinced that this face was indeed climbable, they returned and established *The Great Hot Blast* (II 5.10d), probably the crag's finest face climb. Bald and Motes were joined by Klawin on the first ascent of a bold line right of *Tangerine Dream,* which they named *Tres Hombres* (II 5.10d). The only new route of 1986 that was not a Bald/Motes production was Travis Klawin and Todd Burrill's *Variation B* (5.9+ R), a short, frightening, and poorly protected climb up the blank, vertical wall at the base of the crag's southwest face.

In 1987, Bald was again the driving force behind route development, producing climbs all over the crag. With Roger Dale, he added *Hades* (5.9), a crack line to the top of a small pinnacle at the northwest end of the rock, and climbed *Far Right Trinity Crack* (5.10d). He made a significant variation to *Tangerine Dream* with Greg Laurie, naming their line *Remote Luxury* (II 5.10b). Teamed with Tim Loughlin, he added *Mejito* (5.9) and *Variation A* (5.8) to the wall left of *Variation B*. They went on to tick impressive firsts on the thin crack of *Pinacoidal Cleavage* (II 5.10a) and *Jelly Belly* (II 5.10b). The fractured buttress right of "the belly" became the site of a stampede as Bald and Jim Yates climbed *Post Nasal* (I 5.7 R) and *Exit Right* (I 5.7); Bald and Loughlin added *Exit Left* (I 5.7) and *Digression* (I 5.10a); and Loughlin and Todd Burrill ascended *Bull Terrier* (I 5.9). Not to be outdone by Bald, Loughlin soloed *Birdleg* (5.10b). Returning with Burrill, he added *Agua Dulce* (5.10c) and *Viscous Variation* (5.10a R). They were joined by Rich James on *Easily Amused* (II 5.10c), a tricky off-width hand crack. Loughlin's finest achievement came near the end of the season with his ascent of *Waganupa* (II 5.10c) with Burrill and Stan Miller. Miller and Burrill finished 1987 with the challenging face climb, *Ghetto Blast* (II 5.11a).

With most of the major lines completed, 1988 was a comparatively quiet year. Bald made an early return with Burrill and Loughlin, braving snow to climb *Changing Phases* (5.10a). That summer, Miller and Loughlin climbed *Pyroclastic Pump* (5.11a). In September, Tim and Linda Loughlin added *Heated Discussion* (II 5.9+), a slightly easier, but more direct finish to *Sympathetic Hygiene*.

By 1989, most new route development was restricted to filling-in. The Loughlins put up *Attitude is Everything* (5.9+), Loughlin and Miller climbed a direct start to *Jelly Belly*, naming it *Viva Gorby* (5.11b/c), and added another fine face climb with *Crisis Line* (II 5.11c).

The crag's last significant new routes were climbed in 1990. Rick Harlan and Ron James made a run-out, direct start to *Tangerine Dream,* rating it 5.10b R. To bring things full circle, Rob Settlemire returned with Dave Caunt and Stan Miller and established a fine, independent finish to *Remote Luxury.* Since then, new route development has languished, but Bellybutton is far from climbed out, and considerable scope for new routes remains—especially for sport climbs.

**Rack:** Because Bellybutton offers both traditional and sport climbs, your rack will be determined in part, at least, by your style preference. Sport climbers can get by with a selection of 8 to 10 quickdraws. Traditional routes have essentially the same gear requirements as those at Eagle Cliff. You should bring a selection of 8 to 12 RPs, about the same number of stoppers to 1", and a set of cams to 3", emphasizing the smaller sizes. Tri-cams will help you utilize pockets for protection. Runners, including a few double-length ones, prove useful, even on shorter climbs. Take 2 ropes to facilitate lowering or rappelling. Because the forces of erosion are in full play at this elevation, loose rock is a constant hazard; wear a helmet. Because the weather can be capricious at this elevation on an essentially isolated peak, you should also bring foul-weather gear, just in case.

**Descent:** You can lower off or rappel from anchors atop the sport routes. Most traditional climbs top out, allowing a scramble descent down the northwest or northeast ends of the crag. On the way, beware of loose rock on ledges, and wear your helmet until back on terra firma.

## TRIP PLANNING INFORMATION

**Area description:** Bellybutton is a glaciated satellite plug dome near the top of Lassen Peak. This west-, south-, and east-facing crag offers sport and traditional climbs ranging from 75' to 400', and spanning a difficulty range of 5.7 to 5.11d. The rock is dacite of excellent quality.

**Location:** At an elevation of nearly 10,000' on the southwest flank of Lassen Peak in Lassen Volcanic National Park.

**Camping:** There are numerous campgrounds located within a few minutes drive from the trailhead. The following campgrounds are listed in order of proximity to the trailhead. Southwest, with 21 walk-in sites, lies 6.2 miles south on California Highway 89; the per-night fee is $12. Summit Lake South and Summit Lake North lie 10.5 miles east on CA 89. Summit Lake South offers 48 developed sites and costs $12 per night; Summit Lake North offers 46 developed sites and costs $14 per night. Crags, with 45 developed sites, lies 17.5 miles north on CA 89; the fee is a bargain $8 per night. Manzanita Lake, 20.5 miles north of the trailhead on CA 89, offers 179 developed sites adjacent to the lake for $14 per night.

**Climbing season:** June through October; earlier in dry years. Note that access depends on the amount of snow remaining after the preceding winter. In some heavy-snow years, the trailhead remains inaccessible to vehicles until late July. It is a good idea to call the park to check on road conditions before committing to a long drive early or late in the season. Note also that, due to the crag's elevation, the weather can deteriorate suddenly at any time, bringing lightning, hail, or even snow.

**Restrictions and access issues:** All visitors entering Lassen Volcanic National Park must pay a $10 entry fee per vehicle. A Golden Eagle Pass, good for unlimited admissions for one year from date of purchase, can be obtained for $50—a bargain for frequent visitors.

The approach to Bellybutton requires climbers to cross the bare, gravelly flank of Lassen Peak. Park managers, concerned about erosion and impacts to fragile, high-elevation soils and plant communities urge climbers to approach and leave Bellybutton *by the approach route only. Avoid the temptation to scree-glissade straight down the mountainside to the parking area visible below. Those who do will be ticketed and will jeopardize future access to this quality crag.*

**Guidebook:** The only previous guidebook to this area is John Bald's self-published *Lassen Volcanic National Park: A Climbers Guide* (1989). Check with the personnel at area climbing shops for current route information.

**Nearby mountain shops, guide services, and gyms:** The nearest mountain shops include Hermit's Hut and Sports Ltd. in Redding and Mountain Sports, Overland Equipment, and Sports Ltd. in Chico. Guiding and instruction are available through Adventures Made Easy in Anderson and Shasta Mountain Guides in Mt. Shasta. The nearest climbing gyms are Ascent Climbing Gym/Outdoor Center in Grass Valley and Granite Arch in Rancho Cordova. California State University, Chico has a climbing gym on campus. It is open to non-students most evenings. Contact the university's outdoor center for more information.

**Services:** There are no services available at the crag, although there are vault toilets at the trailhead parking area. The nearest source for food and beverages is Lassen Chalet, located near the Southwest campground.

**Emergency services:** In an emergency, contact park rangers. There are ranger stations at both park entrances and at the Summit Lake North campground. Area hospitals include: Saint Elizabeth Community Hospital in Red Bluff and Mercy Medical Center and Redding Medical Center, both in Redding.

**Nearby climbing areas:** The nearest climbing area is Eagle Cliff, easily visible (end-on) across a small valley west of Bellybutton. To the northeast, two small formations on the south side of Raker Peak offer quality traditional and sport climbing.

**Nearby attractions:** The most obvious nearby attraction is, of course, the giant slag-pile of Lassen Peak. For an unforgettable view, follow the 2.5-mile trail to the summit. South and west of the trailhead lies the park's famous hot springs area, with boiling mudpots, geysers, and fumaroles. To the east of the highway, the eastern half of the park offers backpacking in the Lassen Volcanic National Park Wilderness.

**Finding the crag:** From Redding, drive 48 miles east on California Highway 44 to a junction with California Highway 89. Turn right and proceed to the park entrance. From the park entrance, follow CA 89 (known as Lassen Park Road inside the national park boundary) for 22 winding, scenic miles to the Lassen Peak Trailhead. If approaching from the south, head east on California Highway 36 from its intersection with U.S. Interstate 5 in Red Bluff. After 3 miles, proceed northeast on CA 36 at its junction with U.S. Highway 99. Follow CA 36 for 44 miles to a junction with CA 89. Turn left and drive 4.8 miles to the southwest entrance to the park. From the entrance, drive another 7 miles to the Lassen Peak Trailhead. From the trailhead, follow the broad, dusty, and heavily used trail for about 0.7 mile to a large boulder with a pronounced overhang on the side facing the trail. At the next switchback, leave the trail and follow a faint bench west to large boulders under the southwest face of Bellybutton. Wander up this talus to the rock, arriving near the starting point of *Regular Route* (Route 19).

Routes are listed from left to right, beginning at the upper left (i.e., northwest) end of the crag.

1. **Birdleg** (5.10b) Notice that the top of Bellybutton is serrated into a series of small pinnacles. Begin below the pinnacle at the northwest end of the crag and about 20' uphill and left of a Class 4 ramp/gully that angles up right, then suddenly slants up left. Ascend a series of steep cracks, topping out just right of the pinnacle's high point.
2. **Hades** (I 5.9) Start at the foot of the ramp/gully mentioned in Route 1. Jam cracks up the steep wall, eventually working left to join Route 1 near the top of the face. You can break this route into 2 pitches.
3. **Trinity Crack—Right** (I 5.11a) Down and right from the small pinnacle ascended by the preceding two routes find Trinity Wall, a dark, slightly overhanging face punctuated by four conspicuous cracks. Begin *Trinity Crack—Right,* the second one from the right and the most difficult of the lot, near the right side of a small roof. **Pitch 1:** Pass the roof, then continue up the long and technical hand crack to a semi-hanging belay from gear. **Pitch 2:** Continue to the top. For variety, try the two cracks to the left, *Trinity Crack—Left* and *Trinity Crack—Center;* both are 5.10a.
4. **Far Right** (I 5.10d) Move downhill 65' right of Route 3 to the farthest-right crack that ascends Trinity Wall. **Pitch 1:** Beginning near the edge of the dark stain, work up the thin crack, which gradually widens as you go, to a gear-anchored hanging belay. **Pitch 2:** Switch to handjams and eventually fistjams as you continue to the top. The small roof at mid-height should give you an interesting moment. Take extra cams in the 3"–4" sizes, as well as numerous smaller nuts.
5. **Wanderer** (5.8+) Locate this route and the five that follow on the "pleated" wall that lies right of a pale wall (the scene of recent rockfall) and left of a spectacular orange pillar that stands guard over the crag's west end. Look for a sloping ledge above an L-shaped roof. Beginning below the left end of the roof, face-climb and jam up right toward the angle of the "L." Before reaching the angle, detour up left, then pull over the roof at its upper end. Belay on the sloping ledge. Rappel from here, or continue to the top via *Tangerine Dream* or *Remote Luxury.*
6. **Tangerine Dream** (II 5.9+) Start this classic climb 20' right of *Wanderer.* **Pitch 1:** Jam up to the L-shaped route, pass it by heading up right, then angle up left to the belay spot on the sloping ledge shared with Route 5.

BELLYBUTTON, LASSEN VOLCANIC NATIONAL PARK
6
9
7
20
19
23
7
1
2
3
4
21
22
23
XX
11
70'
5
6
8
9
10
11
XX
70'
12
13
14
15
16

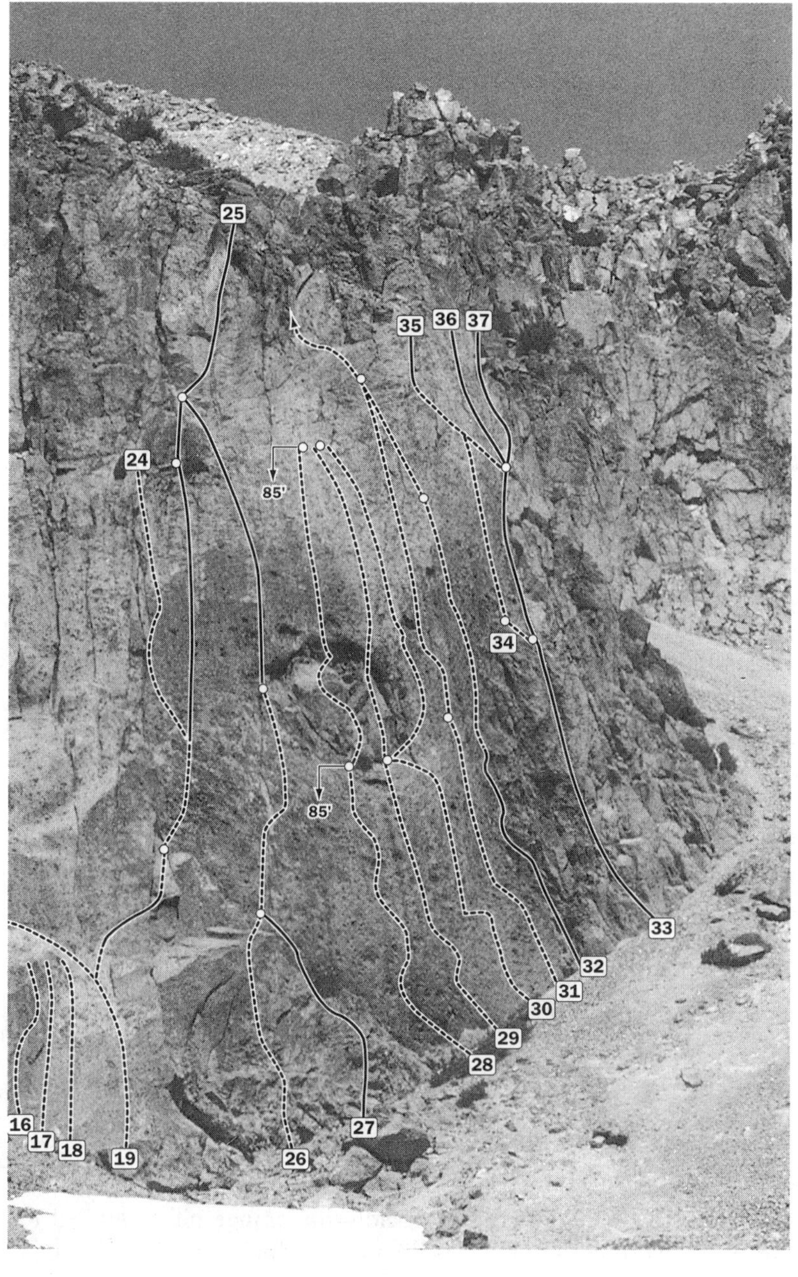
25
35
36
37
24
85'
34
85'
33
32
31
30
29
28
27
16
17
18
19
26

You can also head directly over the roof to the ledge, but this involves run-out 5.10b climbing. **Pitch 2:** From the left end of the sloping ledge, jam a lengthy hand-and-fist crack in a right-facing dihedral to a small ledge on the left. **Pitch 3:** Curve up right to a belay spot in a niche on top of the orange finger of rock above the first belay ledge. **Pitch 4:** Jam a long straight-in crack up the wall above to the top of the crag.

7. **Remote Luxury** (II 5.10b) Begin as for Route 6, ascending its first pitch. **Pitch 2:** Move back to the right end of the sloping ledge and enter a dihedral crack that follows the right side of the orange finger of rock above the ledge. Jam this hand crack to a semi-hanging belay near the top of the finger. **Pitch 3:** Although the route initially went up left to join *Tangerine Dream,* you now switch to face climbing, chasing 7 bolts up the steep face above your belay.
8. **Attitude Is Everything** (5.9+) Be sure you have plenty of strength—and a pair of 60-meter ropes before starting this one. Begin below the right end of the L-shaped roof. Ascend a flake, then face-climb past 2 bolts to a shallow, left-facing dihedral. Follow the thin crack in the dihedral to its end at a semi-hanging belay 15' right of the second belay on Route 7. Rappel the route, or head left and finish via Routes 6 or 7. Take numerous small nuts to 2".
9. **Sporting Chance** (II 5.9) Start 20' downhill and right of Route 8. **Pitch 1:** Work up right, then follow a very long crack pitch to a belay spot level with the top of Route 8. **Pitch 2:** Head up right around a corner, then continue up right to a belay niche where two facing corners converge. **Pitch 3:** Exit the niche via a short, overhanging section, then proceed up much easier jamming to the top. Take extra cams to 4".
10. **Tres Hombres** (II 5.10d) Locate the start of this classic route at a shallow, right-facing dihedral 20' right of Route 9 and immediately below the left side of a spectacular orange pillar. **Pitch 1:** Jam the 5.8 dihedral to a broad, sloping terrace. **Pitch 2:** Continue up the dihedral, following a wider (5.10a) crack that soon curves right to a belay niche at the foot of an impressive offwidth crack. **Pitch 3:** Jam the crux 6-inch offwidth alongside the orange pillar, arriving at the belay ledge atop Route 9's second pitch. **Pitch 4:** Follow Route 9 to the top. Take large cams to 6" for the offwidth pitch.
11. **Unnamed** (5.12a TR) Start directly below the orange pillar flanked by Route 10. Pull crimps and pockets up an overhanging black and orange wall, then proceed up easier—but still tricky—face climbing to the large, blocky terrace just right of the pillar's base. Lower off or rappel from here (75'). Note that you must climb the first 2 pitches of *Regular Route* to reach the toprope anchors.

12. **Pyroclastic Pump** (5.11a) Find this route and the 6 that follow on a 70-foot, orange and gray wall just left of the crag's lowest point. Start around the corner left of the main part of this wall, where the dark-stained rock overhangs. Clip 3 bolts as you pull pockets up the overhanging wall, encountering the crux above the second bolt. Once over the overhanging part, clip one more bolt, then head up somewhat easier rock to the anchors.
13. **Agua Dulce** (5.10c) Starting 15' right of Route 12, climb the right side of the overhanging wall, head up right into a thin, right-facing corner, then follow it to the anchors on a large, sloping terrace. Add small tri-cams to your regular rack to utilize pockets for protection.
14. **Changing Phases** (5.10a) Start 10' right of *Agua Dulce.* Climb steep rock past 2 bolts to a waterstreak, then proceed up the waterstreak to the terrace.
15. **Mejito** (5.9 R) Begin a few feet right of Route 14. Ascend doubtful, marginally protected climbing up pockets and crimps to a bolt, then make the crux mantle and continue to the terrace.
16. **Variation A** (5.8) Six feet right of *Mejito,* climb steep rock to a thin arch that sweeps up right. Undercling, then lieback the arch, which soon bends upward again. Continue up the shallow, right-facing corner to the terrace.
17. **Variation B** (5.9+ R) Start 8' right of Route 16. Use small, shallow pockets to climb the very smooth face, keeping right of the tempting ground on Route 16. Note that although this route can be protected with traditional gear, the placements are tricky and not too secure.
18. **Viscous Variation** (5.10a R) If you enjoy the challenges of *Variation B,* you'll find more of the same on this route. Begin climbing 6' right of Route 17.
19. **Regular Route** (II 5.8) Start just left of the crag's lowest point, at the right-hand edge of the steep, smooth wall climbed by the preceding several routes. **Pitch 1:** Climb steep, enjoyable 5.8 rock up a waterstreak, eventually heading left to the terrace above Routes 13–18. Belay at its upper left corner, at the foot of a right-facing dihedral. **Pitch 2:** Climb the dihedral, then head up left on gray-colored rock to a belay spot at the foot of a prominent, right-facing dihedral that forms the right side of the spectacular orange pillar flanked on its other side by *Tres Hombres.* **Pitch 3:** Instead of following the dihedral, follow the next crack system to the right (5.8). Scramble up left to the top of the crag.
20. **Regular Route—Finish Left** (II 5.9) Climb the first 2 pitches of *Regular Route.* **Pitch 3:** Climb the long, strenuous hand crack in the main dihedral. From its top, scramble up left to the top of the crag.

21. **Busload of Faith** (II 5.11c) Climb the first 2 pitches of *Regular Route.* **Pitch 3:** Chase a series of 7 bolts up the face right of *Regular Route.* From the top of the face, either lower off or scramble up left over blocks to the top.
22. **Easily Amused** (II 5.10c) Climb the first 2 leads of *Regular Route.* **Pitch 3:** Jam the splitter hand crack on the wall just left of the arete right of Route 21. Finish as for Route 21. Take pro to 2½".
23. **Pinacoidal Cleavage** (II 5.10a) Follow *Regular Route* for 2 pitches. **Pitch 3:** Ascend a wild, thin-hands crack positioned on the arete itself. Finish by scrambling up left to the top of the crag.
24. **Heated Discussion** (II 5.9+) Begin as for *Regular Route.* **Pitch 1:** Climb the 5.8 waterstreak. At its top, exit right instead of left, eventually working up right along a terrace, then up a short crack to a belay niche at the left edge of the smooth, bulging face that gives the formation its name. **Pitch 2:** Exit up right out of the niche, face climbing to the foot of a thin crack (Route 25). Don't follow the crack; head up the 5.9+ face to the left, passing two protection bolts before reaching the easier climbing that leads to a belay spot on broken ledges. Scramble to the top from here.
25. **Sympathetic Hygiene** (II 5.9+) **Pitch 1:** Climb the first pitch of *Heated Discussion.* **Pitch 2:** Face-climb up right to the thin crack on the upper left part of the face, then jam to its end at a large, broken terrace atop the smooth face. **Pitch 3:** Move the belay up right to a niche at the foot of a prominent, right-leaning, wide crack, then follow the crack to the top of the crag. Take gear to 3".
26. **Viva Gorby** (5.11 b/c TR) Begin this enjoyable one-pitch route directly below the far-right end of the terrace followed by the preceding two routes. Reach the belay/toprope anchor by either climbing the first pitch of *Jelly Belly* or by traversing right along the terrace reached on the first pitch of Routes 24 and 25. Climb to an obvious, white shelf, then head up right for a few feet, make a sweeping detour left, then curve back right and up to the anchor.
27. **Jelly Belly** (II 5.10b) Locate the starting point of this route 25' right of *Viva Gorby,* at the base of the zone of weakness that defines the left edge of the bulging Bellybutton face. **Pitch 1:** Jam and stem steep grooves past 2 bolts to reach the far-right end of the terrace used by the preceding several routes. **Pitch 2:** Leave the grooves and head up right across the steep, pocketed face to a belay at the left edge of the Bellybutton formation. Use 2 bolts to protect this lead. **Pitch 3:** Climb along the left edge of The Bellybutton, then ascend the face directly to the belay spot at the foot of Route 25's third pitch. Watch for creative tri-cam possibilities in pockets. **Pitch 4:** Finish via *Sympathetic Hygiene.* Take protection to 3".

28. **Crisis Line** (II 5.11c/d) Begin this challenging, classic route a few yards right of *Jelly Belly,* just below the left edge of The Bellybutton. **Pitch 1:** Use large pockets to work up and left on the overhanging wall past 2 bolts. Continue up left to a large pocket, from which you can clip another bolt. Make the crux move, then head pretty much directly up the exposed, vertical face past 6 more bolts to a good belay ledge at The Bellybutton. **Pitch 2:** Climb the cleft that splits the rock inside The Bellybutton, exiting left along an out-sloping ramp to a bolt. Climb up and back right, clip a bolt at the lip of the roof at the top of *The Bellybutton,* pull over, clip another welcome bolt, and face-climb directly up to belay bolts. Make 2 rappels of 85' to reach the ground.

29. **Ghetto Blast** (II 5.11a) Begin 20' right of *Crisis Line* and directly below a point midway between The Bellybutton's center and its right edge. **Pitch 1:** Face-climb up left past 2 bolts (5.11a). Continue up left a few feet, then angle up right before heading up left again to a third bolt. Now proceed directly up the face past 2 more bolts to a good belay spot in The Bellybutton. **Pitch 2:** Climb the face right of the cleft in the center of The Bellybutton, clip a bolt at the lip of the roof, swing over (5.10c), and forge on up the face to the belay bolts of *Crisis Line.* Return via 2 rappels of 85'. For a still more challenging version of this route, begin as for *Crisis Line.* From its first bolt, angle up right, eventually joining *Ghetto Blast* below its third bolt. This variation is 5.11c. Take a range of gear from RPs to 2".

30. **Waganupa** (II 5.10b) Make sure of your gear-placing skills before attempting this route— the first pitch goes without any fixed pro. **Pitch 1:** Starting 15' uphill and right of Route 29, face-climb up and slightly left for 25'. Traverse left to a series of large buckets and climb just right of these. From the highest one, aim for a lone bucket 20' higher. Just beyond, traverse straight left to the belay spot atop *Ghetto Blast's* first pitch. **Pitch 2:** Work back right to a bolt, pull pockets just right of the right edge of The Bellybutton past 3 more bolts, then continue up the face to anchors shared with *Ghetto Blast.* Take pro from very small wires to 3". Top out, or make 2 rappels of 85'.

31. **The Great Hot Blast** (II 5.10d) Begin 15' uphill and right of *Waganupa.* **Pitch 1:** Face-climb up left to a bolt set just above a large pocket. Continue more directly up past 2 more bolts and the crux, then follow 3 more bolts that lead up and slightly right. Head up left, then make a dash for the anchor, which is level with the centerline of The Bellybutton and 15' to the right. **Pitch 2:** Climb up to a bolt, swing left to a large pocket, move up to a still larger one, then tiptoe up steep rock, gradually veering right to the anchor. **Pitch 3:** Top out via a short, easy pitch of friction. Take gear to 2½".

32. **Praeruptus** (5.10b) Locate the start of this long, one-pitch route where the smooth rock of the Bellybutton face meets more broken-looking rock 25' right of Route 31. Climb a left-curving arch, then proceed up the junction of smooth and broken rock until level with The Bellybutton. Move right a few feet, then head directly up the face to the anchors. Take quickdraws for this route's 7 bolts, and a few nuts to 1½". You need 2 ropes to rappel the route; otherwise, you must climb a short, run-out pitch up left to Route 31's anchor, then one more to top out.
33. **Post Nasal** (I 5.7 R) Start at the foot of a prominent, left-facing dihedral 30' uphill and right of Route 32. **Pitch 1:** Climb the dihedral, taking care to avoid knocking any of the abundant loose rock onto your belayer. Belay on a ledge. **Pitch 2:** From the right end of the ledge, climb a shorter and more solid, left-facing dihedral, which curves up right to another ledge. You have your choice of many variations to finish this climb.
34. **Digression** (I 5.10a) **Pitch 1:** Climb the first pitch of *Post Nasal.* **Pitch 2:** From the left end of the ledge, follow a ramp up left and re-establish the belay at a bolted anchor. Face-climb directly up, keeping about 15' left of *Post Nasal's* second pitch and eventually joining *Exit Left* to reach the top of the face. Take numerous small wires to protect this pitch.
35. **Exit Left** (I 5.7) From the top of *Post Nasal,* follow a crack out left, then up to the top of the face.
36. **Bull Terrier** (I 5.9) From the top of *Post Nasal,* climb the central crack to the top of the face.
37. **Exit Right** (I 5.7) From the top of *Post Nasal,* follow the right-hand crack to the top of the face.

## RAKER PEAK

Unlike the plug dome of nearby Lassen Peak, Raker Peak is a shield volcano, built up by successive flows of relatively fluid lava. Subsequent glaciation carved away part of its southwest flank, leaving a 200-foot band of cliffs that can be easily seen and admired from California Highway 89. However, the quality of rock on these cliffs is not nearly as good as that on Eagle Cliff or Bellybutton, and climbers have made few forays into this often brittle and unreliable rock.

As if to make up for the disappointing climbing on the main peak, the Raker Peak area also includes two excellent satellite formations just to the south. Here, harder, more massive andesite forms 120-foot Roadside Distraction Wall and the spectacular, leaning prow of Devastation Pillar. Both formations provide interesting, easily accessible, one-pitch traditional and sport routes ranging in difficulty from 5.6 to 5.12d.

**Climbing history:** Roadside Distraction Wall and Devastation Pillar were "discovered" as possible climbing destinations by John Bald and Steve Lauderdale in the early 1980s. They climbed several recorded routes on the main peak, but the climbing record for the satellite formations is sketchy at best. It is fairly safe to assume, however, that most of these climbs were established by either the Redding-area group of Bald, Yates, Travis Klawin, and Tim Loughlin or by the Chico-based climbers Rob Settlemire, Dave Caunt, and Gary Adams. Neither crag is close to being fully developed, and the author invites climbers to forward new route information.

**Rack:** Because climbs in this area encompass both traditional and sport routes, your rack should include gear for the type of climbing you prefer. Traditional climbs call for a selection of stoppers and hexes from small wires to about 3", as well as sets of TCUs and FCUs from ½" to 6". For the sport routes, add 10 to 12 quickdraws. Be sure to take extra webbing for setting up toprope anchors.

**Descent:** You can descend from the top of either crag by scrambling down the gully that separates the two formations. In addition, several of the sport routes have chain anchors on top, so you could lower off if you prefer.

## TRIP PLANNING INFORMATION

**Area description:** Roadside Distraction Wall is a 60- to 120-foot wall of andesite, offering steep, sporty wall climbs punctuated by wide cracks and troughs. Devastation Pillar is a 150-foot prow of andesite offering traditional and toprope routes. These crags offer climbs ranging from 5.6 to 5.12d on sunny, west- and southwest-facing rock.

**Location:** On the lower southwest slopes of Raker Peak in Lassen Volcanic National Park.

**Camping:** There are several campgrounds located near the crags. The following campgrounds are listed in order of proximity to the parking area. Summit Lake South and Summit Lake North lie 2.6 miles east on CA 89. Summit Lake South offers 48 developed sites and costs $12 per night; Summit Lake North offers 46 developed sites and costs $14 per night. Crags, with 45 developed sites, lies 4.4 miles north on CA 89; the fee is a bargain $8 per night. Manzanita Lake, 7.4 miles north of the trailhead on CA 89, offers 179 developed sites adjacent to the lake for $14 per night. Southwest, with 21 walk-in sites, lies 19.3 miles south on California 89; the per-night fee is $12.

**Climbing season:** June through October; earlier in dry years. Note that access depends on the amount of snow remaining after the preceding winter. In some heavy-snow years, the trailhead remains inaccessible to vehicles until late July. It is a good idea to call the park to check on road conditions before committing to a long drive early or late in the season.

**Restrictions and access issues:** All visitors entering Lassen Volcanic National Park must pay a $10 entry fee per vehicle. A Golden Eagle Pass, good for unlimited admissions for one year from date of purchase, can be obtained for $50—a bargain for frequent visitors.

There is no maintained trail to the crags, but climber traffic has established a couple of easy-to-find paths. To help preserve fragile soils and vegetation (and ensure continued access to the crags), please keep to these trails. Secure temporary toprope anchors to gear whenever possible to avoid damaging clifftop vegetation, and protect any trees used as rappel anchors by using webbing. There are comparatively few bolts in place here, and park managers are likely to take a dim view of large-scale bolting operations. Before you drill, please make sure the line is worth bolting and that you use stainless-steel bolts at least ⅜" in diameter and at least 2½" long with heavy-duty, rustless, and camouflaged hangers. If you find any quickdraws in place, please leave them; climbers working projects are not passing out free gear.

**Guidebook:** The only previous guidebook to this area is John Bald's self-published *Lassen Volcanic National Park: A Climbers Guide* (1989). Check with the personnel at area climbing shops for current route information.

**Nearby mountain shops, guide services, and gyms:** The nearest mountain shops include Hermit's Hut and Sports Ltd. in Redding and Mountain Sports, Overland Equipment, and Sports Ltd. in Chico. Guiding and instruction are available through Adventures Made Easy in Anderson and Shasta Mountain Guides in Mt. Shasta. The nearest climbing gyms are Ascent Climbing Gym/Outdoor Center in Grass Valley and Granite Arch in Rancho Cordova. California State University, Chico has a climbing gym on campus. It is open to non-students most evenings. Contact the university's outdoor center for more information.

**Services:** There are no services available at the crag, so all parties will need to provide their own food and water. The absence of toilets makes the need for sound waste disposal practices obvious. All human waste should be buried, and all toilet paper should be carried out. The nearest source for food and beverages is the small store and gift shop at Manzanita Lake, located near the north park entrance.

**Emergency services:** In an emergency, contact park rangers. There are ranger stations at both park entrances and at the Summit Lake North campground. Area hospitals include: Saint Elizabeth Community Hospital in Red Bluff and Mercy Medical Center and Redding Medical Center, both in Redding.

**Nearby climbing areas:** Bellybutton and Eagle Cliff lie on the far side of Lassen Peak from here, a 13.1-mile drive to the southwest.

**Nearby attractions:** The most obvious nearby attraction is, of course, the giant slag-pile of Lassen Peak. For an unforgettable view, follow the 2.5-mile trail to the summit. South and west of the Lassen Peak trailhead lies the park's famous hot springs area, with boiling mudpots, geysers, and fumaroles. To the east of CA 89, the eastern half of the park offers outstanding backpacking in the Lassen Volcanic National Park Wilderness.

**Finding the crags:** From Redding, drive 48 miles east on California Highway 44 to a junction with California 89. Turn right and proceed to the park entrance. From the park entrance, drive south on CA 89 (known as Lassen Park Road inside the national park boundary) for 8.9 miles and park on the west side of the road in any of a series of pullouts. If approaching from the south, head east on California Highway 36 from its intersection with U.S. Interstate 5 in Red Bluff. After 3 miles, proceed northeast on CA 36 at its junction with U.S. Highway 99. Follow CA 36 for 44 miles to a junction with CA 89. Turn left and drive 4.8 miles to the southwest entrance to the park. From the entrance, proceed 20.1 miles to the previously mentioned pullouts. From the parking area, cross the highway and walk northeast toward the crags. Once the ground slopes abruptly upward, follow a use trail to Roadside Distraction Wall. To reach Devastation Pillar, contour right from the base of Roadside Distraction Wall. Help preserve fragile, easily eroded soils by resisting making new trails or cutting switchbacks.

## ROADSIDE DISTRACTION WALL

Seen from the parking area, this is the left-hand, lower of the two satellite formations immediately south of Raker Peak. You can scramble up and around the right side of the crag to reach toprope anchors on top, or use this as a means of descent. Note that most leaders choose to lower off or rappel to avoid loose rock on the summit.

1. **Vignette** (5.6) Start near the center of a small, triangular face at the north end of the crag. Climb flakes to the upper of two small ledges, traverse left, then lieback up a right-facing dihedral to the top of the wall. For a more interesting finish, face-climb directly up from the ledge's right end (5.7).

2. **Slum Lord** (5.9) Beginning 25' right of *Vignette,* climb a short, overhanging wall, then ascend a crack system that passes through blocky terrain before entering a corner/trough that leads to the top of the wall.

3. **Fruit Stand** (5.11b) Locate the start of this route in the back of an alcove about 60' uphill and right of Route 2. Climb up left out of the alcove, pulling over a blocky overhang. Bridge up a wide groove until the groove splits at a prominent block. Lieback up left to the top. Alternatively, work up right, then up steeper rock to the top. Take pro to 5".

4. **Roadside Distraction** (5.10d) Climb the obvious dihedral that runs all the way up the wall to its highest point. Take pro to 6" for this challenging offwidth exercise.

5. **Fresh Air** (5.11c or 5.12d) Watch for the initial bolts of this route on the wall 20' right of Route 4. Face-climb past 3 bolts to a finger crack. Jam about two-thirds of the way up this crack to a bolt, face-climb up left past another bolt to an arete, then follow it past 3 more bolts to the top of the crag. For the harder finish, continue up the finger crack to its top, then ascend strenuous, technical rock past 3 bolts to the chains at the top.
6. **Unnamed** (5.11d) To find this route, scramble a few yards up the gully between Roadside Distraction Wall and Devastation Pillar, watching for a striking offwidth crack in a shallow, left-facing dihedral. Beginning 8' left of the dihedral, surmount a small roof, then climb the steep, featureless face past 3 bolts to a chain anchor.
7. **Subterranean Homesick Blues** (5.10c) Climb the offwidth crack in a small, left-facing dihedral 8' right of Route 6. Take pro to 6".

## HUNK OF BURNING LOVE

This large boulder lies at the foot of Devastation Pillar and provides both good bouldering and a convenient spot for spectators to watch climbers on Devastation Pillar. The short, overhanging routes on the north side range from 5.9 to 5.11d, while those on the easier south side provide longer climbs from 5.4 to 5.10a. Descend via the short 5.2 face on the uphill side of the rock.

## DEVASTATION PILLAR

This is the impressive tower visible over the treetops when viewed from the parking area. To descend this rock, top out, then scramble down to the north.

1. **Blue Suede Shoes** (5.8) Starting between Hunk of Burning Love and Devastation Pillar, climb the sinuous hand crack at the left end of a prominent, orange-stained wall. Take pro to 3", including some small stoppers and TCUs up high.
2. **Heartbreak Hotel** (5.10b) Begin 10' right of *Blue Suede Shoes.* Make some technical face moves to reach a left-slanting finger crack, or start a few feet farther right near a flake shaped like a shark's fin and begin jamming sooner. Either way, follow the crack as it snakes up the wall, ending at an obvious notch in the skyline. Take numerous small to mid-size pieces of pro.
3. **Sharkfin Soup** (5.10d TR) From the top of the shark fin–shaped flake just right of Route 2, climb the steep, smooth orange wall, passing left of a small overhang, then working up and right to a small ledge. Finish by either joining *Jailhouse Rock* or by climbing the fractured wall to the left.
4. **Jailhouse Rock** (5.7) Climb the obvious, dark, left-facing dihedral at the right edge of the wall ascended by the previous climbs. Take larger pro for the hand-and-fist crack in the corner.
5. **Marginal** (5.10d/.11a R or TR) For this interesting and challenging route, follow the striking arete that forms the upper right edge of the

dihedral climbed by *Jailhouse Rock*. If leading, take pro to 2½". You may occasionally have to detour right to find gear placements.

6. **Chariots of Fire** (5.10c) Begin 30' right of Route 5, where you gain a clear view of the west face of Devastation Pillar. Lieback or finger-jam a short, clean dihedral on the left side of a block-filled trough. From its top, head up left past a bush, then jam a winding, 5.9 finger-to-hands crack. When the crack ends, face-climb (5.10c) to a small notch in the summit skyline.
7. **Bang Bang Bang** (5.11a TR) Scramble up the block-filled gully just right of Route 6. From the highest block, climb a hand crack in a left-leaning dihedral, then, just below its top, exit over an overhang and climb the exposed, technical face above to the top.

DEVASTATION PILLAR
.11d
7
8
6

8. **Nameless** (5.11d TR) Begin just around the corner right of the blocky gully of Route 7. Keep to the arete that bounds the gully's right side. From its top, make a few tricky moves over a smooth, angular bulge, pull crimps and pockets up a short overhanging wall, then finish via delicate but strenuous face climbing up the summit headwall.

## HONORABLE MENTION

### EAGLE PEAK—NORTH BUTTRESS

In addition to the quality climbing on Eagle Cliff, Eagle Peak also boasts superb climbing on its north buttress. The climbs are comparable in length and difficulty to those on Eagle Cliff, but their location on the "back side" of the mountain gives them a definite wilderness atmosphere, and it is easy to imagine being the only people within a hundred miles.

Reach the north buttress by taking the approach route for Eagle Cliff. From the flat area near the foot of the rocky chute leading up to the Eagle Cliff bench, head up right, winding up the slope to a broad saddle east of the peak. Hike north on rocky, but easy terrain, gradually contouring left to reach the base of the north buttress. Most of the climbs ascend a striking fin of dacite. Either rappel the routes or traverse and scramble down.

### THE LOADING ZONE

This excellent small crag lies southeast of Lassen Volcanic National Park, on land managed by Lassen National Forest in scenic Warner Valley. The 70-foot cliff of andesite provides a number of steep and interesting routes from 5.7 to 5.11b. Although some routes have bolts, all require the placement of gear for protection. A standard rack will suffice.

Approach from the town of Chester, which lies 72 miles east of Red Bluff on California Highway 36 (25 miles east of the junction with California Highway 89 leading into the south entrance to the park). Drive northwest on Warner Valley Road, heading for the private resort of Drakesbad. After 6.5 miles, pass Warner Creek Campground on the right, then cross Warner Creek on a bridge 1.8 miles farther on. About 0.25 mile beyond the bridge, park on the shoulder and hike 0.25 mile up to the rock.

# Feather River Country

The Feather River region, comprising portions of Plumas and Butte Counties, is the northernmost bulwark of the granitic Sierra Nevada before it merges into the volcanic rocks of the Cascade Range. Here, on the west side of the range, in the precipitous gorges of the Feather River's north and middle forks, climbers can find domes, walls, slabs, outcrops, and boulders of beautiful, clean, flint-hard granite and diorite, as well as Feather Falls, the nation's sixth-highest. All these treasures lie within an hour's drive of the population centers of Chico, Quincy, and Oroville, while Sacramento lies only a couple of hours away to the south.

The generally easy access and spectacular rock have made this area a favorite of local climbers, and it truly does offer something for enthusiasts of all abilities. Moreover, the areas described here represent only a part of the abundance of rock found in this region. Ambitious new-route developers could climb here for decades without risk of exhausting the supply of unclimbed Feather River rock. All climbs lie outside designated wilderness areas, so access issues are virtually non-existent.

Older routes in the Feather River region consist of traditional lines that follow natural zones of weakness, as well as some exhilarating and run-out slab climbs with bolts placed on-lead. More recent routes display the influence of sport climbing and tend to be generally better protected with more closely spaced bolts. Some of these, however, are undersized, quarter-inch bolts. Local climbers are currently in the process of replacing these with more substantial bolts at Grizzly Dome and Bald Rock Dome.

## Grizzly Dome and Plumas Slab

The deep gorge carved by the North Fork of Feather River is the scene of many marvels. Within the narrow confines of the canyon one finds a major state highway; a trans-Sierra railroad; a scenic river; and a huge complex of hydroelectric dams, penstocks, and flumes. Here, too, climbers find a wealth of climbing opportunities on boulders, outcrops, isolated slabs, and domes. The most spectacular of these crags line the southeast side of the canyon, where a pair of highway tunnels pierce granite bastions. Plumas Slab is a

# FEATHER RIVER COUNTRY CLIMBING AREAS

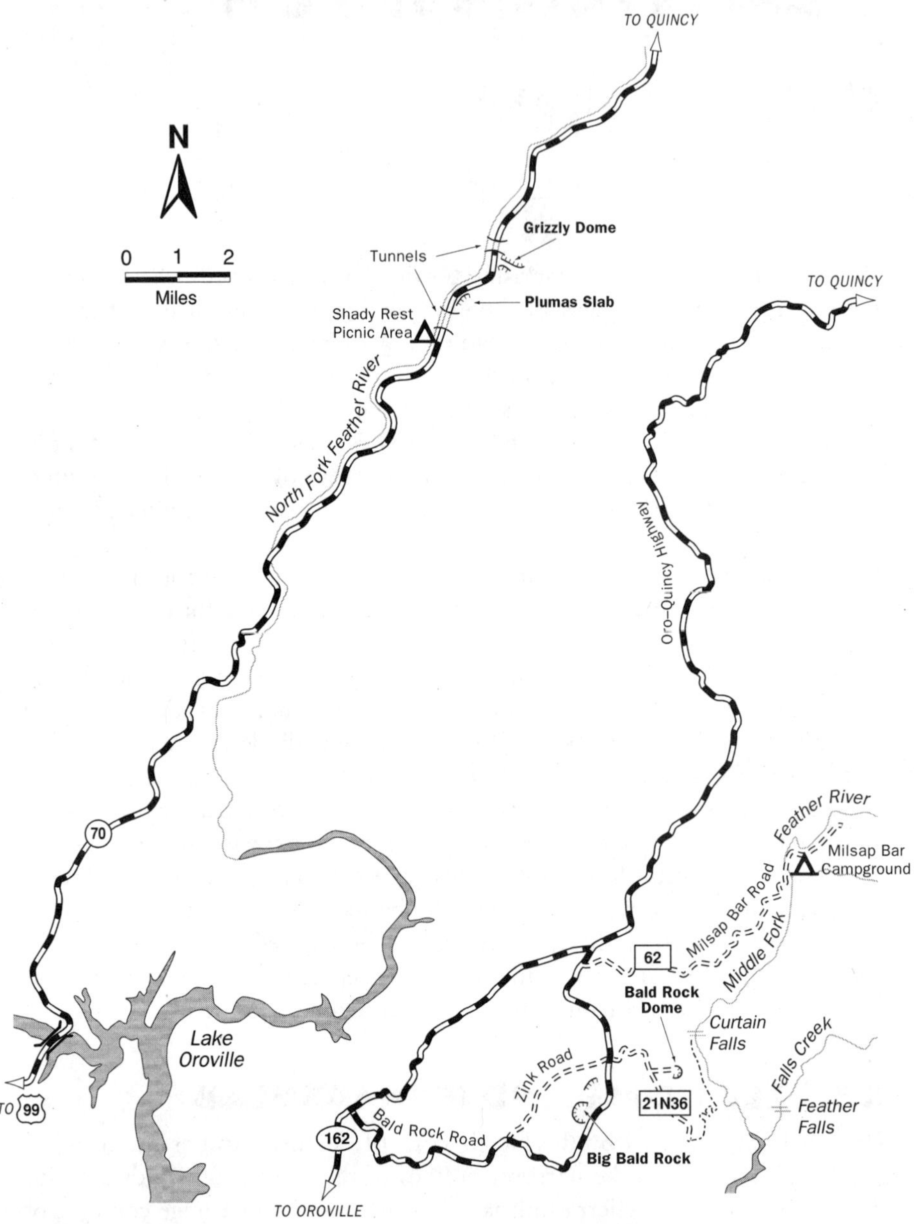

large, generally moderately angled granite slab whose tantalizing upper reaches are guarded by an overhanging 15-foot wall formed by exfoliation. Grizzly Dome is a 350-foot dome of unglaciated granite intermixed with gneiss. Both formations rise directly from the edge of the highway. The resulting easy access and the excellent quality of the rock has made both crags—especially Grizzly Dome—very popular hangouts.

Both rocks offer both traditional and sport climbs of one to three pitches, which range in difficulty from 5.6 to 5.11d. Some projects currently under development at Grizzly Dome promise routes of up to 5.13a. Most climbs involve friction and face climbing, although visitors will also find thin-hand cracks, offwidths, and liebacks. First-time visitors should note that these crags require a cool head and impeccable footwork, even with good protection. Many routes feature sections that yield only to careful planning and clever combinations of movements. The degree of subtlety necessary to succeed often leads the reckless into thinking that the ratings are too conservative.

Most routes are adequately protected with bolts, and nearly all of these are healthy ⅜-inch stainless steel anchors with rustless hangers. Most sport routes at Grizzly Dome are equipped with pairs of stout chains for lowering or rappelling, while those at Plumas Slab have either chains or paired bolts. At Grizzly Dome, there are numerous relics of past engineering, such as dynamite holes and broken rock drills. These can sometimes be used for protection via flexible-stemmed cams or tie-offs.

**Climbing history:** Because of the proximity of Grizzly Dome and Plumas Slab to each other, both formations were explored and developed simultaneously, along with a number of nearby small formations along both banks of the North Fork Feather River. The earliest forays onto the flanks of these rocks were made by the work crews hired to construct the mammoth penstocks, footings, rights of way, and tunnels required by the Feather River Project system of hydroelectric dams and the constuction of California Highway 70 and the route used by the Union Pacific Railroad.

Although the work crews did not establish climbs themselves, they did contribute to the development of climbing in the area in several ways. In many places along the lower portions of rocks in the area one can see numerous holes that were drilled into the rock to either support scaffolding or to contain dynamite for blasting tunnels. These holes provide useful holds on some climbs, and the sawn-off remains of stuck rock drills have been used as landmarks and even as anchors. The Elephant Butte (Grizzly Dome) Tunnel was completed in 1936, as was a smaller tunnel through the rock formation west of the tunnel, which allowed Grizzly Creek to drain into Feather River while avoiding the highway where it crosses the narrow canyon cut by the creek. This small tunnel has become the site of the area's new wave of extreme sport climbs.

Recreational rock climbers discovered the area's potential as early as the mid-1960s, when an unknown party climbed *Regular Route* (I 5.7) on Grizzly

Dome. This route remained the sole climb on either formation for several years, primarily due to the difficult and hard-to-protect nature of other lines on the rock. It wasn't until the early 1970s that another anonymous party climbed the thin crack line right of the prominent arch on Grizzly Dome to establish *Broken Arrow* (I 5.7).

The late 1970s saw the first concerted development of bolted face climbs in the area. On Plumas Slab, John Dewitt and Steve Wong climbed *Vernal Equinox* (I 5.8) in 1974. A party of three known only as "Quentin, Brian, and one other" put up the slab's first 5.10 route, *Solstice,* in 1976. In 1977, Brian Conry and John Cuzio attacked the overhanging wall at the foot of Plumas Slab, continuing up the slab above the overhang to join *Solstice.* Their route, *The Black Eye* (II 5.6 A2), remains the slab's only aided climb. Later that year, Rob Settlemire, one of the region's most active climbers and new route developers, made a solo first ascent of *Side Issue* (I 5.9), then returned with Gary Adams to create *Top Hat* (I 5.8). Both returned the following year to climb *Eclipse* (5.6). Pete Kilbourne and Dave Caunt visited Plumas Slab in 1979 and climbed *Far Left* (I 5.8). Later, they worked out the initial moves and climbed *Grizzly Terrace* (5.8), creating Grizzly Dome's first bolted face climb.

By the 1980s, the Plumas Slab and Grizzly Dome had become destination crags for local climbers, and the search for new routes swung into high gear. Kicking off the decade, Dave Caunt and Steve Schneider climbed the run-out testpiece *Zenith* (5.11a), the area's first climb at this grade. In 1983, Randy Dewees and friends looked over the unpromising wall right of *Regular Route,* decided it could be led, and added *Old Top Rope* (5.9). In 1984, Rob Settlemire and Rick Harlan checked out the face of Grizzly Dome between the two entrances to the highway tunnel and produced *Crutches Are Cheap* (5.9+), returning with Dave Caunt to add *Toy Shop* (5.9). In 1987, Jake Jacobs climbed *Wimps Are People Too* (5.7) with Craig Nielson, adding a second pitch with Bob Kingman for *You Round Table Guys* (5.8). During this period, unknown parties (probably Settlemire, Caunt, and company) put up *Space Bucket* (5.10a), *Fingergag* (5.10c), and *Out of Order* (5.10d), creating three of Grizzly Dome's most popular routes.

**Rack:** Because most routes in the area are bolted sport routes, you can usually rig adequate protection using a selection of eight to ten quickdraws. For the few traditional climbs, or to supplement existing protection, take a few nuts or cams to three inches width, emphasizing smaller sizes.

**Descent:** You have no choice of walking off the tops of any of these climbs. Plan to rappel all multi-pitch routes and rappel or lower off all single-pitch climbs.

## TRIP PLANNING INFORMATION

**Area description:** Grizzly Dome is a 400-foot, unglaciated dome of mixed granite and gneiss situated at the confluence of Grizzly Creek and North Fork

*Climbers on the main wall of Grizzly Dome. The Party in the foreground is on* Bonebreaker *(I 5.10b), while the distant party works on* Grizzly Terrace *(5.8).*

Feather River. Plumas Slab is a smaller slab of granite that rises abruptly from the southeastern edge of California Highway 70 just west of Grizzly Dome. Both crags offer quality climbing on good rock, with the majority of climbs in the 5.8 and harder range, including some projects that promise 5.12–5.13 climbing.

**Location:** Alongside California 70 in the canyon of North Fork Feather River, 35 miles northeast of Oroville.

**Camping:** Both Grizzly Dome and Plumas Slab are essentially day-use areas, due to the lack of suitable camping facilities anywhere nearby. It is possible—but not recommended—to camp at the Pacific Gas and Electric-managed Shady Rest Picnic Area, but note that there are no developed sites.

**Climbing season:** Almost all year; a short warm spell in winter usually dries out Grizzly Dome enough to permit climbing. Note, however, that sport climbs across Grizzly Creek in The Cave do not open until the water level of Grizzly Creek drops in late June of most years. Prior to that time, the rushing water presents a significant safety hazard.

**Restrictions and access issues:** Because both these crags lie immediately adjacent to a paved highway, access is no problem at all; most climbers relish the prospect of park-and-climb cragging. However, there are certain cautions that apply to this area. The California Department of Transportation (CalTrans) forbids climbing within 15' of the highway's edge or above any of the tunnels. A fall that would put you into the path of an oncoming big rig is definitely something to be avoided. Similarly, Pacific Gas and Electric, the owner of all the hydroelectric structures in the area—including the huge concrete penstock that crosses Grizzly Creek just upstream of Grizzly Dome—prohibits visitors from treating these concrete wonders as additional crags. Camping is prohibited at the parking area for Grizzly Dome.

As for considerations of the crags themselves, please keep in mind the fragile nature of the streamside habitat between the foot of Grizzly Dome and Grizzly Creek. Pick up and carry out any trash you create or find. There are no suitable places for disposing of human waste, even if you could find a suitably private spot. Plan to "take care of business" before and after your visit, or make a quick trip down the highway to the restrooms at the picnic area. If you bring kids or dogs, keep a close eye on both; Grizzly Creek is a big stream, and CA 70 is a busy highway. If you plan to establish new routes, always think in terms of those who will follow; use good, stout, ⅜-inch stainless-steel bolts with rustless hangers. Use welded coldshuts or chains for belay/rap stations, and avoid leaving webbing if you rappel or retreat. It is not only unsightly, it can create clipping problems for other parties.

**Guidebook:** The sole guidebook for this area is Robert Stahl's self-published *Feather River Rock—A Trenchant Guide to Rock Climbing in the Feather River Country* (1989).

**Nearby mountain shops, guide services, and gyms:** The nearest sources for climbing gear and information are Mountain Sports and Sports Ltd. in Chico. There are no guide services, although groups from California State University, Chico occasionally use the area for instruction. The nearest climbing gym is Granite Arch in Rancho Cordova. California State University, Chico has a climbing gym on campus. It is open to non-students most evenings. Contact the university's outdoor center for more information.

**Services:** There are no services available at Grizzly Dome or Plumas Slab. The nearest restrooms are located at the Shady Rest Picnic Area 1.8 miles southwest of Grizzly Dome on CA 70. Although the climbing area lies adjacent to both Feather River and Grizzly Creek, visitors should plan to treat all water from these sources or bring their own bottled water or other drinks from home.

**Emergency services:** In the event of an emergency, summon help by calling 911. The nearest hospitals are Enloe Medical Center in Chico, Oroville Hospital in Oroville, and Feather River Hospital in Paradise.

**Nearby climbing areas:** In addition to the excellent climbing on these formations, visitors can also enjoy the challenges offered by small outcrops across the river from the highway, between the Arch Rock and Grizzly Dome highway tunnels. Big Bald Rock and Bald Rock Dome lie southeast from here, on the ridge northwest of the canyon of Middle Fork Feather River.

# PLUMAS SLAB AND GRIZZLY DOME

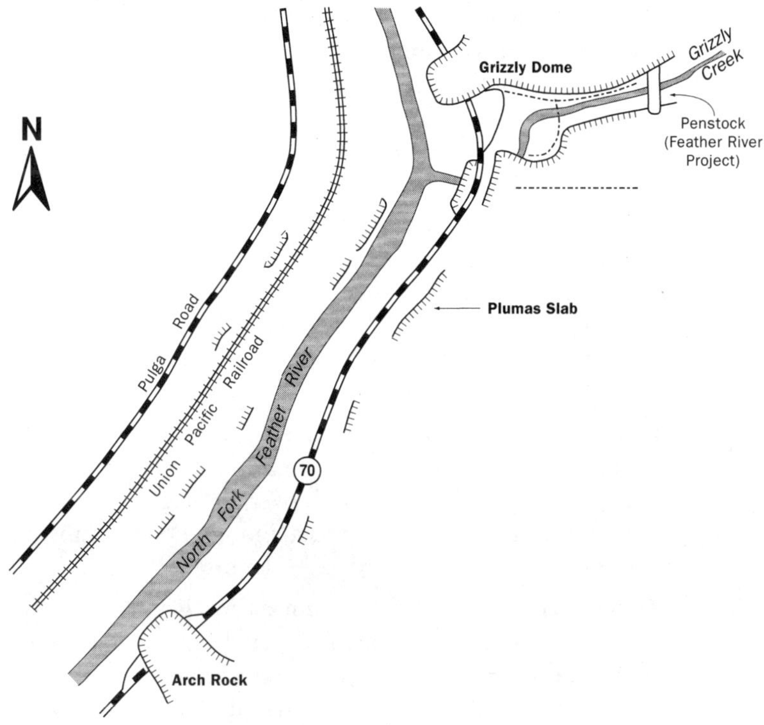


**Nearby attractions:** The nearby North Fork Feather River provides excellent opportunities for swimming (during summer months) and fishing, while the Union Pacific Railroad tracks across the canyon allow visitors to enjoy watching rail traffic. Farther south near Oroville, Lake Oroville offers water-skiing, fishing, swimming, and lakeshore relaxing.

**Finding the crags:** From Oroville, proceed north, then northeast on California 70. At 32.6 miles, pass the Shady Rest Picnic Area just west of the Arch Rock Tunnel. Just beyond the tunnel, where a sign indicates your entry into Plumas County, Plumas Slab rises from the highway's edge on the right. At 34.8 miles, pull off into a sandy parking area just before entering the Elephant Butte Tunnel. The Grizzly Dome climbing area lies on the wall right of the tunnel's entrance. Additional routes can be found on the very steep and overhanging walls immediately across roaring Grizzly Creek. Note that it is easier and safer to reach the parking for Plumas Slab by first going to the Grizzly Dome parking area and turning around, as the Plumas Slab parking pullout lies on the wrong side of the road when you are driving northeast.

## PLUMAS SLAB

This is the very obvious, large granite slab guarded at its base by a short, overhanging wall. For visibility's sake, it is best to walk northeast along the far edge of the highway until you spot the route you want, then cross to the slab. The sign marking the Butte/Plumas county line provides a handy point of reference. Route descriptions run from left to right, beginning at the county line sign. Because there are no walk-off descents, you should plan to rappel all routes on this formation.

1. **Nada Da Narda** (5.10a) Almost directly above the county line sign, notice a left-curving corner. Scramble up to the corner, then work up left to the small ledge where this route begins. Climb up to a bolt, then continue to a small pedestal beneath an overlap. Move up left over the overlap, then friction up very smooth rock past 3 more bolts to the paired belay/rappel bolts. Take pro to 1".
2. **Wimps Are People Too** (5.7) Scramble and climb to the top of a short, left-curving corner directly above the county line sign. From a small ledge, face-climb past 3 bolts, pass over the right end of the overlap crossed by Route 1, then continue past another bolt (and the crux) to the bolts that mark the end of the route. Take pro to 1".
3. **You Round Table Guys** (I 5.8) Begin as for Route 2. **Pitch 1:** Climb *Wimps Are People Too.* **Pitch 2:** Face-climb past 4 bolts, encountering the crux just beyond the second one. From the upper bolt, either head up left to a small tree on a ledge, or diagonal up right, then more directly up to a pair of belay/rap bolts. Take pro to 1".
4. **Eclipse** (5.6) Start at the left-curving corner used by the preceding routes. Halfway up the corner, exit right, then slant up right past a bolt to the belay anchors.
5. **Vernal Equinox** (I 5.8) Begin at the left end of the prominent, overhanging wall formed by the lower edge of an exfoliation slab—the wall comes quite close to the ground at this point. **Pitch 1:** From a narrow ledge, climb to a small, left-jutting flake, above which is a bolt. From the bolt, make a 5.6 move or two before reaching the belay bolts. **Pitch 2:** Head up right on a poorly protected 5.6 lead to another pair of bolts. **Pitch 3:** Continue up right on easier ground to a third pair of bolts. From here, you can choose from three possible finishes: *Vernal Equinox* takes the far-right line. **Pitch 4:** Traverse right, then work up to a bolt. Pass the 5.8 crux just above, and head up to belay anchors at the lower end of a long, left-slanting ramp. Although the climb ends here, you can add another pitch by following the ramp up left, then traversing left to the bolts atop Route 3.

# PLUMAS SLAB

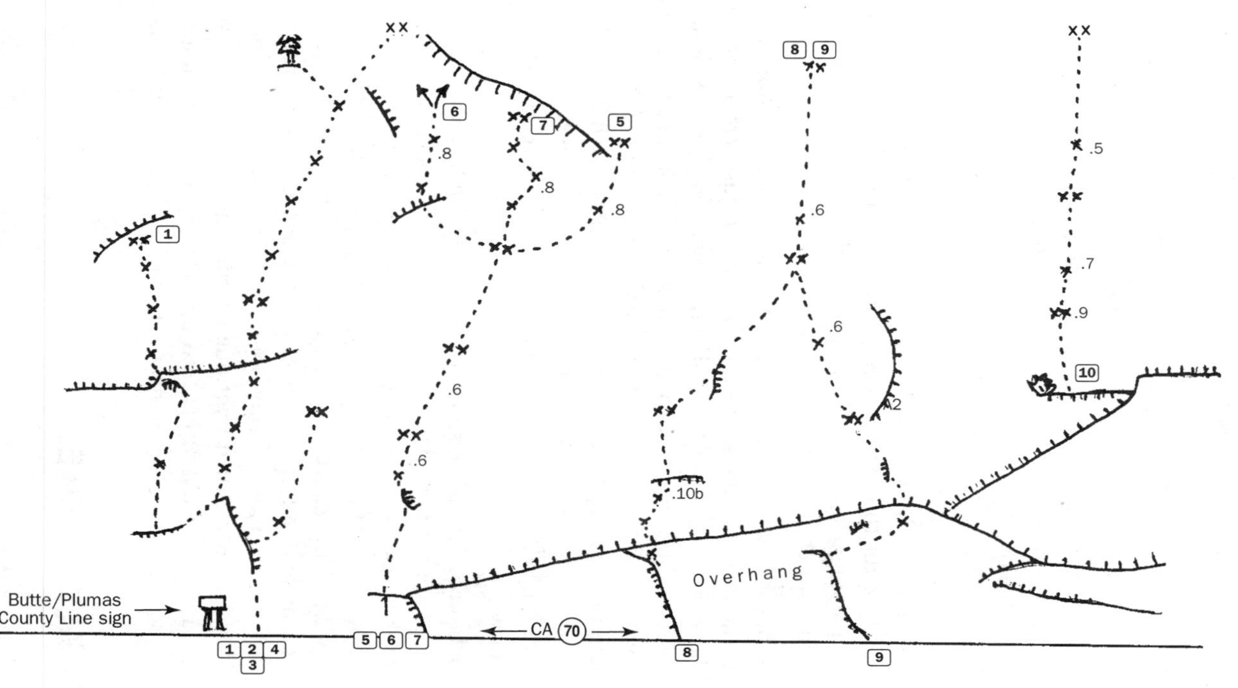

1
6
7
5
.8
.8
.8
.6
.6
8 9
.6
.6
A2
.5
.7
.9
10
.10b
Overhang
Butte/Plumas
County Line sign
CA 70
1 2 4
3
5 6 7
8
9

6. **Far Left** (I 5.8) Begin at the third belay on *Vernal Equinox*. Traverse left and slightly up to an overlap. Pass over, clip a bolt, then ascend the 5.8 face past another bolt to easier climbing that leads either up to the ramp above or up left to the bolts at the end of *You Round Table Guys*.
7. **Top Hat** (I 5.8) Begin by climbing the first 3 pitches of *Vernal Equinox*. From the third set of belay anchors, head up past 3 bolts (crux above the second bolt) to the belay/rap anchors.
8. **Solstice** (I 5.10b) Locate the starting point of this route about 90' right of the left end of the overhanging wall, where a right-facing flake runs up to meet the overhang. **Pitch 1:** Climb the flake to a bolt beneath the overhang, make a 5.10b mantle onto the slab above, then proceed past two more bolts to a narrow ledge. Continue to a pair of belay bolts higher on the slab. **Pitch 2:** Head up right to a left-facing flake. From its top, continue up right to a pair of belay anchors. **Pitch 3:** Climb directly up the slab, passing a bolt and a 5.6 move early in the game. Enjoy the easier, but run-out climbing to the belay bolts.
9. **The Black Eye** (II 5.6 A2) Start this more direct version of *Solstice* at a left-leaning, easy crack that lies below and just left of the highest point of the overhanging wall guarding the lower portion of Plumas Slab. **Pitch 1:** Ascend the easy crack to a small, sloping ledge. Face-climb up right to a bolt, then pass the overhang at its highest point (A2). Continue past a small, right-facing flake to the belay anchors. **Pitch 2:** Work up left to a bolt, then go more directly up past some 5.6 moves to the second belay stance on *Solstice*. Finish via that route. Take several thin pitons or very small wires.
10. **Side Issue** (I 5.9) Take some time to study the face so you can determine the best approach to the starting point of this route; most parties traverse onto the rock from the right. Begin the route proper at a small ledge near the upper end of a right-slanting overlap that takes off from just right of the apex of the short, overhanging wall at the foot of the slab. **Pitch 1:** From the left end of the ledge, climb a short, poorly-protected 5.9 friction pitch to a pair of belay bolts. **Pitch 2:** Head up to a bolt, which protects a 5.7 move, then continue on run-out climbing to a second set of belay anchors. **Pitch 3:** Proceed up easier rock past another lone bolt at a 5.5 section, then forge onward to the final pair of anchors.

# GRIZZLY DOME

## TUNNEL FACE

The following routes lie between the tunnel entrances, on the side of Grizzly Dome that faces Feather River. Approach by either rappelling the first pitch of *Tunnel Vision* from the east end of the tunnel or climbing down from the west tunnel entrance.

1. **Tunnel Vision** (I 5.9) From the outer edge of California Highway 70 at the east end of Elephant Butte Tunnel, traverse right on a ledge to a pair of bolts. Either begin climbing here, or for a longer climb, rappel to the edge of Feather River, where the route actually begins. **Pitch 1:** Face-climb up and slightly left (5.5), clip a bolt, then continue to the belay bolts on the approach ledge. **Pitch 2:** Face-climb up right past a bolt, encountering some 5.9 moves before reaching a small ledge. Continue up right to a second bolt, then proceed more directly upward to the anchors that mark the end of the climb. Rappel from here. You can also climb a somewhat easier alternative to the second pitch by heading up left from the first bolt then angling gradually up right to the anchors. Either way, take pro to 1".
2. **Crutches Are Cheap** (5.9+) Begin 40' right of Route 1, just below a small, curving overhang. Climb up to and past the overhang, then head up right to a bolt. Make a 5.9 mantle and continue to a second bolt. From here, climb directly up to a third bolt, then, after a few more feet, angle up left to the belay chains. For a slightly easier and better protected finish, angle up left from the second bolt. Clip a third bolt and continue up left to a right-leaning overlap. From its upper end, clip a fourth bolt, then make a few 5.9 moves up right to the belay chains. Rappel the route.
3. **Toy Shop** (I 5.9) Start *Toy Shop* at the foot of the cliff, about 65' right of Route 2. **Pitch 1:** Beginning at the base of a right-leaning flake, climb easy ground to a small ledge. **Pitch 2:** Climb easy rock up right to a prominent flake, then angle up left to a bolt. You can also reach the bolt by climbing more directly upward from the ledge, but this involves some poorly protected 5.7. From the bolt, angle up left past 2 more bolts, surmounting the crux moves just below the upper bolt. Head up and gradually right to belay/rap bolts, which are set above an overlap. Carry pro to 1½".

## MAIN WALL

The main, south-facing wall of Grizzly Dome, overlooking Grizzly Creek, is its most popular climbing area. Routes here include both traditional and sport climbs ranging up to 400'.

4. **Ursus Horribilis** (I 5.8) Begin about 25' right of the highway guardrail at the west end of the Elephant Butte Tunnel. **Pitch 1:** Ascend easy rock for 35' to a smoother section. Face-climb directly up past three bolts to belay/rappel chains. **Pitch 2:** Continue your course directly upward, passing several small bulges and 3 protection bolts before reaching the anchors. Surmount the crux between the first 2 bolts. **Pitch 3:** Again,

MAIN WALL, GRIZZLY DOME

# MAIN WALL, GRIZZLY DOME

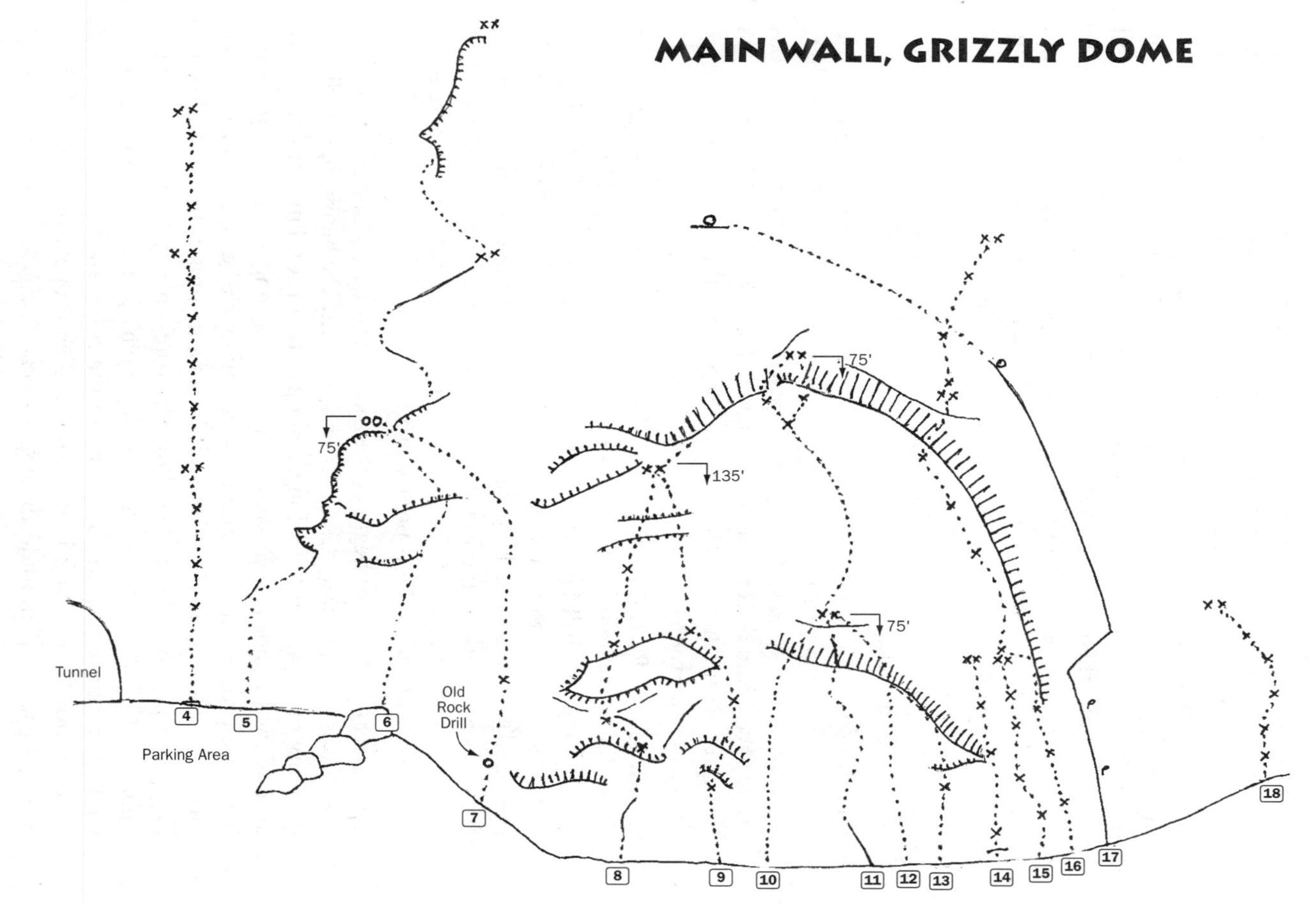

ascend pretty much directly up, clipping 3 more bolts. From the belay anchors, rappel the route.

5. **Regular Route** (I 5.7 or 5.10a) Locate this popular route by looking for a prominent, irregular-shaped, left-facing flake/corner 30' right of Route 4. Begin a few feet right of *Ursus Horribilis.* **Pitch 1:** Ascend easy face climbing for 35' to a smoother section. Make a long move right to enter the left-facing corner at an overhanging section. Pass the 5.6 overhang and follow the flake to belay chains at its top. **Pitch 2:** Traverse right and up to a bolt, then angle up left along a diagonal crack. Where it ends, make a few 5.5 moves upward, then slant up right along another diagonal crack to belay anchors. **Pitch 3:** Angle up left to a bolt, then head up right to an obvious, left-facing dihedral. Climb the 5.7 dihedral, then belay on a ledge at its top. Rappel the route. For a greater challenge, head more directly up from the first bolt on the second pitch, passing 2 more bolts and face climbing of up to 5.10b. Either way, take pro to 3".
6. **Old Toprope, a.k.a. Old Top Route** (5.9 R) As the name suggests, you may want to toprope this one. Begin 30' right of *Regular Route,* where the base of the rock suddenly drops down a bank reinforced with concrete. Face-climb directly up to the chains that mark the end of Route 5's first pitch. Note that this route has no bolts, and the gear placements are rather far apart. Take pro to 1".
7. **Zenith** (5.11a R) Locate the start of *Zenith* near the foot of the steep slope that leads down to the foot of the main face. About 8' up the rock, notice a cut-off drill bit left over from the construction of the Elephant Butte Tunnel. Climb up to the drill bit, which can be tied off for protection, and continue to a bolt. Just beyond, pass the crux, then angle up left, pass an overlap, and eventually work farther left to the chains atop the first pitch of Route 5. Take a few small wired nuts, but note that the upper part of this route is poorly protected.
8. **Bone Breaker** (I 5.10b) Begin at the foot of the steep slope that separates the climbs along Grizzly Creek from those near the highway, and directly below the lower end of a long, right-slanting roof. **Pitch 1:** Face-climb around the left side of a prominent, white overhang 35' up the face, passing three protection bolts and the crux along the way. Higher, clip two more bolts before arriving at the belay chains under the left end of the long, slanting roof. **Pitch 2:** Follow the roof up right until it meets the upper end of a prominent, left-curving arch. Clip a bolt, then make a wild 5.10a move past the overhang to the belay anchors. Rappel to the belay station shared with Routes 10–12, then rappel to the ground. Take pro to 1" if you plan to do the upper pitch.

9. **You're No Warren Harding** (5.8+) Start this route 10' right of *Bone Breaker,* below the left end of an obvious, white roof. Climb steep rock past 2 bolts, surmount the white roof at its left end, then continue up and somewhat left past another bolt to the anchors atop *Bone Breaker's* first pitch.
10. **Pennies from Heaven** (5.10a TR) Rig the toprope for this one by climbing the first pitch of *Space Bucket.* Starting 10' right of Route 9, head directly up to the white roof, pass over it a bit left of center, then angle up right to the anchors.
11. **Space Bucket** (I 5.10a) Begin this popular route—one of the finest on the crag—15' right of Route 10, where a short crack angles up left. **Pitch 1:** Jam the left-slanting crack, then face-climb (5.10a) up right to the white roof. Pass over it near its center, using another short, left-leaning crack, then head up right to the belay chains. **Pitch 2:** Work up right, then head straight up to a bolt 15' below the upper end of a large, left-curving arch. From here, either climb up left and use another bolt to protect the 5.10a move over the tip of the arch, or go directly up to a bolt and pass the arch (5.10b) at a wider spot. Either way, reach the anchors a few feet higher. Rappel the route. Take pro to 1".
12. **Spare Change** (5.10a) From a point 10' right of the initial crack of *Space Bucket,* face-climb straight up to the white roof, then pass over near its right side. Head up left to the belay anchor on Route 11.
13. **He's Got Woody Allen Eyes** (5.10a) Begin below the right end of the prominent white roof. Climb past a bolt (5.10a) to the roof, then join *Spare Change* as you surmount the roof and head up left to the anchors on Route 11. Rap off or continue up the second pitch of *Space Bucket.*
14. **Grizzly Terrace** (5.8) Don't be misled by the comparatively modest rating of this area classic—the intricate combination of moves necessary to maintain the 5.8 rating eludes many climbers. Begin below a small overlap that lies close to the ground and about 10' right of Route 13. Surmount the overlap, clip a bolt, then work up left to a bolt at the right end of the white roof. Angle up right to another bolt, then proceed straight up to the anchors.
15. **Fingergag** (5.10c) Locate the start of this route about midway between Route 14 and the lower end of the prominent, left-curving arch ascended by *Out of Order.* Face-climb past 4 bolts to a 3-bolt anchor, encountering the crux between the first 2 bolts.
16. **Out of Order** (I 5.10d) Begin below the lower end of the prominent, left-curving arch near the right side of the main face. **Pitch 1:** Face-climb past 3 bolts (5.10c/d) to the arch. Follow it until you can step left to the anchors atop Route 15. **Pitch 2:** Follow the arch, or face-climb just left

of it, passing 3 more bolts. From the upper bolt, make the crux move over the arch to reach the 3-bolt belay. **Pitch 3:** Work up right over easier ground, clipping 2 bolts, to the final belay anchors. Rappel the route. Supplement your selection of quickdraws with TCUs and stoppers to 1½".

17. **Broken Arrow** (I 5.7 R) Start this bold, early, traditional classic 20' right of *Out of Order,* where a thin crack slants up left. **Pitch 1:** Climb the crack and adjacent face to a fixed pin. Jog right, then follow the upper crack as it parallels the left-curving arch followed by Route 16. Make a semi-hanging belay near the top of the crack. **Pitch 2:** Reach the top of the crack, then follow a sketchy line of weakness up and far left, crossing *Out of Order*'s third pitch (clip a bolt here) and continuing run-out face climbing to a small ledge located about 70' above the top of the arch. You can rappel from here using a single rope by rappelling to the bolts atop *Space Bucket,* then rappelling that route. Take pro to 1½", including several small wires.
18. **To Bosch or Not To Be** (5.9+) From the base of *Broken Arrow,* walk right 40' to find the start of this quality sport route. Face-climb past 3 bolts, then work up left past 2 more to the belay chains. Pass the crux near the second bolt.

## TUNNEL WALL

The following climbs lie across Grizzly Creek from Grizzly Dome, near the upstream entrance of a tunnel through which Grizzly Creek flows. Despite the sometimes mild appearance of Grizzly Creek, the current can be dangerous. Do not attempt to cross to these routes until mid-summer!

19. **Each Year People Are Killed** (5.10d) Begin this route just left of the entrance to a small tunnel that empties into the main tunnel. Use an obvious eyebolt to anchor the belayer. Ascend the left margin of the side tunnel's opening (2 bolts), then continue up the face above past 2 more bolts to a pair of coldshuts and a bolt. Surmount the crux above the first bolt.
20. **Unnamed** (5.11a R) Start this harder version of Route 19 at a similar eyebolt near the right side of the side tunnel's opening. Climb the right side of the opening, then pass a small overlap and the crux before reaching the first of three bolts. Continue directly up to the anchors atop Route 19.
21. **Lust** (5.11c) Begin this long and strenuous classic at the right side of the entrance to the main tunnel. Ascend the wall at the tunnel's entrance, then work your way up right and out of the tunnel (5.11c). Continue up the face above to the belay/rappel chains. Pass the crux at the fourth of 7 bolts.

# BIG BALD ROCK

Big Bald Rock is one of the great surprises that await climbers exploring Northwest California. Despite the name, Big Bald Rock actually consists of a considerable number of big, bald rocks scattered over a 150-acre expanse of low-angle, bare granite slabs. The slabs themselves are warped and molded into a series of bowls, water pockets, shallow canyons, and elongated domes. As a result, the area combines variety, clean rock, easy access, and textbook rock features in ways reminiscent of both Yosemite and Joshua Tree.

The climbs themselves range from 10-foot boulder problems to 50-foot outcrops, and routes of all descriptions present themselves. Visiting climbers can sample thin cracks, hand cracks, offwidths, edging, friction, and chimneys. Difficulties range from third-class walk-ups to 5.12, and the area offers the potential for literally hundreds of routes.

Surprisingly, Big Bald has seen virtually no development of sport climbs; routes here are either toproped, bouldered, or led using traditional, leader-placed protection. Because of the numbers of non-climbers who also use the area, climbers should restrict any bolted sport route development to areas unfrequented by the general public to avoid creating any impression of defacing the rock. In the same vein, all climbers should use chalk sparingly, choosing rock-colored chalk when possible, and avoiding the temptation to tick holds.

An area as complex as Big Bald Rock defies a straight left-to-right arrangement of route descriptions. In general, directions and route descriptions appear in roughly the order they would to somebody approaching from the trail and heading for a particular formation. It may be necessary to back up to a previous formation's description to clarify the appropriate way to a specific rock.

**Climbing history:** Members of the Maidu and Yana Indian tribes were the first visitors to Big Bald Rock. The high point was at times used for spiritual observances, while hollows in the lower, more easily accessible areas saw duty as grindstones for the abundant local acorns. The history of climbing activity here has been cryptic, or sketchy at best. Sharp-eyed individuals may spot rusting, hangerless, quarter-inch Rawl-drive bolts here and there or the occasional crack-bound shrub with its bark abraded from rappel ropes. These signs attest to the presence of climbers dating back to the early 1970s. This area has received passing mention as a possible bouldering venue in a local guidebook and in two articles in old issues of *Summit* (October 1967 and September 1981). Other than these references and artifacts, little is known for certain, although local route developers such as Rob Settlemire, David Caunt, Eric Mayo, Rick Harlan, Tim Laughlin, Gary Adams, and Ron James probably made the first ascents of many of the obvious lines. There is still ample

# BIG BALD ROCK AND BALD ROCK DOME AREA MAP

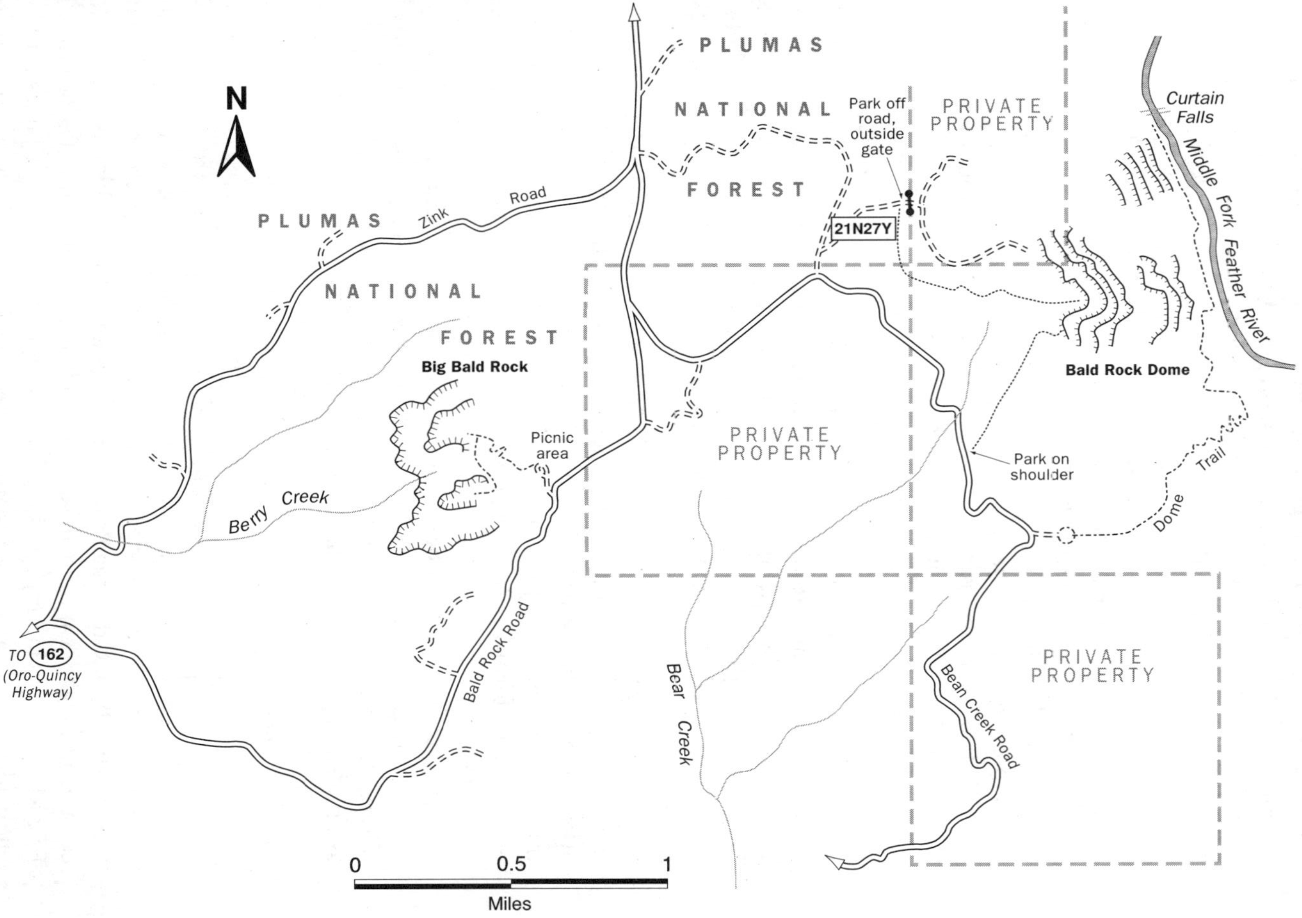

N

PLUMAS NATIONAL FOREST

Park off road, outside gate

PRIVATE PROPERTY

Curtain Falls

Middle Fork Feather River

21N27Y

PLUMAS NATIONAL FOREST

Zink Road

Big Bald Rock

Picnic area

PRIVATE PROPERTY

Bald Rock Dome

Park on shoulder

Dome Trail

Berry Creek

TO 162 (Oro-Quincy Highway)

Bald Rock Road

Bear Creek

Bean Creek Road

PRIVATE PROPERTY

0 0.5 1

Miles

# BIG BALD ROCK AREA MAP

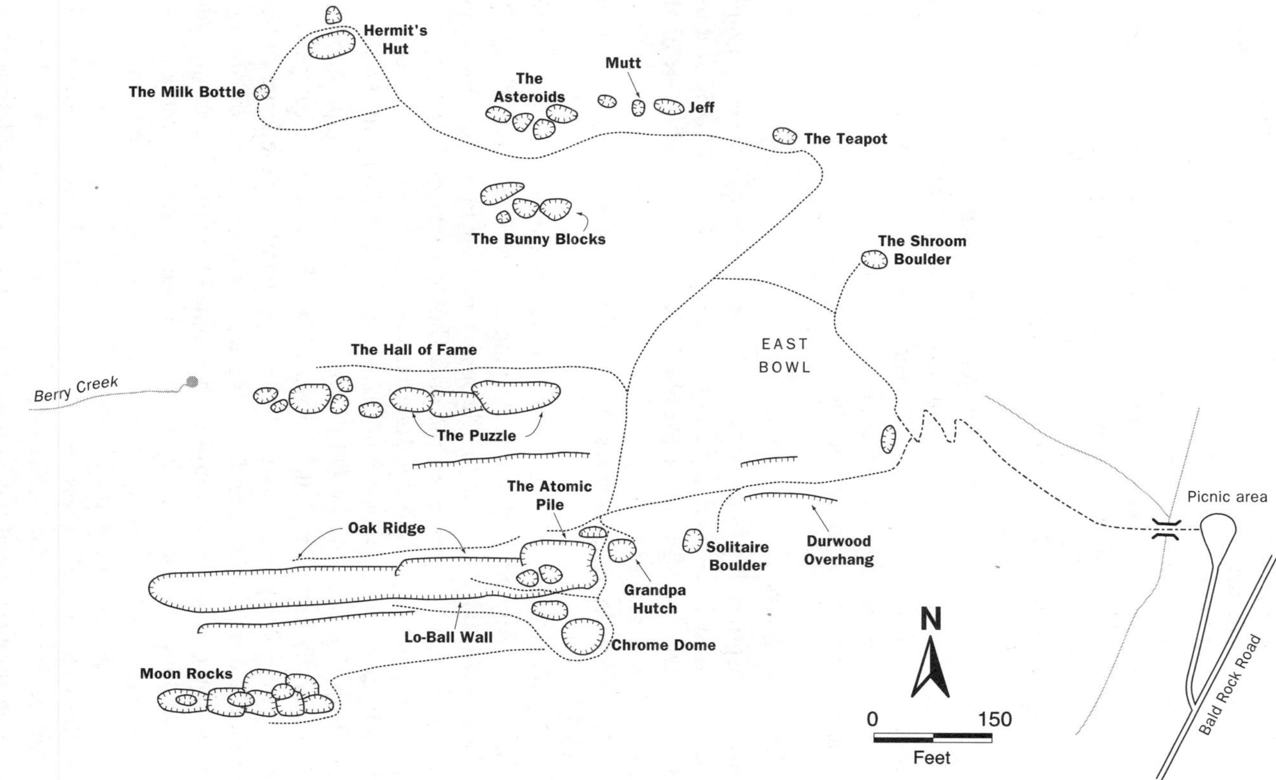

scope for scores of quality routes at all levels of difficulty, and Big Bald Rock remains far from being completely developed or documented.

**Rack:** Because most routes at Big Bald Rock can be toproped, you can get away with a modest rack if you like: several runners, a few quickdraws, and stoppers and hexes from ½" to 2". If you prefer to lead the longer routes, bring whatever you have. Cracks range from ¼" to over 8" in width. There are virtually no sport routes, so plan on placing your own pro. If you come to boulder, be sure to bring a crashpad, as nearly all climbs start from bare granite, and a slip could end your day with a sprained ankle or worse. Although the area generally lacks loose material atop the various formations, wearing a helmet is still a good idea.

**Descent:** You can generally scramble down from most formations. Occasionally, you encounter climbs that lack walk-off descents; most of the more popular ones have rappel/lowering bolts, but in some cases you may have to use some ingenuity to get down safely. If in doubt, scope out all sides of a formation prior to leaving the ground.

## TRIP PLANNING INFORMATION

**Area description:** Big Bald Rock is a 150-acre area of low-angle granite slabs punctuated by large boulders and walls ranging from 10 to 50 feet in height. These provide opportunities for climbs of all types and levels of difficulty from Class 4 to 5.12.

**Location:** In the northern Sierra Nevada foothills, overlooking Lake Oroville.

**Camping:** Although one could conceivably camp at the rock, it would be a bad idea. Any level spots for sleeping tend to be located in runoff gullies. There is virtually no soil for disposing of human waste, and firewood is scarce. Overnight visitors to the area should consider staying at the Milsap Bar Campground. Reach this 20-space Forest Service facility by continuing up Bald Rock Road another 4.9 miles to a signed junction with Forest Highway 62. Turn right and follow FH 62 for 7.2 miles to the campground entrance. Alternatively, return to Lake Oroville State Recreation Area for camping at the Bidwell Canyon or Loafer Bar campgrounds. These large campgrounds are located on the lake, and competition for sites is brisk on summer weekends. You can reserve a campsite by calling DESTINET (See Appendix D).

**Climbing season:** Reliably, March through November, but a dry spell during winter allows the area to open. Generally, if you reach the trailhead without encountering snow, the climbs will be dry.

**Restrictions and access issues:** Big Bald Rock is located on public land administered by the Oroville Ranger District of Plumas National Forest. It lies outside any designated wilderness area, so there are no administrative access issues to consider. All visitors should keep in mind the fragility of the area's vegetation, given the almost non-existent soil and seasonal scarcity of water.

Answering Nature's call anywhere on or near the rock is a bad idea; it's best to stop at a gas station on the way, or at least use the deeper soils near the trailhead. Because of thoughtless sanitation practices by some visitors each year, the water here should be considered unsafe to drink without boiling, filtration, or chemical purification. Visitors are generally better off bringing from home whatever they plan to drink.

In addition to these health and sanitation considerations, climbers must remember that this area receives a *lot* of use by non-climbers, many of whom will base their perceptions of climbing on what they see. It is therefore imperative to put forth a good image by picking up litter, avoiding the urge to use "strong" language, and being willing to patiently explain "how the rope gets up there."

**Guidebook:** Big Bald Rock is mentioned briefly in Robert Stahl's *Feather River Rock* (1989). Robert Hutchinson compiled and distributed—but never published—*Big Bald Rock Picnic Area: A Bouldering Guide* in the early 1980s. One of the few extant copies resides at Mountain Sports in Chico.

**Nearby mountain shops, guide services, and gyms:** The nearest sources for climbing gear and information are Mountain Sports and Sports Ltd. in Chico. There are no guide services, although groups from California State University, Chico occasionally use the area for instruction. The nearest climbing gym is Granite Arch in Rancho Cordova. California State University, Chico has a climbing gym on campus. It is open to non-students most evenings. Contact the university's outdoor center for more information.

**Services:** There are no services available at the rock. Water is available early in the season in several seasonal creeks, but because of the thin soils and relatively heavy visitor traffic, it is best to bring whatever you plan to drink.

**Emergency services:** In the event of an emergency, summon help by calling 911. The nearest hospital is Oroville Hospital in Oroville. The Berry Creek Health Center on Bald Rock Road does not offer emergency room services.

**Nearby climbing areas:** The nearest climbing area is the impressive and somewhat remote Bald Rock Dome. Other climbing can be found in the lower part of Feather River Canyon along California Highway 70.

**Nearby attractions:** Those seeking a break from climbing will find a visit to Feather Falls a rewarding experience. This 640-foot waterfall is the sixth highest in the country. Lake Oroville offers sunbathing and waterskiing, while the lake and the various forks of Feather River provide good fishing. For those seeking risk of another sort, the local Native American community offers two gambling establishments, Gold Country Casino and Feather Falls Casino.

**Finding the crag:** From the junction of California 70 and California Highway 162, drive east through the city of Oroville on CA 162/Oro-Quincy Highway, then head northeast, passing Lake Oroville. At 19.2 miles, turn right at a signed junction onto Bald Rock Road. Follow Bald Rock Road 7.3 miles to a signed spur road leading left a hundred yards to the Bald Rock

Trailhead. Follow the easy, shaded trail 300 yards to the curious moonscape of Big Bald Rock. Once the trail ends, you can reach the various climbing areas by walking and scrambling across acres of granite slabs. Take note of the way back to the trail; it's easy to make a mistake and head back down the wrong bowl.

**Author's Note:** Where and when possible, the original names of climbs here (as given in Robert Hutchinson's pioneer bouldering guide) have been noted; however, many of the routes described by Hutchinson are either unnamed or are all but impossible to identify accurately. Names given are those in current use, followed by their names in the earlier guide.

## SOUTH SUMMIT AREA

The south summit of Big Bald Rock consists of a rising series of narrow, east-west corrugations culminating in the elongated, fin-like dome of Oak Ridge. Because this area is the highest part of the rock and offers the finest view, it has attracted the most visitor activity. The climbs range from 10 to over 50 feet in length and span the gamut of difficulty from walk-up to the most severe tests of climbing skill.

Access this area by passing left of the first large boulder encountered on the approach trail. Once you leave the trees, head up a broad, shallow, slabby ravine. Near the top, you meet the first of many noteworthy problems: Durwood Overhang.

## DURWOOD OVERHANG

Durwood Overhang is the nearly level, eight-foot wall on the left near the upper end of the approach ravine. The impressive six-foot roof that runs most of the length of the wall is unmistakable.

1. **Durwood Left** (5.10c) Ascend the left-hand, narrow, flared crack that splits the roof. If you're a glutton for punishment, try a sit-down start to make the climb 5.11a.
2. **Durwood Right** (5.10d) Climb the right-hand roof splitter. Again, a sit-down start really cranks up the difficulty.
3. **The Lip** (5.11a) Starting 15' right of Route 2, make a difficult pull over the roof.

## SOLITAIRE BOULDER

As a warmup for the ferocious cracks of The Atomic Pile, visit this interesting formation. From the top of Durwood Overhang, head south, aiming for a large boulder near a good-sized liveoak. Route 5 easily identifies the formation.

4. **Left Arete** (5.10a) Pull and balance your way up the arete on the southeast side of the boulder. Save some energy for the final mantle.

5. **Solitaire** (5.10a) Climb the offset, left-leaning hand crack that splits the east side of this triangular formation. For variety, you can also try liebacking the crack.
6. **Right Arete** (5.10a/b) Follow the arete right of Route 5, keeping in mind that the difficulties are largely height-dependent.

## GRANDPA HUTCH

Grandpa Hutch is the huge boulder immediately east of The Atomic Pile. Its smooth flanks all overhang at the bottom, providing interesting entry problems.

7. **Wide World of Sports** (5.10c/5.11a TR) Using a shoulderstand or cheater rock, the northeast face is 5.10c. Without, it's more like 5.11a. The other faces and aretes are harder. The original guide shows a bolt on top and one on the southeast arete, but these were missing in 1999. You may have to throw a rope over the top for protection and rappelling.

## THE ATOMIC PILE, A.K.A. THE HACKY SACK AREA

The Atomic Pile is the impressive collection of large blocks that forms the highest point of Big Bald Rock. This formation offers the finest collection of crack climbs in the area, including a particularly demanding local testpiece. There are 3/8-inch bolts in place atop several of these climbs, offering convenient toprope anchors. Approach this obvious formation by walking up slabs from the north or east. Scramble up the southeast side and pass through a notch to reach the toprope anchors.

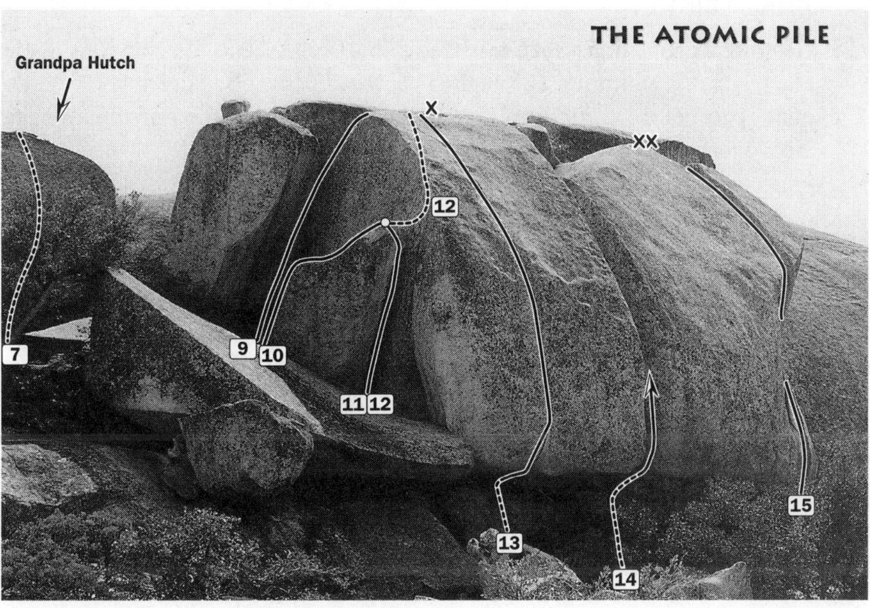

8. **Rockin' It** (5.8) This strenuous offwidth/squeeze chimney on the southeast side of The Atomic Pile is easily identified by the "rock in it."
9. **Above-Ground Test** (5.9+) Begin in a shaded alcove around the corner right of Route 8 and jam the obvious, overhanging, wide crack in the flared corner. Best done with a toprope.
10. **Twinkie Left** (5.7) The Twinkie is the detached block that encloses the alcove on the northeast side of The Atomic Pile. Ascend the offwidth up the formation's left side.
11. **Twinkie Right** (5.9) Grunt up the offwidth/squeezer on the right side of The Twinkie. On either of the *Twinkie* routes, you can lower off with a toprope from higher up. If leading, take a long runner for the rap off.
12. **Got Milk?** (5.10d) Ascend either of the *Twinkie* routes, then make difficult face moves up right, swing up over the arete, and ascend much easier friction to the top. Even with a toprope, there is considerable risk of injury if you fall at the crux—be careful.
13. **Reactor, a.k.a. Hacky Sack** (5.11d/5.12a) This classic off-fingers-to-thin-hands splitter looks like no more than a 5.9 from a distance. Up close, however, you find that the start is a tips-only roof. Even bridging out to the lip from the shelf underneath, you face an appalling pull up on loose finger-jams. The crack widens higher up, so once past the lip, enjoy the cruise. If leading, take wired nuts and cams from ⅜" to 2½".
14. **Critical Mass** (5.8) From the shelf below the north side of The Atomic Pile, launch upward into the flared squeeze chimney 10' right of *Reactor* and thrutch your way to the top. You can anchor a toprope by tying off a large bollard.
15. **Ground Zero, a.k.a. Slice and Dice** (5.10b) Ascend the obvious wide crack/squeeze chimney 20' right of *Critical Mass*. Be sure to place adequate pro before committing to the overhanging middle portion and the crux overhang. Take cams to 4".
16. **Gone Fission** (5.8) Lieback or face-climb the big, right-facing dihedral that forms the right side of The Atomic Pile. Belay at a trio of bolts under the summit block. Either walk off up right, or finish up left via a short, easy crack.

## OAK RIDGE

Oak Ridge, named for the abundant live oaks in the area, is the long, finger-like dome extending west from The Atomic Pile. In contrast to the Pile's ferocious cracks, climbs on Oak Ridge are mostly face routes. In general, difficulties ease the farther west (i.e., downhill) you begin. A use trail skirts the foot of the formation. There are numerous walk-off descent routes, or you can lower off or rappel from paired bolts under the summit block.

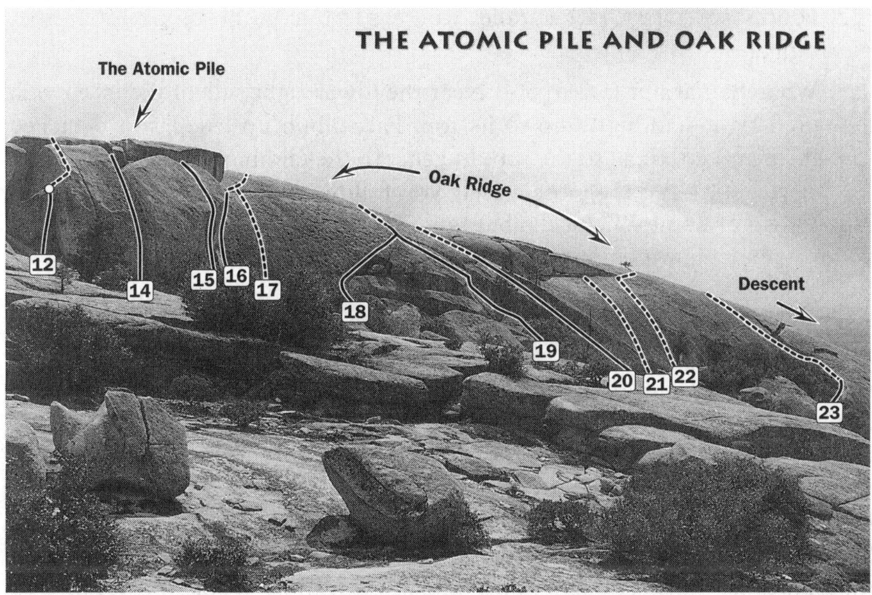


17. **Shadow of a Doubt** (5.10a TR) Using a pair of bolts under the summit block for toprope protection, climb almost anywhere up the bulging face right of *Gone Fission.*
18. **Squirrel Nut Zipper** (5.8) Begin below the left end of a prominent ledge atop a huge detached block right of Route 17. Climb a tricky, right-leaning crack up right to the ledge. Follow a thinner continuation of the crack to its end on the face above, then friction to the top. Take pro to 3". You can also reach the ledge via an easy scramble from its right end. In case you were wondering, the name commemorates a popular New England candy bar.
19. **Double Cracks** (5.5) Locate the start of this popular route at the foot of an obvious crack system that slants up left to meet the top of the crack followed by Route 18. Follow the wide crack up to a small tree, then continue up left along your choice of cracks until they end. From here, friction to the top of the rock.
20. **Garden Party** (5.0) Beginning 25' right of *Double Cracks,* follow a wide crack/ramp system up left to the top. Runners around small trees provide adequate protection.
21. **Pick Your Poison** (5.9+ TR) From the foot of a ramp that slants up left a few yards right of Route 20, ascend the broad white streak up the steep wall above. Use cracks in the exfoliation slab atop the face to anchor your toprope.

22. **Footloose** (5.10a TR) Parallel Route 21, but begin about 15' farther right.
23. **Whatchamacallit** (5.2 to 5.4) Near the lower right side of the face, walk up a right-slanting ramp to its top. Face-climb up left past a detached flake and continue to the top. In general, the climbing is easier the higher you start and the more closely you follow the flakes.

**Note:** Right of Route 23, the climbing generally reverts to easy slab-walking, but you may find a few interesting problems near the far west end of the ridge.

## LO-BALL WALL, A.K.A. EASY WALL

Lo-Ball Wall is the long, low, south face of Oak Ridge. Starting as a short wall near its eastern end, it becomes a gully wall toward its western terminus. Many short face climbs ranging from 5.6 to 5.11a ascend this wall.

## CHROME DOME

Chrome Dome is the small, dome-like formation southeast of The Atomic Pile and due south of Grandpa Hutch. Its steep flanks offer many opportunities for enjoyable, toproped face climbs (and a few lead climbs) in the 5.6 to 5.11 range.

24. **Out of It** (5.9 R) Locate this interesting face climb by watching for its protection bolt 15' off the deck on the south side of the formation. Ascend a wide, shallow groove, clip the bolt, then face-climb to the top. Do not attempt this route if you are new to climbing at this level; missing the clip could have dire results.

## MOON ROCKS, A.K.A. MUSCLE BUTT AREA

This impressive pile of large boulders lies southwest of Lo-Ball Wall and is best approached by walking around the east and south sides of The Atomic Pile, passing below the south side of Chrome Dome. As the area's name suggests, the large, rounded stones bear a striking resemblance to you-know-what. Most routes follow the cracks formed where adjacent rocks come together. It is possible to scramble off the formation, or you can rappel from anchors on top. Routes not shown.

25. **Muscle Butt** (5.10a) This is the classic, flaring, overhanging corner crack just right of the westernmost rock's south face. Follow awkward thin-hands jamming to great finger jams at the top.
26. **Pain in the Butt** (5.8) Climb the off-width crack right of Route 25 to a pair of bolts under a boulder atop the formation.
27. **Baywatch** (5.8) Mimic Route 26, using off-width and face-climbing techniques to climb the right-hand crack on the south side of the formation. There may still be a pair of bolts on top.

## THE ATOMIC PILE, OAK RIDGE, AND THE HALL OF FAME

28. **One-piece** (5.10a) On the north side of the formation, ascend the crack and face that lead to the easternmost erratic on top.

## THE HALL OF FAME

The Hall of Fame is the narrow, secluded gully that separates the major ridges of the north and south summits. In addition to numerous boulder problems, it offers challenging short climbs on The Puzzle, a.k.a. Steep Wall, a wooded, three-part, north-facing wall near its upper end.

29. **Eileen** (5.10c) Beginning below the left end of the prominent roof that crosses the left end of The Puzzle, face-climb up to the roof, then follow a wide, left-leaning crack through the roof and up the face above. Take pro to 3".
30. **Streakers' Ball** (5.11b TR) Start as for *Eileen,* but ascend the crux roof directly and continue up a pale waterstreak to the top.
31. **Hanging Teeth** (5.12a TR) From a light-colored area of rock below the central part of the roof, surmount a small overhang, then work up right onto a right-slanting ramp (crux). From the ramp, make a scary, difficult mantle onto the face above the roof and friction to the top. It may be possible to lead this route, but it's a dangerous proposition.
32. **Jigsaw** (5.10b) Beginning near the right side of the left section of The Puzzle, jam a left-leaning crack, which eventually curves sharply left along the bottom of a flake. Follow it to the top. Take pro to 2½".
33. **Corner Piece** (5.8) Ascend the crack that separates the left and middle portions of The Puzzle. Nuts or cams to 2" provide adequate protection.
34. **Meddle** (5.12a TR) Face-climb the center of The Puzzle's middle block.
35. **As If** (5.9) Follow the deep, nearly vertical corner separating the middle and right-hand blocks of The Puzzle. Take pro to 3".
36. **Clueless** (5.11d TR) Ascend the arete that forms the right-hand edge of the far-right block of The Puzzle.
37. **Restless** (5.9) Climb the deep, narrow chimney 30' right of Route 36.

## THE NORTH SUMMIT AREA

In contrast to the south summit of Big Bald Rock, the north summit is a vast, low-angle slab dotted with numerous large boulders. Where the south summit attracts crack climbers and those interested in its wall climbs, the north is the realm of the boulderers. Climbs on the outbuilding-size blocks range from two- or three-move warmups to longer problems best attempted with a toprope. Climbs here span the gamut from about 5.5 to 5.12d, and there is considerable potential for many quality new routes. Most of the boulders lack walk-off descents, so climbers must be prepared to either downclimb or lower

SOUTH SIDE OF BIG BALD ROCK'S NORTH SUMMIT
The Asteroids
Mutt
Jeff
50
51
49
46
44
43
41
40
The Bunny Blocks
John Gill
Memorial
Boulder
62
61
58

off. This may in some cases involve being let down the opposite side of the rock from one's belayer.

Access this area by keeping right once you come to the first large boulder blocking the route of the approach trail. Follow the path through liveoaks and arrive at the foot of East Bowl, a broad, shallow hollow that leads up to the ridge connecting the north and south summit areas. Head north along the ridgetop, then walk west on the pavement-like top of the ridge to the first pair of boulders. Route descriptions for the north summit proper begin here.

## EAST BOWL

Although East Bowl contains little to interest most climbers, a notable exception is The Shroom Boulder, a conspicuous rock shaped like an inverted cone, situated about halfway up the north side of the bowl.

38. **Shroom** (5.9) You may find the mantle onto the top of the boulder's south side harder than it appears. Definitely use a crashpad and a spotter.

## THE TEAPOT

The Teapot, named for its distinctive shape, is the first large boulder encountered on the north summit's ridgetop.

39. **Spouting Off** (5.8) Make a lunge or off-balance face moves to reach the "spout," then mantle onto the top.

## MUTT AND JEFF

This conspicuous pair of large boulders lies less than 100 yards west of The Teapot. The origin of Mutt and Jeff, like that of numerous other boulders here, is somewhat of a mystery: they are not glacial erratics, nor are they debris from some higher, larger formation. In any case, they provide excellent bouldering. Jeff, the larger, egg-shaped boulder, presents short, fierce problems that generally involve passing its overhung base via thin edges. Mutt offers more distinct routes up its more angular faces. It is possible to rig a toprope by throwing a rope over the top of either boulder.

40. **Jeff—Southeast Arete** (5.10c) Use sometimes subtle combinations of face holds to ascend the bulging, rounded, outside corner.
41. **Jeff—South Face** (5.11a) Climb the left side of the boulder's south face, incorporating a small dish high on the rock.
42. **Valley View** (5.10a-5.10d) Start at the northwest corner of the rock. Leave the ground, then head out left onto the north face. Head up for easier going, or continue farther left for more of a challenge.
43. **Mutt—Southeast Face** (5.9-5.10b) Ascend the nearly vertical face, finding the most challenging moves near its center.

44. **Mutt Arete** (5.9) Begin as for Route 43, but work up left along the lip of the overhanging base of the boulder's south side. From a bucket at the apex of the overhang, follow the fun 5.7 arete between the southeast and south faces.

45. **Mutt Arete—Direct** (5.10d) Start below the overhang on the rock's south side. Using a heel hook, mantle into the bucket at the apex of the overhang. Finish via Route 44.

46. **Mongrel** (5.11b) Climb Route 45 to the bucket, then step left and ascend the steep, smooth face above, resisting the temptation to use holds on the arete.

## THE ASTEROIDS

Immediately west of Mutt and Jeff lie The Asteroids, a group of several closely spaced, large boulders. In addition to face climbing, these also offer short, flared chimneys between the rocks.

47. **The Birdbath** (5.9) Notice a large bucket at the top of the overhanging east face of the boulder nearest Mutt and Jeff. Starting below this feature, ascend flakes and thin cracks, then make a tricky mantle into the bucket and scramble to the top.

48. **Fingerbowl** (5.11a) Climb *The Birdbath,* but instead of making the mantle into the large bucket, work up right and mantle into a smaller, higher bucket. The earlier you head up right, the harder the climbing becomes.

49. **Hit and Miss** (5.10c) Start this face climb just right of a wide, shallow rib on the south face of the largest of The Asteroids. As you climb, stay on or right of the rib.
50. **Mars Bars** (5.8) Begin in the flared chimney 10' left of Route 49. Face climb up and slightly right.
51. **Sandy Claws** (5.7) Follow the flared chimney 10' left of Route 49. You can also use this route as a means of descent.

Locate the following several routes on the north side of The Asteroids, beginning with *Eros,* a deep corner, which is actually the "back side" of *Mars Bars.*

52. **Eros** (5.10b) Use the wide crack/squeeze chimney if you dare; otherwise, face-climb until you can pull over the roof to the top.
53. **Meteor** (5.10a TR) Using liebacks, ascend the left side of the arete between *Eros* and the deep squeeze chimney to the right. Use a bolt at the top for a toprope anchor.
54. **Meat-Eater** (5.10c TR) Climb this mirror image of Route 53, using liebacks to go up the right side of the same arete. Anchor to the bolt at the top.
55. **Maneater** (5.10d TR) On the arete just right of the deep squeeze chimney right of Routes 53 and 54, use the same lieback techniques to ascend the blunt arete. Use a bolt on top to anchor your toprope.
56. **Mantichore** (5.11a TR) If you haven't yet had enough, climb the right side of the *Maneater* arete. Anchor to the bolt on top.
57. **Asteroid Bash** (5.8) Climb the steep, juggy arete on the northwest end of the formation.

## THE BUNNY BLOCKS, A.K.A. BREAD LOAF BOULDERS

The Bunny Blocks is the isolated cluster of angular boulders 100' downhill toward The Hall of Fame from The Asteroids. Strenuous mantles, thin edges, slopers, and clean-cut aretes typify the climbs here. The following four routes climb John Gill Memorial Boulder, the easternmost of these blocks.

58. **Mission Impossible** (5.12a) This is one of the best routes at Big Bald. Climb the difficult face and arete on the northeast side of John Gill Memorial Boulder.
59. **Mission Improbable** (5.11c/d) Begin near the right side of the uphill face of the boulder, then face-climb to the top, using tiny edges and "improbable" slopers.
60. **JGMB Arete** (5.9) Follow the northwest arete of the boulder.

61. **Hare-d Out** (5.10a) On the south (downhill) side of the formation, jam the difficult off-width where John Gill Memorial Boulder nearly touches the other Bunny Blocks.
62. **Hugh Hefner** (5.10a) Jam or face-climb the wide crack 15' left of Route 61.

## HERMIT'S HUT

Near the northwest end of the high ridge that forms the north summit, some enterprising person has used blocks of local stone to wall-in the severe overhang on the northeast side of a giant boulder to form a rude shelter. The Hermit's Hut boulder provides a number of excellent problems. These are lengthy, however, and should not be attempted without a crashpad and spotter or a belay.

63. **Flea on a Hippo** (5.9) On the opposite side of the boulder from the stone hut, surmount the overhang on rounded holds and proceed up much easier climbing to the top. Use this route as a means of descent—best with a crash pad.
64. **El Hermano** (5.10d) Follow the arete that separates the *Flea* face from the vertical northwest face.
65. **Not Fade Away** (5.11b/c) Begin 10' left of Route 64. Use small slopers to climb the overhanging face, then edge or dyno to the arete of *El Hermano*. Follow that route to the top.

66. **Ramblin' Recluse** (5.9) Start under the sharp overhang just right of the stone hut. Pass the overhang on its left side, then follow knobs and shallow cracks up left. Where the cracks end, face climb to the top.
67. **Reckless Recluse** (5.11a) Begin as for Route 66. At the overhang, head left along an overlap, then move up left to a thin crack. follow it to its end, then connect with Route 66 to finish.

### THE MILK BOTTLE

About a hundred yards or so southwest of Hermit's Hut stands a small, isolated pinnacle with a distinctive, milk-bottle shape. The uphill side requires only a short scramble, but the other faces provide interesting bouldering up to 5.10a.

## BALD ROCK DOME

*(See Big Bald Rock Dome area map on p. 234)*

High above the yawning chasm of the Middle Fork Feather River stands formidable-looking Bald Rock Dome. Like its many cousins found in river canyons all along the west side of the Sierra Nevada Range, Bald Rock Dome is an unglaciated crag of exfoliating granite, steep near its base and gradually easing in angle higher up. The dome is particularly attractive, with its tawny orange stripes and an extensive system of thin, raised dikes, which give the rock the appearance of having a giant net draped over it. The rock is clean, and even the few moderate routes are very aesthetic. The granite itself is rather curious; in many places, it has weathered into a sort of "lizard skin" of coarse crystals protruding from a smoother background.

Bald Rock Dome consists of the 600-foot main dome, divided into two lobes by a major system of openbooks and cracks; a lower-angle formation immediately to the south; and a large and complex series of walls and slabs that lead from the sandy ledge at the foot of the main dome all the way down to the roaring, green water of Feather River. Stairmaster Slab, a huge, comparatively low-angle apron capped by a 50-foot headwall, is the most accessible of these and offers much new route potential.

Routes on Bald Rock Dome generally use face climbing to link other features, such as flakes, intermittent cracks, dikes, and small ledges. Nearly all were established using traditional climbing techniques, which means that all protection bolts were placed on-lead, wherever and whenever it was feasible to do so. This ethic has led to the rather unfortunate characteristic of most of these climbs: long runouts, sometimes on very tricky ground. On some climbs, the leader faces the sobering prospect of a potential 200-foot fall. Visitors should be aware that most of the bolts on older routes were of the quarter-inch Rawl-drive variety and would be of questionable value in holding a fall. Bruce Hart of Mountain Sports in Chico is currently spearheading a local effort to replace these old bolts with stout new bolts and hangers. Bolt

*Bald Rock Dome.*

replacement is a slow process, so visitors may not find bombproof anchors on all routes. Difficulties range from 5.7 to 5.11a, and, although most major lines on the main dome have been climbed, much unclimbed rock remains, both on the dome and on the faces beside and below it.

Route descriptions listed follow the traditional, left-to-right arrangement, beginning near the top of the approach gully immediately south of the dome. Climbers approaching from below should note that they first reach the main dome near the start of *English Breakfast Squirrel.*

**Climbing history:** Bald Rock Dome was well known to members of the Yana and Maidu Indian tribes in the old days. They knew it as "*U-I-No,* the Monster of the Middle Fork." Its reputation as the abode of a local demon kept prehistoric visits to an understandable minimum.

The crag's climbing history began with Joe Kelsey's 1967 ascent of the huge corner system that splits the east face of the dome. Kelsey, who is generally credited with the discovery of Bald Rock Dome as a climbing resource, later climbed one of the dome's longest routes, a classic face-and-crack route he named *The Grove* (II 5.9). On a 1971 visit to repeat Kelsey's classic, Craig Neilson and Richard Waller added a direct start to the route, giving it its now-accepted line of ascent. Word of the crag's potential spread, and in 1977, Brian Conry, Mark Turner, and Bob Reimer put up *Fear and Loathing* (II 5.9 R) near the east edge of the south face. Their route was the first to challenge the dome's largely crackless face, relying almost entirely on leader-placed bolts for protection. In 1978, Neilson returned with Gary Adams and Rob Settlemire to establish what would become one of the rock's most popular routes, *Moroccan Roll* (II 5.7). That same year saw a return visit from Conry, who, with Howard Paul, established *Uncle Ben's Fine Line* (I 5.10a R) high up on the dome's left side.

The 1980s was the golden age of route development on Bald Rock Dome, and the most important climbing figure of this era as Rob Settlemire, who established nearly all the new routes. An exception to the Settlemire reign was the 1980 classic *Bit of Honey* (II 5.10c R), established by Eric Mayo and Stan Miller. Settlemire responded with *Foxtrot* (II 5.9), teaming with Steve Schneider for the job. The following year, Settlemire produced a direct variation to *Fear and Loathing—Paradox* (II 5.11a)—with Dave Caunt. That fall, a Settlemire/Mayo collaboration (with Rick Harlan) put up *Fleet Street* (I 5.10a), a more direct and logical start to *Bit of Honey.* In 1982, Settlemire and Caunt created the first sport route on Bald Rock Dome, naming their new route *Order Yours Now* (5.10c). Within days of *Order Yours Now,* Tim Sorenson and Jim Thoen put up the impressive and popular *Burning Giraffes* (II 5.9 R), which follows a line just left of the nose of the dome. Mayo and Harlan came back in 1983, establishing *Flying Lizards* (I 5.9) near the top of the approach gully. In 1985, Settlemire and Caunt accounted for three new sport routes: *Nuns for Fun* (5.10d), *Praying Mantle* (5.11a), and *Smooth Operator* (5.10a). Quiet returned to the dome for two years, then Settlemire and Ron James climbed *All You Can Eat* (5.9+) and *Twyla* (I 5.9). *Twyla* was Settlemire's last new route, but an impressed and inspired James came back in 1989 and climbed the bold and run-out *English Breakfast Squirrel* (I 5.9 R) with Tim Laughlin.

The early 1990s marked the last period of significant new route development. Laughlin became the dome's torchbearer, putting up the run-out dike-walk *Right of the Grove* (II 5.9 R/X) with Gary Jacobs in 1990 and its direct start, *Jolly Rancher* (II 5.9 R), with Linda Ryan in 1991. Since that time, access problems have caused route development to languish, but the established routes explore only a portion of Bald Rock Dome's wealth of slabs and walls. The Monster of the Middle Fork is far from vanquished.

**Rack:** Because most of the climbing on Bald Rock Dome ascends bolted slabs, your rack should include eight to ten quickdraws. Add to these an assortment of RPs, stoppers, hexes, and cams to 2½ inches, emphasizing sizes one inch and smaller. Be sure to include several runners to reduce rope drag. You may wish to bring a bolt kit, or at least a few hangers, just in case. A number of old bolts on some routes need replacing, but don't add more protection bolts to established routes. Considering the potential for really long falls on some climbs, your helmet should not stay at home or in the car.

**Descent:** Descend from the top of Bald Rock Dome by either scrambling off left under a short wall at the summit, or making multiple two-rope rappels. If you took the upper approach, you can head out from here; otherwise, descend the slabby gully left of the dome and make the long scramble down to the Dome Trail approach route.

## TRIP PLANNING INFORMATION

**Area description:** Bald Rock Dome is a complex assemblage of granite walls and slabs, culminating in a beautiful, Yosemite-like dome nearly 600' high. The summit elevation of only 3,902' promises generally mild weather and nearly year-round access.

**Location:** In the northern Sierra Nevada foothills, overlooking the Middle Fork of Feather River.

**Camping:** Although one could conceivably camp at the dome, it would be a bad idea. Campfires are out due to the risk of fire in this brushy area; most level spots for sleeping tend to be located in runoff gullies; there is no readily available water; and there is virtually no soil for disposing of human waste. Overnight visitors to the area should consider staying at the Milsap Bar Campground. Reach this 20-space Forest Service facility by continuing up Bald Rock Road another 4.9 miles to a signed junction with Forest Highway 62. Turn right and follow FH 62 for 7.2 miles to the campground entrance. Alternatively, return to Lake Oroville State Recreation Area for camping at the Bidwell Canyon or Loafer Bar Campgrounds. These large campgrounds are located on the lake, and competition for sites is brisk on summer weekends. You can reserve a campsite by calling DESTINET (See Appendix D).

**Climbing season:** Reliably, March through November, but even in winter, a dry spell allows the area to open for climbing. Generally, if you can reach the trailhead without encountering snow, the climbs will be dry. Early in the season, you can often get in and out via the Dome Trail before most of the poison oak leafs out.

**Restrictions and access issues:** Bald Rock Dome is located on public land administered by the Oroville Ranger District of Plumas National Forest. It lies outside any designated wilderness area, so there are no administrative access issues to consider. However, much of the land in this general area—signed or not—is private, and some landowners have reportedly greeted unwanted visitors with gunfire. To maintain a healthy relationship with landowners, please respect their privacy and choose an approach route that keeps you well away from all private property. Be sure to park as far off the traveled way as you can when heading into the woods; don't ruin your welcome by blocking anyone's right-of-way. Respect the fragility of the area's vegetation, as well as its community of animals. Do not disturb any nest you may find on the crags. Considering the thinness of soils adjacent to most climbing areas, you should consider all surface water unsafe to drink without boiling, filtration, or chemical disinfection.

**Guidebook:** Robert Stahl's *Feather River Rock* (1989) provides good, concise coverage of climbs in the Feather River region. If you are using Stahl's guide, however, note that the Bald Rock Dome access route listed is out-of-date. Bald Rock Dome was also described to some extent in *Summit* (October 1967 and September 1981).

**Nearby mountain shops, guide services, and gyms:** The nearest sources for climbing gear and information are Mountain Sports and Sports Ltd. in Chico. There are no guide services, although groups from California State University, Chico occasionally visit the area. The nearest climbing gym is Granite Arch in Rancho Cordova. California State University, Chico has a climbing gym on campus. It is open to non-students most evenings. Contact the university's outdoor program for more information.

**Services:** There are no services available at the rock. Water is available in spring in several seasonal creeks and springs, but these water sources dry up later in the summer. It is best to bring whatever you plan to drink.

**Emergency services:** In the event of an emergency, summon help by calling 911. The nearest hospital is Oroville Hospital in Oroville. The Berry Creek Health Center on Bald Rock Road does not offer emergency room services.

**Nearby climbing areas:** The nearest climbing area is popular Big Bald Rock. Other climbing can be found in the lower part of Feather River Canyon along California Highway 70.

**Nearby attractions:** Continuing on the Dome Trail past the staircase to trail's end, hikers come to picturesque Curtain Falls. The cool green of the Feather River roaring below provides a pleasant ambiance for hiking or climbing. A very worthwhile side trip off California Highway 162 on Forbestown Road leads to Feather Falls. This 640-foot waterfall is the sixth highest in the country. Lake Oroville offers sunbathing and waterskiing, while the lake and the various forks of Feather River provide good fishing. For those seeking risk of another sort, the local Native American community offers two gambling establishments, Gold Country Casino and Feather Falls Casino.

**Finding the crag:** From the junction of California 70 and California 162, drive east through the city of Oroville on CA 162/Oro-Quincy Highway, then head northeast, passing Lake Oroville. At 19.2 miles, turn right at a signed junction onto Bald Rock Road. At 2.7 miles, pass an intersection with Zink Road on the left. Meet Zink Road again at a four-way intersection at 8.6 miles and turn right onto an unmarked forest road. From here, you have your choice of two routes.

To reach the crag from above (formerly the shortest route, but now complicated by private land ownership and the need to avoid trespassing), proceed for 1 mile to a dirt road leading left. Turn left onto this road (Forest Road 21N27Y) and drive a few hundred yards to a locked gate. From here, your challenge is to head east-southeast to the crag, keeping a respectful distance from the private property line. As recently as the early 1990s, it was possible to drive to the end of this road, which terminates at an overlook a few hundred yards north of the summit of Bald Rock Dome. A subsequent change in ownership now requires visitors to bushwhack through giant manzanita and dense forest interspersed with boulders and gullies. In general, head for the edge of the deep gorge of Feather River, get your bearings, and proceed from there. Reach the foot of the dome by descending a steep, slabby gully situated between the main dome and a lower-angled subsidiary formation to the south. Note that this gully is prone to seepage well into spring, creating dangerously slick footing.

You can avoid the risk of trespassing by taking the lower approach. Once you turn onto the unmarked forest road at the four-way intersection, proceed past the junction with FR 21N27Y and proceed a total of 2.7 miles, keeping left at all major intersections, to the parking area for the Dome Trail, a Forest Service scenic trail. Follow the track down the crest of a ridge, then turn left and begin an amazing and seemingly endless series of switchbacks. At 1.7 miles, come to a rock streambed—the lower extension of the upper approach route's gully. Leave the trail here and scramble up the left side of the gully for hundreds of feet to the foot of the dome. If that seems like too much work, continue down the trail another 0.3 mile to an incongruous flight of stairs with metal railings. Just above and east of here is Stairmaster Slab, a relatively low-angle apron surmounted by an impressive headwall. Neither has seen any serious development, although both offer potential for many interesting climbs. Although the lower approach is on trail most of the way, keep in mind that returning via this route involves close to 1,000 feet of elevation gain! Also, the trail is flanked by a particularly populous community of poison oak. Take your pick.

The following routes are described from left to right, in the order they are encountered on the upper approach.

1. **Flying Lizards** (I 5.9) Notice a pair of parallel cracks about 25' apart that slant up and right from the access gully at a point about 300' from its top. **Pitch 1:** Head up right along the upper crack to a belay spot atop a flake. **Pitch 2:** Face climb up left to a bolt, then proceed more directly

upward (5.9) to a second bolt. Angle left to a flake. From its far end, angle up right past another bolt to a long, left-slanting crack. Follow it up left to a belay spot where the crack jogs. (There is reportedly a fixed pin here, but don't count on it.) **Pitch 3:** Continue up the crack, encountering some 5.8 climbing before passing over a small overhang. Continue along the intermittent crack until you reach a more fractured, water-streaked area, then friction up right to a belay on lower-angled slabs. **Pitch 4:** Ascend easy slabs to the top. Take protection up to 2".

2. **Uncle Ben's Fine Line** (I 5.10a R) Begin 25' right of Route 1, at the foot of the lower of the two parallel, right-slanting cracks. **Pitch 1:** Head up right along the crack to a two-bolt belay on a sloping ledge. **Pitch 2:** Follow the crack (5.7) past a bolt, jogging up left along an intersecting crack that offsets the main crack system. Continue along the upper crack (5.5) to a two-bolt anchor. **Pitch 3:** Leave the crack, heading straight up the dome and passing two protection bolts (5.9). Cross the upper of the two parallel cracks, encountering unprotected 5.10a moves higher up as you follow a prominent orange streak. Belay at the foot of a deep groove. **Pitch 4:** Ascend the 5.7 groove, exiting onto easy slabs near the top of the dome. Take pro to 1".
3. **Nuns for Fun** (5.10c) Locate the starting point 75' downhill and right of the crack system of Route 2, and directly below where its crack system makes a pronounced jog left. Here, find a ledge about 10' off the ground, on which are a small tree and a small rock pedestal. From the top of the pedestal, face climb past 4 bolts to a two-bolt belay, encountering the crux just beyond the second bolt. Lower off, or make a few more moves upward and join Route 2 at the top of the 5.7 crack on its first pitch.
4. **Praying Mantle** (5.11a) Begin 75' down and right of *Nuns for Fun,* and a few feet left of 2 short cracks that meet near the bottom of a prominent, orange streak. Edge up very steep rock, passing the left-hand crack to reach the first bolt (5.11a). From the second bolt a few feet higher, gradually work up left past 3 more bolts, encountering 5.10c/d moves above the second bolt and below the last one. Belay at a pair of bolts. Rappel from here. Pro to 1¼" will help.
5. **Order Yours Now, a.k.a. Cast Your Fate** (5.10c) Starting 30' right of Route 4, near where the short cracks meet, climb partway up the right-hand crack, then exit right onto the face. Clip a bolt, then face-climb up and over a small overhang and past 3 more protection bolts. Pass the blank section ahead via a 5.10c jog right, then back left and up to the belay bolts.
6. **Fleet Street** (I 5.10a) Seventy-five feet down and right of the start of *Order Yours Now,* notice a left-leaning column about 20' off the ground.

Begin *Fleet Street* just below this feature. **Pitch 1:** Diagonal up right, then jam a right-slanting crack that passes through an overlap. Belay at a bolt near the top of the crack. **Pitch 2:** Make a few 5.9 moves to a bolt, then follow a devious path up right, then up left past 3 more bolts. Proceed more directly upward to the last bolt, then pass the crux on a short traverse left to a pair of belay bolts shared with *Bit of Honey.* Descend via 2 rappels, or go to the top via Route 7. Take pro to 2".

7. **Bit of Honey** (II 5.10c R) Begin this popular classic 50' downhill and right of *Fleet Street,* where a short, right-slanting crack leads to a thin, right-facing flake/corner. **Pitch 1:** Ascend the slanting crack, then, instead of following a vertical continuation just left of the flake/corner, face-climb up left to the right end of the overlap crossed by *Fleet Street.* Undercling left, then ascend the left-leaning pillar left of the overlap and belay at a pair of bolts. **Pitch 2:** Face-climb up left (5.9) to a left-slanting crack, which suddenly angles sharply right. From its top, friction up right to a right-slanting ramp. Face-climb up left from the top of the ramp to belay bolts at a small ledge that marks the end of Route 6. **Pitch 3:** Climb the face above to a bolt, then angle up right to 2 more bolts, passing the crux at the second of these. Continue up and slightly left to a 2-bolt belay. **Pitch 4:** Climb up right to a bolt, then pass an overlap and make a very long runout, which involves much 5.9 and 5.10a edging, to another bolt. Head up right to a 2-bolt belay station, joining *Foxtrot* for the rest of the way to the top. Note that, although this route is not extreme, a slip on the fourth lead could result in a fall of over 100'. Take pro to 2".
8. **Foxtrot** (II 5.9 R) Start just a few yards right of *Bit of Honey,* directly below the right-facing flake/corner. **Pitch 1:** Edge up to and ascend the 5.9 corner, then face-climb past 3 bolts, encountering more 5.9 moves above the second one. Belay a bit higher at a 2-bolt stance. **Pitch 2:** Face-climb up and gradually left past 3 bolts (5.9), then head more directly up to the belay bolts. **Pitch 3:** Make a few friction moves, then follow a 5.7 dike. Where moderate climbing ends, head up left to a bolt, then face-climb up to the double-bolted belay that marks the end of *Bit of Honey.* **Pitch 4:** Ascend moderate, though unprotected friction directly up to belay bolts. **Pitch 5:** Climb another long, unprotected—but much easier—friction pitch to the top. Pro to 1" will suffice.
9. **Paradox** (II 5.11a) Begin this excellent and challenging route about 70' downhill and right of the start of *Foxtrot,* and about the same distance uphill and left of the parallel cracks that mark the start of *Fear and Loathing.* **Pitch 1:** From a point a few feet left of a short, vertical crack, edge up to the crack, climb it, then exit (5.9) up right to a pair of belay bolts. **Pitch 2:** Face-climb up left past two bolts (5.8), then follow a dike a few feet up right to a sloping belay ledge with a bolt. **Pitch 3:** Climb up

# SOUTH AND EAST FACES, BALD ROCK DOME

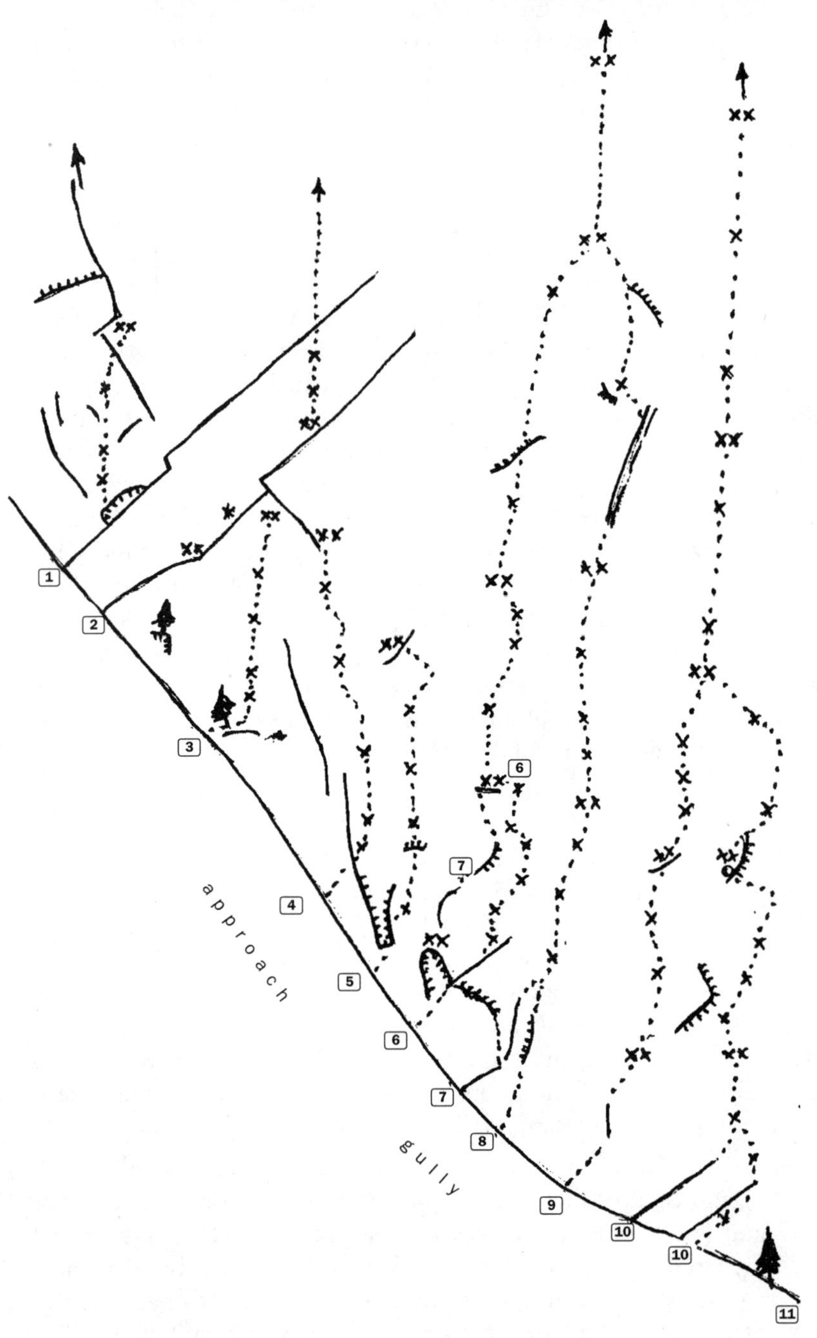

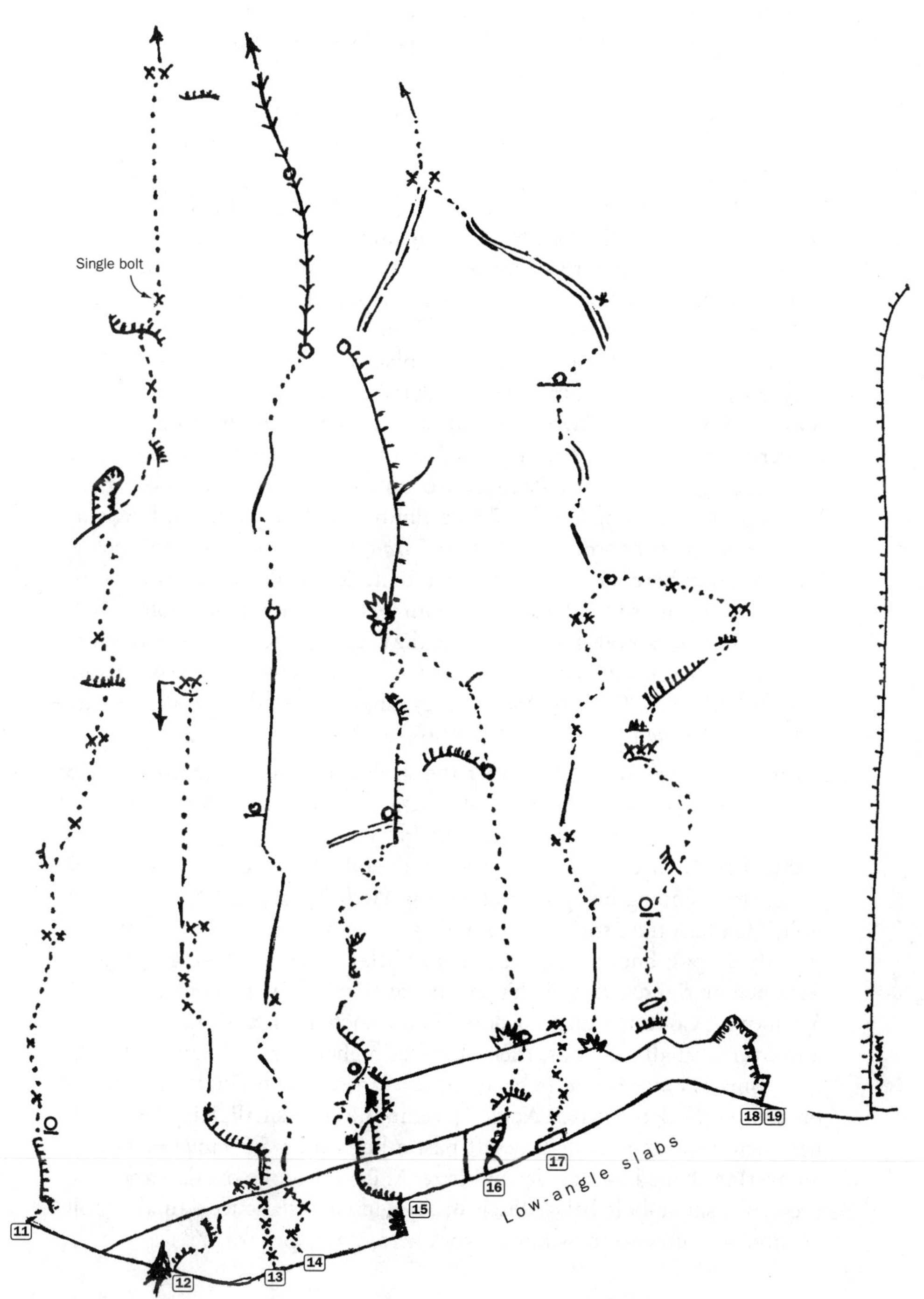
Single bolt
11
12
13
14
15
16
17
18
19
Low-angle slabs

right to a bolt, then proceed up continuous 5.10c/d face moves past 2 more bolts, encountering the 5.11a crux between them. From the top bolt, head up, then right to a double-bolt belay shared with *Fear and Loathing*. Finish via that route. Take pro to 1".

10. **Fear and Loathing** (II 5.9 R) About 75' downhill and right of the start of *Paradox,* notice a pair of right-slanting, parallel cracks about 30' apart. You can use either one to begin the first pitch, but most climbers agree that the lower crack is more interesting. **Pitch 1:** Follow the lower of the two cracks up right past a bolt. From its upper end, climb directly up to a bolt, then angle up left to another, situated up and right from the upper end of the upper crack. (If you choose the upper crack, this bolt is the only one you clip.) From the bolt, climb the 5.6 face above to a two-bolt stance. **Pitch 2:** Angle up left to a bolt placed right of a prominent flake shaped like a letter V on its left side. From here, head up right past a bolt, make a 5.8 move or two, and clip a third bolt. Climb more directly upward for about 10', then traverse left and up to a double-bolt belay at a left-facing flake/corner. **Pitch 3:** Go up right again, clip a bolt, then head up, encountering some 5.7 face climbing before making a long traverse up left past another bolt to join *Paradox* at its final two-bolt belay. **Pitch 4:** From here, face-climb 10' to a bolt, then make a long runout on moderate ground to another bolt. Continue to a pair of belay bolts. **Pitch 5:** Climb 15' to a bolt, then negotiate the crux 5.9 face moves. Continue up easier but run-out face climbing past another bolt, and arrive at the final bolted belay. **Pitch 6:** Ascend easy, unprotected slabs to the brushy ledges just below the summit. Take pro to 1".

11. **Burning Giraffes** (II 5.9 R) Locate the start of this classic about 200' up and left from the major system of cracks and grooves followed by *The Groove,* just below a left-facing dihedral that begins about 20' off the deck. **Pitch 1:** Face-climb to the foot of the dihedral, then lieback the 5.9 corner to a sloping belay spot at its top. **Pitch 2:** Face-climb up left to a bolt, then negotiate some 5.8 moves as you work up left and eventually directly up past another bolt to a 2-bolt belay. **Pitch 3:** Make a sweep up left, then up right to this pitch's sole protection bolt, which protects some 5.8 moves. Continue up to a double-bolt anchor. **Pitch 4:** Climb up to, and over a small 5.9 roof, then, 15' feet higher, head up left to a bolt. Pass some 5.8 moves before belaying at a large, thumb-like flake perched on a sloping ledge. **Pitch 5:** Angle up right (5.8) to a small, left-facing corner, then head up and slightly left past a bolt and a 5.9 move or two to an overlap shaped like a sideways letter S. Pass over the overlap and proceed to a single-bolt belay. **Pitch 6:** Ascend easy slabs to a final 2-bolt anchor. Scramble to the summit from here. Carry pro to 2½".

12. **English Breakfast Squirrel** (I 5.9 R) Begin at a small, right-curving arch located about midway between the dome's lowest point and the left end of a long, right-slanting crack. **Pitch 1:** Ascend the arch, then face-climb up right (5.9) to a shallow, left-facing corner. Climb a crack just right of the corner, then angle up right to the prominent, right-slanting crack. Follow it up right to a 2-bolt anchor below a left-curving arch. **Pitch 2:** Undercling and lieback the 5.7 arch, then jam an easy crack to its top. Face-climb up left to a bolt, then head up to a second bolt (5.9). Work up right, then ascend discontinuous cracks to a double-bolt belay on the right. **Pitch 3:** Climb a short crack, then ascend a very run-out 5.7 face to the bolts at a small ledge that marks the end of the climb. Rappel the route. Take pro to 2".
13. **Smooth Operator** (5.10a) Use this enjoyable sport route as an alternate first pitch to *English Breakfast Squirrel.* Beginning at the lowest point of the dome's southeast face, face-climb past 4 bolts to Route 12's first belay anchors.
14. **The Grove, a.k.a. The Nose, a.k.a. The Groove** (II 5.9) Begin this, Bald Rock Dome's original, surprisingly moderate, and deservedly most popular route, 30' right of Route 13, at the foot of the prominent system of shallow corners and cracks that splits the center of the dome. **Pitch 1:** Angle up left to a bolt, jog back right to another (5.8), then go up left to a third, belaying just below the long, right-slanting crack described in Route 12. **Pitch 2:** Face-climb past the diagonal crack, then ascend a short 5.9 crack. Friction up left, jam another short crack, then face-climb directly up to a belay bolt near the foot of a long crack. **Pitch 3:** Jam a long, 5.6 crack nearly to its top, exit up left to the foot of another long crack, and follow it to a belay ledge on the left. **Pitch 4:** Continue up the long crack (5.6) to a belay spot at its top. **Pitch 5:** Face-climb directly up, then veer left and climb a 5.7 crack. From its top, friction up right to a belay at the foot of a prominent trough. **Pitches 6 and 7:** Follow the trough to the summit slabs. Take pro to 2½", including extras of the middle and larger sizes.
15. **Jolly Rancher** (I 5.9) Locate this more direct start to Route 16 about 75' right of *The Grove,* where the base of the rock jogs upward above low-angle slabs, following a right-slanting course parallel to the obvious, diagonal cracks on the face above. **Pitch 1:** Beginning just below the lower end of a prominent, sickle-shaped overhang that shoots out left from the jog, face-climb parallel to the overhang until you can use it to make a 5.9 undercling and eventually lieback up to the lower of two major, right-slanting crack systems. From the crack, ascend small corners, broken flakes, and some 5.7 friction, then work up right to a sloping belay stance partway up a left-leaning, left-facing dihedral. **Pitch 2:**

Lieback up the 5.9 dihedral, then work up and right to a small, left-facing corner. From its top, zigzag up 5.7 friction, heading generally up right to a shallow, left-facing corner. Belay where a dike comes in from the left. **Pitch 3:** Ascend intermittent, left-facing openbooks, crossing a gap via some 5.8 face climbing. Climb partway up a large, left-curving dihedral, belaying at the small oak tree that marks the junction of *Jolly Rancher* with *Right of the Grove.* Finish via that route, or rappel. Take pro to 3", including several cams.

16. **Right of the Grove** (II 5.9 R/X) Start about 75' up and right of *Jolly Rancher,* where a small pedestal stands below the uphill end of the lower of two prominent, right-slanting crack systems. **Pitch 1:** Climb up right past a bolt (5.9) to the upper end of the slanting crack. From here, head directly up, passing over a small roof, and continuing up run-out face climbing to a belay bush at the upper slanting crack. **Pitch 2:** Face climb straight up poorly protected 5.7 rock to a belay at the right end of an arch. **Pitch 3:** Continue upward on run-out climbing until nearly level with the foot of a large, left-curving dihedral, then traverse up left (5.6) to the dihedral and belay at an oak tree. **Pitch 4:** Ascend the 5.7 dihedral and belay at its top. **Pitch 5:** Follow a wide 5.4 dike up right to a 2-bolt belay anchor shared with *Moroccan Roll.* **Pitch 6:** Ascend easy slabs to the short summit wall, then jam a short 5.9 hand crack to the top. Carry pro to 2½". Be careful on this route: there is considerable groundfall potential.
17. **All You Can Eat** (5.9) Begin at an angular block 75' up and right from Route 16. Work your way past a series of 4 bolts that lead gradually up and right. Pass the crux just above the fourth bolt. Find the belay bolts just above where the long, right-slanting crack described in Routes 15 and 16 forms a small overlap. Rappel the route.
18. **Moroccan Roll** (I 5.7) Start this popular route 100' right of Route 17, where the sloping base of the dome levels out. Scramble to a small oak growing at the far left end of a jagged flake/ledge. **Pitch 1:** Face-climb to a short crack, climb it, then ascend 5.7 friction up left to a pair of belay bolts. **Pitch 2:** Jam a short 5.7 finger crack, then friction up to a bolt. Angle up right, then head up left to belay bolts. **Pitch 3:** Face-climb up right to a left-leaning crack, climb it, then friction up right and climb the left-hand of two parallel, curved cracks. Ascend a short 5.5 face to a belay ledge. **Pitch 4:** Traverse up right to a prominent dike, follow it up left until above the belay ledge, then face-climb up to a 2-bolt belay shared with *Right of the Grove.* **Pitch 5:** Climb easy slabs to the summit wall and walk off left. Take pro to 1¼".
19. **Mute Testimony** (I 5.5) For an easier version of the lower half of *Moroccan Roll,* try *Mute Testimony.* Begin 75' right of Route 18, where

the flake/ledge rises to a point near its center. **Pitch 1:** Face-climb past a small overlap and a conspicuous hole, then head up to a fixed pin. Angle up right to a belay spot at a sloping ledge. **Pitch 2:** Climb a 5.5 face, then traverse left and slightly up to a belay ledge with 3 bolts. **Pitch 3:** Ascend the face above the ledge to a right-leaning corner, then follow it up right and continue (5.5) to a two-bolt belay. **Pitch 4:** Make a long, rising traverse left past a bolt, eventually joining *Moroccan Roll* at the foot of the diagonal crack on its third pitch. Take pro to 1½".

## HONORABLE MENTION

### ARCH ROCK TUNNEL

Arch Rock's north face borders the North Fork Feather River, and, like its neighbor Grizzly Dome, it is penetrated by a tunnel for California Highway 70. Several short climbs have been established on its north face. These are best approached from a small parking area immediately east of the tunnel, on the north side of the highway. One climb [*Bobbing for Poodles* (5.10a)] lies on the narrow face right of the east entrance to the tunnel, while the remainder require a short scramble down to a slab that leads back west along the base of the face. These routes, most of which are in the 5.10–5.11 range, end on a large, sloping ledge equipped with rappel bolts.

### NORTH FORK OUTCROPS

Between the tunnels of Arch Rock and Grizzly Dome, you can see several interesting-looking small outcrops across the river and situated above and below the Union Pacific Railroad tracks. These offer numerous interesting and scenic boulder problems, topropes, and short lead climbs. Approach by turning north from California 70 onto signed Pulga Road about 6 miles downcanyon from the Shady Rest Picnic Area, then heading back northeast parallel to, and across the river from, CA 70. Park on the shoulder when you draw opposite Arch Rock, then cross the railroad tracks and scramble down to the edge of the river, from which the rocks are fairly easy to access. Do not attempt to cross the river; its calm appearance here is deceptive.

# APPENDIX A: FURTHER READING

**Climbing Guides**

Bald, John. *Castle Crags: A Climbers Guide* (1989), self-published (out-of-print).

_____. *Lassen Volcanic National Park: A Climbers Guide* (1991), self-published.

Chemello, Eric. *Sandstone Supplement: Topographic Maps of Rock Climbs on The Northcoast* (1998), self-published.

Davis, Laird. *Classic Rock Climbs Number 18: Castle Crags California* (1997), Chockstone Press, Conifer, CO.

Humphrey, Paul and Eric Chemello. *Bigfoot Country Climbing: Guide to the Limestone of the Klamath Knot* (1997), M. Humphrey Publications, Arcata, CA.

LaFarge, David W. *Climbing Notes for the Humboldt County Coast* (1996), self-published.

Mackay, Steven. *California's Trinity Alps: A Climber's Guide* (1994), self-published.

Selters, Andy and Michael Zanger. *The Mt. Shasta Book: A Guide to Hiking, Climbing, Skiing, and Exploring the Mountain and Surrounding Area* (1989), Wilderness Press, Berkeley, CA.

Stahl, Robert. *Feather River Rock: A Trenchant Guide to Rock Climbing in the Feather River Country* (1989), self-published.

**Geology**

Alt, David D. and Donald W. Hyndman. *Roadside Geology of Northern California* (1975), Mountain Press Publishing Company, Missoula, MT.

Guyton, J. William and Frank L. DeCourten. *Introduction to the Geology of Bidwell Park* (1978), University Foundation, California State University, Chico, Chico, CA.

Pough, Frederick. *A Field Guide to Rocks and Minerals* (1960), The Peterson Field Guide Series, Houghton Mifflin Company, Boston, MA.

Talbitzer, Bill. *Lost Beneath the Feather* (1963), Las Plumas Publications, Oroville, CA.

# APPENDIX B: RATING SYSTEM COMPARISON CHART

| YDS* | NCCS** | UIAA*** | British**** | Australian | French |
|---|---|---|---|---|---|
| 5.0 | F4 | III | V. Diff. | 5–6 | |
| 5.1 | " | III+ | " | 7 | |
| 5.2 | " | IV- | " | 8 | |
| 5.3 | F5 | IV | Mild Severe | 9 | |
| 5.4 | " | IV+ | " | 10–11 | |
| 5.5 | F6 | V- | Severe 12 | | |
| 5.6 | " | V | " | 13 | |
| 5.7 | F7 | V+ | Very Severe (4b) | 14 | 5a |
| 5.8 | F8 | VI- | VS (4c)-Hard VS (5a) | 15 | 5b |
| 5.9 | F9 | VI+ | HVS (5a) | 16–17 | 5c |
| 5.10a | F10 | VII- | E1 (5a) | 18 | 6a |
| 5.10b | " | VII | E1 (5b) | 19 | 6a+ |
| 5.10c | " | " | E2 (5b) | 20 | 6b |
| 5.10d | " | VII+ | E3 (5c) | 20–21 | 6b+ |
| 5.11a | F11 | " | E3 (6a) | 22 | 6c |
| 5.11b | " | VIII- | E4 (6a) | " | " |
| 5.11c | " | VIII | E4 (6b) | 23 | 6c+ |
| 5.11d | " | VIII+ | E5 (6b) | 24 | 7a |
| 5.12a | F12 | IX- | E5 (6b) | 25 | 7a+ |
| 5.12b | " | IX | E6 (6c) | 26 | 7b |
| 5.12c | " | " | E6 (7a) | 27 | 7b+ |
| 5.12d | " | IX+ | E7 (7a) | 28 | 7c |
| 5.13a | F13 | X- | | " | 7c+ |
| 5.13b | " | X | | 29 | 8a |
| 5.13c | " | " | | 30 | 8a+ |
| 5.13d | " | X+ | ? | 31 | 8b |
| 5.14a | F14 | XI- | | 32 | 8b+ |

*YDS = Yosemite Decimal System
**NCCS = National Climbing Classification System. This system was employed in the Tetons and in the early Joshua Tree climber's guides.
***UIAA = Union International d'Associations d'Alpinism (The International Union of Alpine Clubs). This system is widely used by Continental climbers.
****The British system started by using adjectives to describe climbs, then became more and more confusing as English climbers exhausted their abundant supply of descriptors. The result was a two-part system intended to rate both technical difficulty and severity. Unlike the rating system used in this book, however, the British ratings have a substantial degree of overlap among adjacent grades, making absolute comparisons virtually impossible.

# APPENDIX C: MOUNTAIN SHOPS, GUIDE SERVICES, AND CLIMBING GYMS

## MOUNTAIN SHOPS

**Arcata**

Adventure's Edge
650 Tenth Street
Arcata, CA 95521
707-822-4673

Moonstone
1563 G Street
Arcata, CA 95521
707-826-8970

**Chico**

Dynamic Gear
13267 Contractors Drive
Chico, CA 95926
530-895-1035

Moonstone Factory Store
256 East First
Chico, CA 95928
530-893-6190

Mountain Sports
176 East Third
Chico, CA 95928
530-345-5011

Overland Equipment
2145 Park Avenue
Chico, CA 95926
530-894-5605

Sports Ltd.
240 Main Street
Chico, CA 95928
530-894-1110 or 800-875-4LTD

**Eureka**

Northern Mountain Supply
125 W. Fifth Street
Eureka, CA 95501
707-445-1711

**Mount Shasta**

The Fifth Season
300 North Mount Shasta Boulevard
Mount Shasta, CA 96067
530-926-3606

**Redding**

Hermit's Hut/Basecamp 1
3184 Bechelli Lane
Redding, CA 96002
530-222-4511

Sports Ltd.
950 Hilltop Drive
Redding, CA 96002
530-221-7333

## GUIDE SERVICES

**Anderson**

Adventures Made Easy
18974 River Ranch Road
Anderson, CA 96007
530-241-4907

**Arcata**

Center Activities
Humboldt State University
Arcata, CA 95521
707-826-3357

**Lewiston**

Rush Creek Enterprises
P.O. Box 1376
Weaverville, CA 96093
530-623-3182

**Mt. Shasta**

Mike Zanger/Shasta Mountain Guides
1938 West Hill Road
Mt. Shasta, CA 96067
530-926-3117

Sierra Wilderness Seminars
P.O. Box 988
Mount Shasta, CA 96067
888-797-6867

**Norden**
Bela and Mimi Vadasz
P.O. Box 8
Norden, CA 95724
916-426-9108

CLIMBING GYMS

**Chico**
California State University
Chico, Climbing Wall
Chico, CA 95928
530-898-5462

**Grass Valley**
Ascent Climbing Gym/Outdoor Center
717 Auburn Street
Grass Valley, CA 95949
916-272-0170

**Mt. Shasta**
Mount Shasta Ski Park
California 89 at Ski Park Highway
Mt. Shasta, CA 96067
530-926-8600

**Rancho Cordova**
Granite Arch
11335 Folsom Boulevard, Building G
Rancho Cordova, CA 95742
916-638-4605

# APPENDIX D: SERVICES AND RESOURCE MANAGEMENT AGENCIES

## GOVERNMENT AGENCIES

California Department of Transportation (CALTRANS)
Road Condition Information 800-427-7623 or 916-445-7623

### California State Parks

Information 916-653-6995

Special Services Information 916-653-4272

State Park Reservations (DESTINET) 800-444-7275
Cancellations 800-695-2269

State Parks Store 916-653-4000

Lake Oroville State Recreation Area, Oroville, CA 95966; 530-538-2200
Bidwell Canyon Campground 530-538-2218
Loafer Creek Campground 530-538-2217

Castle Crags State Park
20022 Castle Creek Road
Castella, CA 96017
530-235-2684

Patricks Point State Park
Trinidad, CA 95570
707-677-3570

Prairie Creek Redwoods State Park,
Orick, CA 95555
707-488-2171

### USDA-Forest Service

Lassen National Forest
Butte Meadows Station
7288 Humboldt Road
Butte Meadows, CA 95942
530-873-0580

Plumas National Forest (Forest Headquarters)
875 Mitchell Avenue
Oroville, CA 95965
530-534-6500

Shasta-Trinity National Forest
Forest Headquarters
2400 Washington Avenue
Redding, CA 96001
530-244-2978

Shasta-Trinity National Forest
Big Bar Ranger District
Highway 299 West
Star Route 1, Box 10
Big Bar, CA 96010
530-623-6106

Shasta-Trinity National Forest
Hayfork Ranger District
Highway 3
P. O. Box 159
Hayfork, CA 96041
530-628-5227

Shasta-Trinity National Forest
Mt. Shasta Ranger District
204 West Alma
Mt. Shasta, CA 96067
530-926-4511

Shasta-Trinity National Forest
Weaverville Ranger District
210 Main Street
P. O. Box 1190
Weaverville, CA 96093
530-623-2121

### National Park Service 415-556-0560

Campground Reservations
800-365-2267

Lassen Volcanic National Park
P. O. Box 100
Mineral, CA 96063
530-595-4444

## PRIVATE NON-PROFIT ORGANIZATIONS

The Access Fund
P.O. Box 17010
Boulder, CO 80308
888-863-6237

The American Alpine Club
710 Tenth Street, Suite 100
Golden, CO 80401
303-384-0110

American Mountain Guides Association (AMGA)
710 Tenth Street
Golden, CO 80401
303-271-0984

Promotional materials can be requested via voice-mail by calling 800-784-AMGA.

# APPENDIX E: EMERGENCY SERVICES

**Arcata**
Mad River Community Hospital
3800 Janes Road
Arcata, CA 95521
707-822-3621

**Chico**
Chico Community Hospital
560 Cohasset Road
Chico, CA 95926
530-896-5000

Enloe Hospital
1531 The Esplanade
Chico, CA 95926
530-891-7300 or 800-822-8102

**Crescent City**
Sutter Coast Hospital
800 East Washington Boulevard
Crescent City, CA 95531
707-464-8511

**Eureka**
General Hospital
2200 Harrison Avenue
Eureka, CA 95501
707-445-5111

Saint Joseph Hospital
700 Dolbeer Street
Eureka, CA 95501
707-445-8121

**Marysville**
Rideout Memorial Hospital
726 Fourth Street
Marysville, CA 95901
530-749-4300

**Mt. Shasta**
Mercy Medical Center
914 Pine Street
Mt. Shasta, CA 96067
530-926-6111

**Oroville**
Oroville Hospital
2767 Olive Highway (California 162)
Oroville, CA 95966
530-533-8500

**Paradise**
Feather River Hospital
5974 Pentz Road
Paradise, CA 95969
530-877-9361

**Red Bluff**
Saint Elizabeth Community Hospital
2550 Sister Mary Columbia Drive
Red Bluff, CA 96080
530-529-8000

**Redding**
Mercy Medical Center
2175 Rosaline Avenue
Redding, CA 96001
530-225-6000

Redding Medical Center
1100 Butte Street
Redding, CA 96001
530-244-5400
RMC AirMED 800-432-9944

**Willow Creek/Hoopa**
Hoopa Health Association
41130 Highway 299
Willow Creek, CA 95573
707-625-4261
Ambulance (Emergencies only) 707-625-4180

**Yuba City**
Fremont Medical Center
970 Plumas
Yuba City, CA 95991
530-751-4000

# INDEX

N



O

U

*The author, scoping out the route possibilities along the Middle Fork, Feather River.*

## ABOUT THE AUTHOR

Steven Mackay has been a rock climber and mountaineer for the past thirty years, during which time he has logged hundreds of climbs throughout California, including first ascents at Suicide Rock, Tahquitz Rock, Mount Williamson, the High Sierra, Tuolumne Meadows, Joshua Tree National Park, Mount Rubidoux, and many of the formations in this book. He holds a graduate degree in Wilderness Management and lives with his wife Cara Lou and cats in a solar-powered home at the edge of the Trinity Alps Wilderness. This is his first FalconGuide.

# ACCESS: It's every climber's concern

**The Access Fund**, a national, non-profit climbers' organization, works to keep climbing areas open and to conserve the climbing environment. Need help with closures? land acquisition? legal or land management issues? funding for trails and other projects? starting a local climbers' group? CALL US!

Climbers can help preserve access by being committed to leaving the environment in its natural state. Here are some simple guidelines:

• **STRIVE FOR ZERO IMPACT** especially in environmentally sensitive areas like caves. Chalk can be a significant impact on dark and porous rock–don't use it around historic rock art. Pick up litter, and leave trees and plants intact.

• **DISPOSE OF HUMAN WASTE PROPERLY** Use toilets whenever possible. If toilets are not available, dig a "cat hole" at least six inches deep and 200 feet from any water, trails, campsites, or the base of climbs. *Always pack out toilet paper.* On big wall routes, use a "poop tube" and carry waste up and off with you (the old "bag toss" is now illegal in many areas).

• **USE EXISTING TRAILS** Cutting switchbacks causes erosion. When walking off-trail, tread lightly, especially in the desert where cryptogamic soils (usually a dark crust) take thousands of years to form and are easily damaged. Be aware that "rim ecologies" (the clifftop) are often highly sensitive to disturbance.

• **BE DISCREET WITH FIXED ANCHORS** *Bolts are controversial and are not a convenience*–don't place 'em unless they are *really* necessary. Camouflage all anchors. Remove unsightly slings from rappel stations (better to use steel chain or welded cold shuts). Bolts sometimes can be used pro-actively to protect fragile resources–consult with your local land manager.

• **RESPECT THE RULES** and speak up when other climbers don't. Expect restrictions in designated wilderness areas, rock art sites, caves, and to protect wildlife, especially nesting birds of prey. *Power drills are illegal in wilderness and all national parks.*

• **PARK AND CAMP IN DESIGNATED AREAS** Some climbing areas require a permit for overnight camping.

• **MAINTAIN A LOW PROFILE** Leave the boom box and day-glo clothing at home–the less climbers are heard and seen, the better.

• **RESPECT PRIVATE PROPERTY** Be courteous to land owners. Don't climb where you're not wanted.

• **JOIN THE ACCESS FUND!** To become a member, make a tax-deductible donation of $25 or more.